PRAISE FOR *LEADING A CHURCH IN A TIME OF SEXUAL QUESTIONING*

"Bruce Miller is a wise guide in one of the most practical books I have read on this subject. A thoroughly biblical, thoughtful, and grace-filled book, you will find yourself returning to it again and again."

—DEBRA HIRSCH, PASTOR AND AUTHOR OF *REDEEMING SEX: NAKED CONVERSATIONS ABOUT SPIRITUALITY AND SEXUALITY*

"As someone well acquainted with the confusing isolation of feeling the need to choose between being gay and being a Christian, I find [this] to be a carefully written book full of meticulous, thoughtful research, but most of all full of love. Miller's heart to show the radical love of God to all people, especially the marginalized, is apparent through every chapter as he challenges church leaders to employ their ministries as effective instruments of God's healing love."

—MALLORY CHAPPELL, ADJUNCT HISTORY PROFESSOR, BOXING TRAINER, AND NAVY VETERAN

"If you're serious about dealing with the sexual issues of our day in a Christlike way, Miller will guide you as a theologian, a pastor, and a fellow sexual being into a much needed balance of grace *and* truth."

—C. GARY BARNES, ThM, PhD, LICENSED PSYCHOLOGIST; BOARD CERTIFIED SEX THERAPIST; PROFESSOR, DALLAS THEOLOGICAL SEMINARY

"It's honest, challenges the genuineness of our biblical conviction of real (Christlike) love and the level of inclusiveness we are willing to embrace. Thought provoking and cutting edge, great depth, well covered, balanced. Disturbing for some because it challenges established leadership habits and some stereotypical teaching. Reflective of our heavenly Father's heart, convicting. Well done."

—TERRY PRESCOTT, RETIRED BUSINESSMAN

"I am grateful for your courage to make bold statements. . . ."

—KARI, RETIRED FIREFIGHTER

"I believe this book is a game changer! It is a powerful guide for church leaders and entire congregations. I think it will also be encouraging for parents of LGBT+ kids. Awesome job!"

—BILL HENSON, FOUNDER AND PRESIDENT, LEAD THEM HOME

"I read every word of your manuscript. My response is *amen*! This book is so needed and I think you've done an incredible job addressing the issue(s), and providing a process and real help for the church. I'm going to take my staff through your book ASAP. It's the best book I've ever read on the subject."

—DOUG WALKER, LEAD PASTOR, FELLOWSHIP OF THE PARKS

"Irenic, compassionate, and pastorally astute, this book is a timely entry in an increasingly antagonistic conversation. Instead of getting lost in debates, Bruce Miller returns us again and again to the Christian necessity of love: love for Christ, love for Scripture, and love for people—all people—regardless of sexual orientation or sexual ethics or sexual expression. I pray that many more church communities with a historic Christian sexual ethic come to resemble the church envisioned in this book."

—GREGORY COLES, AUTHOR OF *SINGLE, GAY, CHRISTIAN*

"This is a book that needed to be written and I can't think of a better person for the job. You are going the love the way Bruce tackles this super-sensitive topic with skill, passion, balance, and grace. Anybody who plans to step outside into the world we live in today needs to take in the message of this book."

—RANDY FRAZEE, PASTOR AND AUTHOR OF *THE HEART OF THE STORY*

"This book needed to be written. As Christians who believe the Bible is the infallible Word of God, we cannot—we must not—look the other way. Bruce Miller has not! As a pastor-theologian, he has probed deeply into the Scriptures to discover God's mind on sexual issues that have surfaced in our present culture. Caution! Read this book carefully from cover to cover. Evaluate the author's conclusions and his total perspective."

—Dr. Gene A. Getz, professor, pastor, author

"In this book [Bruce Miller] applies his God-given gift of clarity to one of the most difficult topics we face today. This is a must-read for pastors, parents, and students facing the difficult task of navigating the topic of sexual identity in today's culture."

—Brad Smith, president, Bakke Graduate University (BGU.edu)

"There has been a need for a book like this for a long time. Bruce has wrestled long and hard with questions related to LGBTQ people and the church. With biblical fidelity and a pastoral heart, he addresses the practical and difficult issues churches are facing today. He doesn't always give easy answers. And you may disagree with him at times, as I do. But I am not aware of any other book that addresses such challenging questions with sensitivity, honesty, and biblical wisdom."

—Sean McDowell, PhD, speaker, professor at Talbot School of Theology, and author of more than eighteen books, including Same-Sex Marriage

"A must-read for church leaders. Bruce's treatment of a controversial topic is done with grace and biblical truth. . . . I encourage readers to dive in with an open mind, allowing God to change your heart, knowing God's truth will remain forever."

—Mark Wilson, church elder and engineering manager

"If you are a busy church leader who cares about these issues but does not have the time to read all the books on the topic, Bruce just saved you time. If you only have time for one book, read this one. . . . You may not agree with everything you read, but you will find guidance and wisdom to make your own decisions for your context."

—STEVE STROOPE, LEAD PASTOR, LAKEPOINTE CHURCH

"With compassion and generosity [Bruce Miller] brings biblical theology into the arena of one of the thorniest topics facing the church in this present culture: human sexuality. I promise you will be challenged!"

—MICHAEL FLETCHER, SENIOR PASTOR, MANNA CHURCH

"A book that walks you through the full array of scenarios a church leader must consider when thinking through issues tied to sexuality. It does so with sensitivity, skill, and clarity. . . . the gift of this book is it will force you to think carefully through this discussion and its myriad possibilities, a real service to us all."

—DARRELL BOCK, EXECUTIVE DIRECTOR FOR CULTURAL ENGAGEMENT, HOWARD G. HENDRICKS CENTER FOR CHRISTIAN LEADERSHIP AND CULTURAL ENGAGEMENT; SENIOR RESEARCH PROFESSOR OF NEW TESTAMENT STUDIES

"I'm so thankful that a book has finally been written from a pastoral perspective that treats faith and sexuality as the truly nuanced subjects that they are. Bruce asks informed, thought-provoking questions that allow you to lean into this conversation and discern what is right for your church in your context—all within sound, biblical theology."

—TY WYSS, EXECUTIVE DIRECTOR OF WALLS DOWN MINISTRY

"Dr. Miller does a great job handling the relevant biblical texts but also interacting with research, sharing stories of those wrestling with all the related issues, and describing productive ways of having meaningful discussions, even with those who may disagree on the myriad issues to address. I commend it highly to pastors and leaders to help them address LGBT+ issues both with their words and with their lives in the coming years."

—DAVE TRAVIS, DIRECTOR, STRATEGIC COUNSEL TO PASTORS AND CHURCH BOARDS AT GENERIS; FORMER CEO, LEADERSHIP NETWORK

"As a pastor who has for thirty-one years been leading a large metroplex church through an intense time of sexual questioning, I am deeply grateful to my long-time friend and colleague Dr. Bruce Miller for providing us more than just a new book. This is actually balm for my pastoral soul! . . . You'll also breathe a sigh of relief as you read Bruce's commonsense answers for pastors attempting to lead wisely through the many seemingly intractable LGBT complexities in their churches."

—Dr. E. Andrew McQuitty, Irving Bible Church
pastor at large; author of *The Way to Brave:
Shaping a David Faith in Our Goliath World*

"As a pastor who is responsible to help our church navigate a whole new sexual and cultural landscape, I've found this to be the most helpful book written on the topic to date. Bruce is a pastor/theologian who is able to bring the best of both worlds to this topic. He breaks down very complex issues in ways that are deeply thoughtful, biblically accurate, appropriately humble, and extremely helpful."

—Jeff Jones, senior pastor, Chase Oaks

OTHER BOOKS BY BRUCE B. MILLER

LEADERSHIP NETWORK

LEADING
A CHURCH
IN A
TIME OF
SEXUAL
QUESTIONING

Grace-Filled Wisdom for Day-to-Day Ministry

BRUCE B. MILLER

THOMAS NELSON
Since 1798

Published in Nashville, Tennessee, by Thomas Nelson. Thomas Nelson is a registered trademark of HarperCollins Christian Publishing, Inc.

Thomas Nelson titles may be purchased in bulk for educational, business, fund-raising, or sales promotional use. For information, please e-mail SpecialMarkets@ ThomasNelson.com.

Scripture quotations are taken from the Holy Bible, New International Version®, NIV®. Copyright © 1973, 1978, 1984, 2011 by Biblica, Inc.® Used by permission of Zondervan. All rights reserved worldwide. www.Zondervan.com. The "NIV" and "New International Version" are trademarks registered in the United States Patent and Trademark Office by Biblica, Inc.®

Any Internet addresses, phone numbers, or company or product information printed in this book are offered as a resource and are not intended in any way to be or to imply an endorsement by Thomas Nelson, nor does Thomas Nelson vouch for the existence, content, or services of these sites, phone numbers, companies, or products beyond the life of this book.

ISBN 978-1-4002-1091-6 (eBook)
ISBN 978-1-4002-1090-9 (TP)

Library of Congress Control Number: 2018964220

Printed in the United States of America
19 20 21 22 23 LSC 10 9 8 7 6 5 4 3 2 1

About Leadership ✳ Network

Leadership Network fosters innovation movements that activate the church to greater impact. We help shape the conversations and practices of pacesetter churches in North America and around the world. The Leadership Network mind-set identifies church leaders with forward-thinking ideas—and helps them to catalyze those ideas resulting in movements that shape the church.

Together with HarperCollins Christian Publishing, the biggest name in Christian books, the NEXT imprint of Leadership Network moves ideas to implementation for leaders to take their ideas to form, substance, and reality. Placed in the hands of other church leaders, that reality begins spreading from one leader to the next . . . and to the next . . . and to the next, where that idea begins to flourish into a full-grown movement that creates a real, tangible impact in the world around it.

NEXT: A Leadership Network Resource
committed to helping you grow your next idea.

leadnet.org/NEXT

CONTENTS

FOREWORD

Questions about faith and sexuality are among the most pressing ethical concerns facing the church today. It is therefore pastorally irresponsible for Christian pastors and leaders to remain unstudied and silent on this topic. Yet, few pastors are willing to engage the topic with truth and grace.

This is why I'm so thankful for Bruce's courage and compassion in not only engaging this conversation with truth and grace, but for doing so in the context of real-life ministry. Bruce is a pastor. Bruce is also a scholar. He's well-studied on the topic of faith and sexuality, but he has also been living out what he preaches, while preaching what he's living out. While there are many books written on the topic, few are written at the intersection of scholarship and ministry. Even fewer are written from one pastor to another, rather than lobbing bombs from one ivory tower to the next.

When I first met Bruce, the first word that came to mind was: *humility*. The second: *authenticity*. Though Bruce is older and wiser than I am, and though he has many more years of pastoral experience under his belt, he immediately wanted to know what I thought about various aspects of how the historically Christian perspective on sexual ethics applies to nitty gritty pastoral questions. He was slow to speak and quick to ask questions. And when he spoke, his words dripped with humility and grace. Bruce is a pastor with a massive heart for people, and it's that heart that saturates every word of this book.

Bruce is also a scholar and a theologian. He's not *just* a pastor who loves people; he's a pastor who loves to study *because* he loves people. You may not agree with everything written in this book. (And you probably shouldn't agree with every word written in any book, save the Bible.) In fact, Bruce, being the humble pastor that he is, does not intend for you to agree with everything in this book. *Leading a Church in a Time of Sexual Questioning* is a discussion starter, not a discussion ender. It's a guide, not a rule book. It's filled with wisdom, not ex-cathedra commands. It's a conversation from one pastor to another about how to go about discipling your people in the most complex and pressing issues of the day. And Bruce is the right person to lead us in this discussion.

You probably picked up Bruce's book because you know you need to start having this conversation in your own church. Or, perhaps, the conversation is already happening and you are looking for guidance. Maybe some gay couples have been showing up at your church, or perhaps a family has come to you asking for help since their child just came out. Maybe you're realizing that there are more gay or same-sex attracted people in your church than you had realized, and you're trying to figure out how to best care for them. Perhaps you're trying to update your policy on marriage and sexuality, or maybe this conversation is much closer to home: your own son or daughter just told you they're gay. Whatever is going on in your life and ministry, this book will help you engage the conversation about faith and sexuality with theological faithfulness and courageous love.

I'm very excited about the journey you're about to embark on as you move your way through Bruce's book. My hope and prayer is that after reading this book, you will consider how you can implement the wisdom you will have gleaned from it. This book is not designed to be read and then left alone. It's designed to help leaders lead well in a cultural moment when Christians are in desperate need of solid, compassionate, truth-seeking, leadership.

Preston Sprinkle
President of the Center for Faith, Sexuality & Gender

PREFACE

Language Matters

L anguage can invite a conversation or shut one down. While we must all be sensitive to the hurtful power of words, on all sides of any issue, there are those eager to pounce on a certain word and use it as leverage for condemnation. Sadly, identity politics and the political correctness movement have so charged language with moral voltage that it actually discourages dialogue by verbal intimidation. It seems that these days no matter how carefully people choose their words, one side or another attacks those words. The emotive power of words changes, and in this sexual arena, often the changes are rapid. So please give me grace in my language. By the time you are reading this book, words that are fine now could have become words some people no longer want to use. And in the event my language offends you, I am still accountable. If that happens, I offer you my sincere apology. I would never want to hurt or offend anyone or cause confusion or misunderstanding with my words.

Let's give each other linguistic grace to hear the heart behind our words. I've chosen to use the acronym LGBT+ (lesbian, gay, bisexual, transgender, and other [+] sexual and gender minorities), however, my focus is more on lesbian and gay people, and those who might describe themselves as same-sex or same-gender attracted (even the term "same-sex attracted" and its acronym, SSA, have been embraced by some and rejected by others). The transgender conversation involves another set of complexities that deserves its own book, so out of respect for the nuances and feelings of those involved, I've chosen not to include transgender issues in this book.

INTRODUCTION

As church leaders, we've all sat across from someone in the middle of a difficult, even heartbreaking situation.

"Pastor," in tears, "my daughter just came home from college and told me she thinks she is a lesbian. We don't know what to do."

You know these stories. And you have tried to help as best you could.

"Pastor," with downcast eyes, "I'm over thirty and not married. Am I doomed to a life of singleness?"

You have tried to encourage her.

"Pastor," in anger, "my son just put on Facebook that he is gay and dating some guy—for all the world to see. We are so ashamed. People will ask me about it. What do I say?"

You have seen this pain and given your best spiritual guidance.

"Pastor," in confusion, "a seventh-grade girl told her small group she is bisexual and has a crush on another girl in the youth group. Should we let her come on the overnight retreat next month?"

You have counseled this youth pastor and sought wisdom from your leaders.

"Pastor," in hope and trepidation, "my partner and I would like to dedicate our beautiful one-year-old daughter, Charis. Would the church let us do that?"

You have wrestled with how to show grace and stand for truth, and you have agonized over potential perceptions of the congregation and the meaning of a baby dedication.

"Pastor," with evident frustration, "it has been more than a year since my wife and I have been intimate, and I have no idea what to do. Do I have to stay married to her?"

You have offered all the solutions you know to try.

"Pastor," in fear and concern, "I think one of the children's workers is gay. Should we let him continue to volunteer in our children's ministry?"

You have prayed hard over how to appreciate the servant's heart of this dear children's worker while being sensitive to your church member's concerns. You've also worried about the precedents you might set no matter what decision you make.

It would not be hard to list dozens more "Pastor, . . ." questions like these that test our spiritual discernment on how to lead our churches well through this time of sexual questioning. If you have been in church leadership for long, you have already had to address complicated, sensitive, and soul-wrenching issues arising out of sexual differences, orientations, and dysfunctions. These come up in youth groups, small groups, children's classes, newcomer classes, and leader meetings.

Our responses to such sexually charged questions are amplified, and potentially become explosive, in our combative public discourse. As church leaders, we are keenly aware that our church could face a lawsuit. We also fear that the social media backlash from Facebook and Twitter could be almost as damaging, especially if we put our response in writing. It might be picked up by a reporter who smells controversy, and before we know it we are on the local news. You know someone in the church will get upset no matter what stance you take, and even a well-intended conviction to protect your church could transform into a backlash against your church.

Ultimately the gospel of Jesus Christ is at stake because the unchurched, especially millennials and Generation Z (those under thirty-five years old), are keenly watching how churches respond to LGBT+ people and their concerns.

My heart is that I might help you navigate your church in these sexually turbulent waters. My hope is that by the power of God local churches will become

- loving communities where LGBT+ people can feel wanted and welcomed and can flourish in the life that Christ offers them by the Spirit.[1]
- spiritual bodies where all of us can unite in our common cleansing baptism in Christ, joining our hands and hearts as members of one body.
- spiritual families where *all* of us as blood brothers and sisters in Christ, adopted by the Father into his eternal divine family, can love and be loved.
- pillars of truth where the foundations of marriage are respected as being a lifelong one-flesh bond between a man and a woman.
- lights to the world who shine brightly with love and justice for all people because we are compelled by Christ to radically love family, friends, neighbors, and coworkers despite our belief differences.

My hope in writing this book is to advance the goal of better navigating our churches with spiritual wisdom and Christlike love. Depending on where you are with these issues, certain chapters of this book may be more relevant to you than others.

Our most powerful act of leadership comes in our example (1 Peter 5:3). It's essential for us to wrestle with our own past and present sexual issues, including our prejudices and wounds, sins, and confusions. When we have personally received the grace of Christ and felt the Father's loving hands cleansing our sin, then we can lead our churches as wounded healers and washed sinners. But sharing our examples raises questions of how vulnerable we need to be with our own stories as we speak, teach, and counsel others. Equally as sensitive, we wrestle with the appropriate level of transparency as we consider sharing stories from our own families: stories about our kids, parents, and extended families. I struggled with these very questions while deciding what to share in this book.

People look to their spiritual leaders to give them truth. On many theological issues, you likely have strong convictions, but you may also have thorny questions about some issues around sexuality. Church leaders need to provide clear theological leadership about sexuality. But few pastors have a robust theology of sexuality beyond the simple moralism: don't have sex before you are married, and when you marry, do it well but only with your spouse, and no porn for anyone.

With this approach, we have made sexual intimacy a bigger deal than it really is. By presenting a brief biblical theology of sexuality, I hope to show that *sex is a good gift, but it is not essential for a good life*. I will develop a brief holistic biblical theology of sexuality as a framework for you to use in your church. In the end, intimacy with the triune God is better than sex.

As we counsel married couples and teach those who might marry someday, we tend to rely on recent evangelical teaching on sex in marriage that has focused on how to have pleasure and not be prudish about it. We have lost the fuller theology of the purposes of sex in marriage that was developed early in the history of the church. As we unfold the richer biblical purposes for marriage, we will learn that sex is not the heart of marriage, but it is important. Sadly, our sexuality in marriage is rarely free of sin, such as when we use sex as a weapon to get what we want.

True Love Waits campaigns (while encouraging purity) build up the wedding night to be such a big deal, which it rarely is. They also have the unintended consequence of signaling to singles that they are missing out on the "big deal." How can the church help singles steward their sexuality? I invite Christian leaders to rethink a biblical theology of singleness and its implications for our churches. The perspective of much recent Christian teaching has been that a few rare people have the unusual gift of lifelong celibate singleness, but most people should get married. Although I long held this view, I have recently come to a different conclusion. We have so romanticized and idolized sex that we have duped ourselves into thinking it is essential for a good life. So we sideline singles as second-class people.

Working from these foundational insights on marriage and singleness, we will also take a closer look at same-sex sexuality. We need to find clarity on what the Bible does and does not say about same-sex sexuality. As pastors, it's important we develop our own convictions about being both a Christian and gay. Here we will consider five different ways the term *gay* is commonly used: sexual roles, behavior, identity, attraction, and orientation. The chapter will call us to broaden our view of masculinity and femininity—more than men's ministry for hunters and high teas for women. Beyond addressing causation, we will dive deeply into the concept of being gay and consider how we can think biblically about the idea of an "orientation." Then we will consider wise pastoral options to offer people who identify as LGBT+.

While I cannot adequately address the complicated and subtle issues around identifying as transgender, most church leaders will minister to, and with, transgender people and to the important people in their lives, their family members and partners. The broad and confusing issues of gender dysphoria relate to *gender* issues that are categorically different from *sexual* issues. A biblical view of gender affirms the uniqueness and beauty of each gender without either subscribing to culture-specific depictions of maleness and femaleness or denying that sexual differences exist. As spiritual leaders, we face practical issues, such as what pronoun do we use to refer to people who are in transition? What do we do about access to church bathrooms? Those important issues require another book. Many of the principles in this book, however, will apply to transgender people and other gender and sexual minorities.

As you help your church have conversations about sexuality, and in particular, same-sex issues, we will find guidance from three conversations Jesus had related to sexuality and what we can learn in terms of how to have real-life conversations on these issues: the woman at the well (John 4), the woman caught in adultery (John 8), and the "sinful" woman who anointed Jesus' feet at the Pharisee's house (Luke 7). Who we are talking with makes a difference, whether the listener is a mature Christian, a new believer, or someone exploring Christianity.

Many church leaders are caught between two factions. Those in our churches from the most conservative backgrounds (often older boomers) can have a hard time showing grace, and those formed by today's progressive sexual ethic (often millennials) can have a hard time standing for truth; as a result, they judge each other. Spiritual leaders need to shepherd those in our church families who struggle with a deep discomfort with gay and lesbian people. Many books focus on how to show grace to LGBT+ people, which is crucial, but we also need grace for those struggling with LGBT+ people. We will consider how to shepherd our entire faith community well. We can empathize with fears, especially those stoked by conservative Christian radio, blogs, and newsletters. How can we lead all the people in our churches to become more like Jesus in both showing God's amazing grace and holding to God's firm truth as unified church families?

Going further than that, how do we build a church family for much more diversity than the traditional American nuclear family with mom, dad, and 2.5 kids? We will consider "gracious spaciousness"—focusing on the center, which is Jesus Christ and not the boundaries. The major biblical metaphor for the church is family—so who do we include in our family? From here we will move to a theology of hospitality, welcoming the "stranger." Our culture makes little space for non-eroticized relationships, so I will call us to a refreshed vision for church "families" that encourage all people, whether married or single, to form deep, spiritual friendship bonds. We will talk about different kinds of living situations with multiple generations and genders. This will include a brief treatment of "fellowship" (*koinonia*) and close relationships, building on Wesley Hill's recent work on spiritual friendships, and Nate Collins's suggestions for a wider view of kinship relationships.

I have found that to lead a church through these turbulent waters, it helps to bring us all back to the cross, where the ground is level and where we can all be washed in the cleansing waters of grace in Christ. In our churches we are leading sexual sinners, starting with ourselves, our leaders, and then all members. You can guide your people by helping them understand why the results of sexual sin are so painful and so serious. In unpacking the connections of sexual sin to show how it violates each member of the Trinity, we will gain insights. Then we will move to divine sexual healing in Jesus Christ. Confession and repentance invite refreshing grace that heals and restores.

All the ground we have plowed to this point prepares us to address how we can practically lead churches to show grace and stand for truth in the messiness of a fallen world. We will address tone as well as theology, our personal posture as well as our theological positions. We will focus more on loving people than on writing policies, more on individual stories than on generic position papers. We will point to practical wisdom principles, such as "welcoming all and affirming none." We will apply theological principles to practical questions related to LGBT+ people, such as how to lead your elders and staff, the use of language, preaching and teaching, employment, and issues around same-sex weddings.

Finally, we will look at sexual questions and common issues, such as membership, baptism, the Lord's Supper, baby dedications, overnight retreats, and ministry to and inclusion of LGBT+ students.

We will look at who—gay or straight—can serve and lead in the church based on their past experiences and present handling of personal temptations. And I'll address what's been called "church discipline," how to handle sin in the church for all people.

My prayer is that the Holy Spirit will use this book to provide practical, theologically sound wisdom for how to wisely navigate your church through sexually turbulent waters. In Christ there is no tension between grace and truth, so my confidence is that by the Spirit we can show amazing grace without compromising truth and provide space for people to differ and to grow while focusing on Jesus Christ and his gospel to honor the triune God.

Discussion Questions

1. Why are you reading this book? What are you hoping, praying, to gain from it? What are you fearful about as you start to read it and discuss it?

2. What are some of your personal connections to the topics of this book? How would you describe your own sexuality? Who among your family or friends are you hoping this book might help you minister to and encourage?

3. What questions have you been asked in this arena that have challenged you, provoked you, or stumped you? What questions do you hope this book will help you answer?

4. Why do you think this topic may be important for your church? For you?

CHAPTER 1

YOUR SEXUALITY

Setting an Example

You probably picked up this book to help you deal with other people's sexual issues. While we are called to do that as spiritual leaders, we must start with ourselves. If you preach or teach, you've experienced that terrible feeling that you are not living what you're teaching. Inside your head, you hear the Spirit's conviction: "Hypocrite, how can you tell others to do what you are not doing?"

Healthy church leaders honestly face their own sexuality. Spiritual leaders' first job is to "keep watch over themselves" (Acts 20:28) in order to set an example. A leader sets the pace. When we courageously face our own sexual sin, embrace the Father's gracious forgiveness, and forgive others, we grow in Christ ourselves and are able to lead with humble authenticity as we invite people to follow our example.

Paul told the spiritual leaders of the Ephesian church: "Keep watch over yourselves and all the flock of which the Holy Spirit has made you overseers. Be shepherds of the church of God, which he bought with his own blood" (Acts 20:28). The Holy Spirit gave you spiritual leadership over the people to whom you are ministering, so your calling is to shepherd the blood-bought people of God. This is weighty! This is not *your* class, group, or church. It is God's, bought by Jesus' blood, and for whom the Spirit gave you responsibility for his people.

In all arenas, including the sexual realm, we are to be examples to the flock, to those who are entrusted to us (1 Peter 5:3). The Greek word used in 1 Peter 5:3 for "examples" is *typoi*, which refers to types or patterns, so we serve as models for the people to follow. How can we serve as *typoi* in the sexual arena?

Face the Truth About You

As in other areas of our lives, we start with confession, facing the truth about ourselves. In twelve-step recovery programs, the fourth step is to make a searching and fearless moral inventory of ourselves. Whatever your view of such programs, this advice is consistent with a biblical perspective. King David prayed,

> Search me, God, and know my heart;
> test me and know my anxious thoughts.
> See if there is any offensive way in me,
> and lead me in the way everlasting. (Ps. 139:23–24)

Ask God to know your heart in sexual matters, to test you and know your thoughts in this realm. See if there is any sexually offensive way in you. And ask him to lead you in his ways about sex.

Obviously, this can be a painful process, but a necessary one for divine healing, like opening the wound and cleaning out the infection. As I look back over my sexual history, I regret things I did as a teenager. Even decades later some of my sexual behavior with girlfriends remains among the greatest regrets of my life. It's helpful to me in helping others to face how deeply those actions scarred my person, even though I was a virgin when I married.

Growing up I saw almost no pornography, but when we were on the verge of planting our church, I remember scanning through channels on the TV late at night. In those days people called it Picasso porn because, however the technology worked, bits of the images would come through on a channel that wasn't part of our TV package. The images grabbed my eyes and I looked, and looked again. I'd bounce back to other channels and then go back and glance again. Even now I can recall the experience and feel ashamed of it, despite the fact that I know God has forgiven me.

Your sexual history almost certainly contains sin over which you feel horrible. And, not to make you feel worse, but let's widen the lens to include how we have treated sexual minorities. Phrases like "that's so gay" may have filled your conversation. Thinking back, have you used slurs like "faggot," "homo," and "dyke"? Did you ever laugh at or ignore a gay peer as he or she was ruthlessly teased? What about how you have treated women or men? Have you whistled at them? Lusted after them? Seduced them? To one extent or another objectified them as sex objects? Or perhaps you have judged those who judge others in this arena. None of us are without sin.

And it's crucial to face what's going on with us sexually right now. If you are in any role of spiritual leadership, your responsibility before God as a leader is greater (James 3:1). So, if you are caught in a sexual addiction or immoral relationship, repent and take strong action to kill (mortify) that sin. Jesus called us to severe action when he said to metaphorically pluck out our eye or cut off our hand (Matt. 5:29–30). The point is not that you are sexually perfect in this life, but that you are currently clear with God. Since it's almost impossible to break sexual sin by yourself, it is likely that you will need to get professional help.

To set the example by honoring Christ with our bodies requires facing our own temptations and prejudices. You have likely told others to hold themselves accountable and set up safeguards, but have you done this in your own life? I use Covenant Eyes on my electronic devices that access the Internet. My accountability partners who get the report of everywhere I have been online include my wife, a fellow pastor, an elder, and one of my sons. Believe me, I do not want to let them down! My decades-long friend Jeff Jones, pastor of Chase Oaks Church, and I meet every Monday morning to encourage each other to run the race for Christ, including in the sexual realm. I have cameras in my office and am open with my wife and assistant about my calendar, who I am meeting with and where. Openness and transparency are vital.

Since many pastors speak from a raised platform, springtime is dangerous when we are looking down at female attendees. I've had to confess, in my mind, during a sermon. One Sunday I went a little too far by asking women not to reveal their cleavage. My request revealed my own problem more than a problem with anyone's mode of dress. Really, I want everyone to be comfortable and welcome no matter what they are wearing, so I need to focus on dealing with my own temptation.

Our sexual histories form larger narratives when we include our families. And here we must be even more careful what we share. My sisters struggled with their own sexual issues, including a rape, teen pregnancy, and abuse. My brother is married to his male partner. And if I went beyond my immediate family, the range of sexual issues grows wider. These family experiences have shaped me whether I want them to or not. They impact my spiritual leadership in this arena.

You Know What to Do with It

As a spiritual leader, you know what to do with your sexual sin, but have you done it? Have you repented of your immorality, your abuse of others, your slander, your objectification? Seriously! We give the advice to everyone else, but have we done it ourselves? When you live in sexual shame and guilt, you cripple your spiritual influence for Christ.

Do what you tell others to do: repent and receive God's amazing grace for you. Let me remind you of what you know already. The Father loves you unconditionally, unfailingly. Jesus Christ died for you not because you are a good person or a spiritual leader, but he died for you when you were a sinner and because you were a sinner, including being a sexual sinner.

While I've known God loves me since I was a little boy and sang the song, "Jesus loves me this I know, for the Bible tells me so," it was in 2017 that the Father vividly impressed on me the reality of his unconditional love. After I'd served our church for twenty years, the elders gave me my first sabbatical, just over four months long. It was filled with wonderful times, but the most amazing experience was an encounter with God in which he appeared to me as my Father and I was a five-year-old boy. He held me and assured me that he loved me regardless of my performance, productivity, accomplishments, or lack of them. In my mind, I protested that I sinned and I knew he did not like that. He laughed and hugged me tighter, assuring me not just that I was already forgiven in Christ but that my sin did not diminish his love in the slightest bit, and to think otherwise was simply laughable. I delighted, danced, and reveled in the Father's unconditional love for me. I want you to experience again his love for you, the precious love that you already know is real. When you freshly experience the Father's love for you, you want to shower it on others.

Our personal journeys include not only a long stop to ponder our own sin but also a second stop to remember how others have sinned against us. You may have been the object of sexual slurs or, worse, been abused. Sexual intimidation and all kinds of unwanted sexual behavior can have lasting effects. When the #MeToo movement on social media was everywhere in the fall of 2017, my wife looked at me and said, "You too." At first I had no idea what she was thinking of, until she reminded me of a summer in high school when a girl tried to seduce me, including taking off her shirt. I had not even recognized that I, too, was a victim, although my situation involved no power differential or violence.

Depending on what has been done to you, you may have much harder forgiveness work to do to forgive your abuser, a family member, or even to forgive someone for what they did to your spouse or your child. As hard as this forgiveness work may be, it is crucial to your ministry because bitterness will block the power of the Spirit as you try to help others spiritually. I know this from painful personal experience.

Early in our marriage, problems in our sexual intimacy took us to counseling where we discovered my wife's repressed memories of sexual abuse. When I first found out, I wanted that man to go to hell. I actually had thoughts of killing her abuser for wounding her so deeply. It took me more than a year to begin the process of forgiving him. Decades later there has been much healing. I forgave the perpetrator, who has since passed away. For me to minister freely, I had to face what was done to the one I love the most, and how it impacted us as a couple.

How Vulnerable Should You Be?

When you courageously face your own sexual sin, embrace the Father's gracious forgiveness, and forgive others, you not only grow in Christ but are free to speak and lead with humble authenticity. But as you lead out in this arena, the question of appropriate vulnerability presses hard.

While you want to be transparent and real, how much do you share and with whom? The apostle Paul confessed publicly, "Here is a trustworthy saying that deserves full acceptance: Christ Jesus came into the world to save sinners—of whom I am the worst. But for that very reason I was shown mercy so that in me, the worst of sinners, Christ Jesus might display his immense patience as an example for those who would believe in him and receive eternal life" (1 Tim. 1:15–16). His audience was as broad as it could be, but his specifics were quite vague. While he did not minimize his sin, he did not describe it in lurid detail. As you prayerfully think through what to share, consider the following:

- *Your audience:* Will it be the entire church on a Sunday morning, a small leadership team, a single-gender retreat, or a counseling situation? What's their maturity level and background?
- *Distance in time:* How long ago did the experience you might share happen? General wisdom is not to share something very recent—"Last night . . ." You want to have dealt with the matter with God before you share it.
- *Level of detail:* There is no need to be salacious, which can tempt others and put the focus on your sin rather than on Christ's grace.
- *Who else is in this story?* Do you have permission(s)?
- *Reason for sharing:* What are your motives? What do you gain? It's good to show humility and authenticity, to model transparency and confession. But it's not good to scandalize, get attention, shock people, or try to soothe your conscience at the expense of another. The focus should ultimately be drawn to the redemptive power of Christ and not to you.

People cannot follow your model if you do not share your life, so even in this sensitive area, it is important to be transparent when you share appropriately. In the right settings, your level of vulnerability will set the pace for everyone else.

When we are transparent and authentic, we invite others into the open where they, too, can encounter God's amazing grace that heals and restores, his unconditional love that embraces us unfailingly. Encourage others to follow your example in facing their own sexual history and dealing with present temptations. Encourage them to confess their sin, repent, and receive God's total forgiveness that washes them clean. As you forgive others who have sexually sinned against you, you can lead people to forgive as well. As you guard yourself in the present, you model practical steps they can take for their own sexual purity. As you seek God's restoration and receive God's grace, you give hope to others in their journeys.

As a spiritual leader, your first job is to watch over your own life, to set the example as a Christ-follower. The most important gift you can give your church is to be transformed by the Spirit yourself so that you radiate the Father's loyal love to the people God has entrusted to you.

Discussion Questions

1. Why is it important for spiritual leaders to set an example in the area of sexuality for the people in your church?
2. What sexual sins do you need to confess to God? Then, to the extent appropriate in your setting, what sins could you confess to one another?
3. What practical actions have you taken, or could you take, to guard yourself against sexual sin?
4. What have you done, or do you need to do, to forgive those who have sinned against you sexually?
5. Given your leadership role in your church or ministry, how wise do you believe it would be to share your own sexual past and to what extent? How would different contexts affect your answer?

CHAPTER 2

BETTER THAN SEX

Providing Theological Leadership

W hat does the Bible say about sexuality?" Those who look to us for spiritual leadership want to know. They are rightly looking to us to make sense of the sexual discourse in today's world and to sort out the conflicting voices they hear from all sides.

After setting an example, the second major way we lead is through our teaching. Church leaders need to provide clear theological leadership, but most of us—whether we realize it or not—have not formed a robust biblical theology of sexuality.

Our society distorts sexuality into monetary transactions, friends with benefits, and the erotic fantasies of *Fifty Shades of Grey*. Our culture has deified desire and exalted the right to choose as inviolable. We believe people should have the right to do what they want to do— right or wrong. Tragically, we also believe that people will be happy if they fulfill their desires—sexual or otherwise—and that to restrict those desires is wrong and harmful. Many today are convinced that if it is consensual, it is fine, no matter what it is, especially if it is not illegal.[1]

While most Christians aim to live pure lives, in an increasingly sexualized culture, navigating this world proves difficult. Moms and dads want to protect their children from sexual corruption, but how do we move beyond moralizing? Sometimes our theology boils down to something as simplistic as this: don't have sex before you are married and then as soon as you get married, enjoy it to the fullest. We buy our teens promise rings, and then when they get engaged, we give them Christian sex manuals. Beyond these noble efforts, could there be a bigger, more robust, biblical story of sexuality that we have missed?

My hope is to offer at least a basic framework that you can use to cast a grander vision of sexuality. A few evangelical theologians have developed theologies of sexuality that help us think about it more holistically. In Todd Wilson's recent *Mere Sexuality*, he said, "We've lost sight of a positive Christian vision for why God made us as sexual beings in the first place. We've lost our grip on the deep logic that connects our created nature as male and female with how we ought to live relationally and sexually with one another."[2] The implications of this more holistic theology of sexuality are huge for how we minister to singles, marrieds, and LGBT+ people, whether single or married, and especially for the picture we give our teenagers.

What Is the Role of Sex?

Humans are sexual beings. God created sex as a good gift, but it is far from the most important feature of our lives. It is not essential to life. Obviously, sex is essential for humanity to continue, but that does not mean that sexual activity is essential for every individual person to live a good life before God. If you are married, before you get too tense, let me assure you that in marriage sex is important. A husband and wife should care for each other sexually. Sex is not essential, however, for a great marriage.

By contrasting biblical theology with current Christian cultural reality, we can see that Christian leaders have generally overplayed sex. We have often made sexual intimacy a bigger deal than it really is. Ironically, we have bought into cultural distortions, essentially making sex an idol, treating it as if it will bring us true happiness. By presenting a brief biblical theology of sexuality, I hope to show that *sex is a good gift, but it is not essential for a good life.*

One way of thinking through a topic biblically is to look at the progress of God's work from beginning to end, through four major phases: creation, fall, redemption, and new creation.[3] A closer look at the biblical progress of revelation has given me new insights into sexuality's place in our lives.[4] Seeing through this powerful lens opens important windows of understanding that have been obscured in many Christians' thinking on this topic. We will discover that the role of sexuality shifts over time.

Creation

In creation, God made sex, and he made it to be good. When he looked at *all* he made, God said, "It is good." In contrast, God said it is not good for the man to be alone, so he made a helper suitable for him (Gen. 2:18).[5] When Adam saw Eve, he became the first poet when he said:

> This is now bone of my bones
> and flesh of my flesh;
> she shall be called "woman,"
> for she was taken out of man. (Gen. 2:23)

The Bible then affirms: "That is why a man leaves his father and mother and is united to his wife, and they become one flesh. Adam and his wife were both naked, and they felt no shame" (Gen. 2:24–25).

God told the original couple to be fruitful and multiply, implying in this first command that they should engage in a sexual relationship. God designed us as sexual beings in the complementary genders of male and female. This truth is fundamental. Human sexuality manifests itself in maleness and femaleness, the mystery of our biological uniqueness, from chromosomes to hormones to anatomy.[6] Today, that simple binary is being challenged by some who argue that sexuality itself is socially constructed or at minimum that there is a continuum between maleness and femaleness. On transgender issues, I recommend the balanced treatment by Mark Yarhouse in *Understanding Gender Dysphoria*[7] and the clarifying pastoral paper by Preston Sprinkle, "A Biblical Conversation About Transgender Identities."[8] For now let's simply note that sexuality and gender are not the same.

In creation God designed sexual intercourse as a physical, intimate act so that in our sexual union, we are able to reproduce offspring according to our kind.[9] Our complementary external anatomy and internal biology enable us to be fruitful and multiply. God created Eve as a "helper suitable" for Adam so that they could fill the earth with their offspring (Gen. 2:18). The word *suitable* (*kĕnegdô*, lit., "like what is in front of him") indicates a *correspondence* between the man and the woman,[10] which can imply both similarity and difference.[11]

Gender itself, however, can be a confusing concept. While some people use gender and sex as synonymns, as Sprinkle points out, "many people typically use gender to describe one (or all) of the following: (1) Your own internal sense of self, (2) how you express yourself (clothing, mannerisms, interests, etc.), or (3) cultural expectations for what it means to be a man or a woman."[12] For instance, according to Ryan Anderson, "Sex is a bodily, biological reality, and gender is how we give social expression to that reality."[13]

While the creation account clearly teaches that there are two, and only two, biological sexes, male and female, we must be careful about going beyond that to suggest that the Bible prescribes certain cultural roles or personalities as male or female. Many gender roles are culturally specific and vary widely across the spectrum of historical human cultures.

In my own marriage, my wife, Tamara, and I do not fit typical twenty-first-century American patterns. I like to talk more than she does and am more romantic. She is better at fixing things around the house than I am, and she does not value gooey love notes, but I do. There is nothing wrong with men being good at needlework and arranging beautiful flowers, and nothing wrong with tomboys who are jocks. Many of our assumptions about what it means to be feminine or masculine are in fact culturally constructed. Often our evangelical subculture tries to make gender norms prescriptive, leaving those who don't fit them feeling doubt and shame about their own masculinity and femininity. This tendency is just one of the many ways the goodness of our sex and sexuality has been distorted from God's design. The God-created goodness of male and female sexuality was marred when humanity sinned against our Creator.

Fall

In the fall, sexuality was distorted, along with every other area of our lives. When Adam and Eve disobeyed God, they brought death into the world. Our desires were twisted in the fall, so we are inclined to do what's wrong. While this does not mean every sexual act is distorted, the pervasiveness of distortion is obvious both from our own lives and from seeing what goes on in the world. As church leaders, we hear far more than we want to hear.

Sexual sin is not new. Just consider the opening chapters of Genesis. Not long after Adam and Eve, God flooded the earth because of sexual immorality and violence (Gen. 6). Then Noah's son committed an immoral act with his father (Gen. 9). Abraham had sex with Hagar (Gen. 16). His nephew Lot got into a mess in Sodom that included attempts of same-sex rape and the offer of his daughters to be raped (Gen. 19). Right after they escaped, Lot's daughters got dad drunk and had sex with him. Since the fall, sex has been sadly distorted.

Like Adam and Eve, many people assume they know better than God what is good for them. We don't want boundaries or limitations on what we can do. Like Adam and Eve, we hide and we blame. We need a Redeemer. In redemption, the role of sexuality shifts. This new insight for me, that the role of sexuality might be different through the progress of revelation, has broadened my perspective on sexuality.

Redemption

In redemption, singleness is honored in a way that it previously was not. I do not mean that marriage is dishonored or unimportant in the New Testament, but that singleness is elevated in a way it was not in the Old Testament. Marriage is no longer considered essential for human flourishing. Ever since the promise of the seed that would crush the serpent (Gen. 3:15), the Old Testament is filled with stories of that seed, the line from which the Messiah, the ultimate seed, would come (Gal. 3).

After the flood dissipated in Genesis 9, God repeated to Noah the creation command to multiply. Main characters such as Sarah (Abraham's wife) had to overcome infertility to bear the seed. A wife had to be found for Isaac. Once we enter the New Testament, after the nativity stories of John the Baptist and Jesus, we find no more such stories of finding a wife, overcoming infertility, or bearing children.

Jesus' Life—the Gospels

Jesus' example is striking. He was single. He did not have sexual intercourse. And yet, I think you will agree that Jesus lived a fulfilled human life. Jesus had the testosterone of a male. He had male sexuality, but he never had sex. Nevertheless he lived the best life. Focused on his Father's will, he lived a life full of peace, joy, purpose, and satisfaction. Jesus modeled the goodness of a single life.

Christ's Church: Acts and the Epistles

When the Father and the Son sent the Holy Spirit at Pentecost (Acts 2), God's people moved from a single ethnic tribe (Israel) to a multinational new humanity (the church, Eph. 2–3). In the New Testament, the command to be fruitful and multiply (Gen. 1:28) shifted the focus from biological reproduction to spiritual reproduction in Jesus' Great Commission (Matt. 28:18–20). We are to multiply and fill the earth with disciples of Jesus. Rather than build a holy nation as a light to the other nations, we are to build Christ's church as a light to the world.

Between the resurrection and the return of Christ, the focus shifts from the family to the church. You can find only a few passages in the New Testament on marriage or parenting but many on relationships in the church body. When Jesus' family came to see him, he looked to his disciples and addressed them as his family: "'Who is my mother, and who are my brothers?' Pointing to his disciples, he said, 'Here are my mother and my brothers. For whoever does the will of my Father in heaven is my brother and sister and mother'" (Matt. 12:48–50).

When describing the greatest love, Jesus did not point to marriage but to the love of a person who would lay down his life for his *friend* (John 15:13). Often New Testament writers used *brother* and *sister* to describe fellow believers. The church is the family of God in which members are related as blood brothers and sisters in the blood of Jesus Christ in whom we all share eternal life.

A search of the New Testament yields very few examples of married couples commended for their great service to God. Peter had a mother-in-law, so he was married. Ananias and Sapphira are not a great example, but we do have passing positive references to Priscilla and Aquila. In contrast, many early leaders were single (or no spouse is mentioned), including the great apostle Paul and, of course, Jesus himself.[14]

In 1 Corinthians 7, the longest biblical passage on marriage and singleness, Paul commends singleness as better than marriage. Many,

including me previously, have misread Paul here as if he were affirming marriage and offering singleness only to those rare, few, unusual
people with the lifelong "gift" of celibacy. While Paul does mention a
gift, his main point is that in this time before Christ returns, singleness offers a better life for many, even most, people.[15]

These biblical realities help us see that while sex is a good gift, it
is not essential for a good life. The final phase in God's work leads
to another challenging thought as we look at sexuality in the new
creation.

New Creation

In the new creation, sex will be surpassed. If you are shocked and
dismayed by this statement, you may need to review the value you
place on sex. I've had to myself. I've come to see that I had given sex
too high a priority in comparison with its biblical place in our lives.
Jesus said, "At the resurrection people will neither marry nor be given
in marriage; they will be like the angels in heaven" (Matt. 22:30).

At this point you may not be sure you want this kind of afterlife!
Seriously, we have a distorted view of sexuality and romance. We have
exalted it. We have made it an idol.[16] We know being with God will be
the greatest experience—or do we really believe that? Better than sex?
Ultimate intimacy with the triune God will surpass sexual intimacy.
Sexual union points forward to the greater union we will experience
with God. So life without sexual intimacy is not a deficient life. Life
without Jesus is a deficient life.[17]

While sex can give intense pleasure, sexual union on earth is
always partial and never ultimate. It is a false god that cannot deliver
on its promise of ultimate fulfillment. It points to something more,
something better. Pastor Ed Shaw put it bluntly: "God has put sex on
this planet to make us want to go to heaven."[18] As a celibate pastor,
he draws the powerful implication: "I know there are many today
who think that it is a great tragedy to die a virgin. But I hope I will.

Because I know that I will not have lost out on anything too significant. Because the Bible teaches me that I will have missed only the brief foretaste that sex is meant to be of the eternal reality of the perfect union between Christ and his church that I will one day experience forever (Rev. 21:1–5)."[19]

Through our union with Christ by the Spirit, we are entering into fellowship with the Trinity. Dennis Hollinger, the author of *The Meaning of Sex*, wrote, "Sex pales in comparison to the heavenly marriage in which we will be fully one with the God who created and redeemed us in Christ."[20] Sex is a good gift, but it is not a god. It is a blessing, but not a necessity. Sex is a good gift, but not essential for a good life. So, what is the purpose of sex? Why have sex?

Discussion Questions

1. Describe our culture's general view of sex. What do most secular people tend to believe about sex?
2. What are most Christians' views of sex? What is taught in our churches about sexuality?
3. In your own words, how does the Bible depict sex in the creation? The fall?
4. In a biblical theology of sex, what changes in redemption?
5. What is the role of sex in the new creation?
6. In your experience, how does this biblical theology of sex compare and contrast with typical Christian thinking?
7. How has the brief survey on the progression of biblical theology about sex challenged your thinking?

CHAPTER 3

MORE THAN PLEASURE

Leading Married Couples and Singles

Much recent evangelical teaching on sex in marriage has focused on how to have pleasure and not be prudish about it. And while that's been a good corrective, we have lost a fuller theology of the purposes of sex in marriage developed early in the history of the church. And many of us have a less than fully biblical view of single sexuality. Singleness is not a lesser life. And sex is not the heart of marriage, but it is important.

When the purpose of sex is reduced to pleasure, it might make sense to enjoy that pleasure in various kinds of relationships, but a more full-orbed understanding of sex reveals why it's reserved for marriage. You can lead the people in your church theologically by teaching them about the purposes of sex in marriage. With time this teaching helps build a solid foundation on which they can think through sexually confusing issues arising in their lives and families, including choices about living together unmarried and marriage between two people of the same gender.

Broadly speaking, Christians in older traditions have recognized four biblical purposes for sex in marriage. Sex celebrates the couple's union, creates children, brings joy, and displays God's exclusive love. If each partner is physically capable, the Bible says they should bless each other sexually (1 Cor. 7:1–7). If physical limitations prevent sex, a married couple can have a great marriage without sexual intercourse. However, our sexuality in marriage is rarely free of sin of any kind. We can use sex to punish or reward, manipulate, or coerce and dominate our partners. Whenever it is focused more on my needs and desires than my spouse's, sex in marriage becomes a selfish act. Most sex in marriage is tinged with selfishness, focused more on my pleasure than my spouse's or on controlling my spouse. What might happen if we call couples to live out 1 Corinthians 13 love in the bedroom? Realizing the sin involved in our sexual activity, even in a heterosexual marriage relationship, helps level the playing field for how we view sexual sin outside of marriage.

Given that sex is a gift from God, distorted in the fall, let's explore God's purposes of sex in marriage. Sex offers much more than merely bodily pleasure. Sex is something we enter into with our whole beings and that connects to cosmic, divine realities.

Biblical Purposes of Sex

Affirms Your Oneness, Celebrating Your Union

Married couples can celebrate their union through sex to affirm their oneness. In Matthew 19 Jesus quotes Genesis 2, which confirms that a husband and a wife are united as one flesh.[1] This purpose has been called the "unitive purpose," to express and celebrate being united as one. Sexual intercourse reaffirms and symbolizes the one-flesh union of a husband and wife.

Whether married or not, something changes in a relationship when a couple has sex (1 Cor. 6:15–16). It unites a couple in a unique way. This act consummates a marriage in a profound way that both symbolizes and manifests a couple's union as persons. This union connects not just their bodies but their souls—all that they are.

We see this reality in reverse in our intuitive sense that to have sex with someone other than our spouses is to be unfaithful, to cheat. It breaks something fundamental. Sexual intercourse confirms our marital vows and reinforces our commitment to be exclusively one for life. It is not merely an arbitrary rule to assert that sex is reserved exclusively for marriage; there is a strong spiritual basis.

Procreation, Celebrating Children

This core unitive purpose is matched by the purpose of procreation, to have children. Only God is the ultimate giver of life, but he invites us to be cocreators with him. We get the privilege of giving life to a child in the miracle of conception and birth, to cocreate one in our image and in his image. God blessed Adam and Eve with the privilege and responsibility of being fruitful and multiplying in order to fill the earth. The Bible teaches that children are a blessing (Ps. 127:3). When we bring children into the world, we share in God's creative, life-giving work.

Procreation forms a central facet of sexuality and thus of marriage itself. One implication of this purpose is that marriage should be between a male and a female. This does not mean that every couple must have children or that birth control is wrong, but rather that children are a blessing.[2] As a result of the fall, some couples are grieved by infertility. Thankfully many can enjoy the blessing of fostering or adopting children. God desires "godly offspring" (Mal. 2:15), which is one reason we are to be sexually faithful to our spouses, so we can provide an atmosphere most conducive to raising "godly offspring." Marital unfaithfulness damages children. Through our marital sexual intercourse, most of us are given the lofty privileges of both celebrating our union and potentially cocreating children, so it's unfortunate that our culture has adopted only one biblical purpose of sex: experiencing bodily pleasure.

Pleasure, Celebrating Joy

God is full of joy. He created Eden as a beautiful place to enjoy and made our bodies to find pleasure in sex (Prov. 5:18–19).

Elaborating on Proverbs, the Song of Solomon celebrates the pleasure of sex in marriage. And the God-intended pleasure in sex is more than physical since we are holistic beings. As Richard Foster put it in a provocative quote: "The problem with [our media] . . . and the pornographic literature of our day is not that they emphasize sexuality too much but that they do not emphasize it enough. They totally eliminate relationship and restrain sexuality to the narrow confines of the genital. They have made sex trivial."[3] Because we are whole beings, sex offers richer pleasures than merely bodily pleasures. We can find intense joy in our oneness, our intimacy, the years of togetherness, our transparency and vulnerability, and our sacrifices for each other. And to these three purposes for sex, we add one more.

God's Exclusive Loyalty, Celebrating His Love

The loyal exclusivity of sex between a husband and wife manifests God's loyal, exclusive love. This is why adultery is so terrible. It mars the picture of God that marriage is designed to show. Marriage pictures God's relationship to Israel and Christ's relationship with the church as his bride. As God is both three persons and yet one, so a couple is both two people and yet one flesh. Paul compared marriage to Christ and the church when he wrote: " 'For this reason a man will leave his father and mother and be united to his wife, and the two will become one flesh.' This is a profound mystery—but I am talking about Christ and the church" (Eph. 5:31–32). In marriage we mirror Christ and the church. Our exclusive sexual relationship shows the loyal devotion of God to his people.

In summary, sex is not the heart of marriage, but it is important. Sex affirms our oneness, creates children, brings joy, and displays

God's exclusive love. Sex outside of marriage between a man and woman cannot fulfill all these purposes.

Against the backdrop of this robust vision of sex in marriage, it's easier to see why sexual sin is so devastating and terrible. As all those who are married know, being married does not remove sexual temptation, nor does it always (or automatically) yield the passion and satisfaction portrayed in Song of Songs. There are many forms of sexual sin in a marriage. Being open about sexual sin in marriage and admonishing couples in our congregations is crucial, and it's a place where LGBT+ people have rightly challenged evangelicals with hypocrisy and double standards. It's tragically common to hear the sadly familiar story: "My dad was a deacon and was a womanizer, but they let him stay in church leadership. But when they found out I was gay, I got kicked out." To many it looks like the church winks at heterosexual sin and in contrast takes extreme measures at even the hint of same-sex romantic tendencies.

While there are other forms of sexual sin in marriage, the classic and all-too-common marital sin is adultery. Adultery is forbidden in the Ten Commandments: "You shall not commit adultery" (Ex. 20:14). For a vivid picture of adultery's horror, review Proverbs 6. Adultery betrays the one to whom you vowed your lifelong, faithful love and violates all the purposes of sex. It wrecks your unity. It can result in children outside of marriage. It reduces pleasure to the fleshly and carnal. And adultery mars the picture of Christ and the church because marriage is to display the loyal, exclusive love of God.

But just because you are married and don't commit adultery, it does not mean your marital sex is sinless. As horrible as adultery is, an equally destructive but less talked about marital sexual sin is abuse. From the fall forward, men have dominated women to gratify their sexual desires, and women have manipulated men with sex, and at times vice versa. Sadly, couples use sex as a weapon to punish the other person by withholding it or to get their way by giving it as a reward or enticement. "If you want to get some tonight, you'd better . . ." or "you'd better not . . ."

Paul gave clear instructions to married couples. When you are married, your body is not your own (1 Cor. 7:3–5). As in other areas, in the sexual realm you should love your spouse sacrificially focused more on blessing him or her than on pleasing yourself. Husbands, listen to the following in relation to your sexual relationship with your wife: "Husbands, in the same way be considerate as you live with your wives, and treat them with respect as the weaker[4] partner and as heirs with you of the gracious gift of life, so that nothing will hinder your prayers" (1 Peter 3:7).

Men are to be sensitive to our wives, considerate of them sexually. Husband, far from objectifying your wife as a sex object, you are to respect her. You are never to force yourself on her. It is possible to rape your own wife. Short of that, you abuse her when you use your physical strength or relational power to make sexual demands against her will. When you don't treat your wife with respect sexually, you can hinder your prayers.

The word *deprive* carries the idea of robbing. When a spouse withholds sex from a husband or wife, the spouse is robbing the other. This does not mean you cannot say no. You can have a headache, but if either husband or wife has a "headache" for an extended period of time, it could be a problem. Both husbands and wives are to yield their bodies to each other. When young wives complain about stress and irritation in their marriages, my wife asks them when they last were intimate. Often, it's been a long time. She exhorts them to push past all the excuses and bless their husbands in this way. "Yes," she says, "your husband will appreciate it even if you are not fully engaged." Many times, wives have been pleasantly surprised at the result, because sexual intimacy impacts much more than merely the physical. And yet, while husbands and wives should give their bodies to each other sexually, if that is not possible physically or emotionally, a couple can have a great marriage without sex. For my wife and me, even though scars from her past prevent us from engaging in a Song of Solomon–like passionate sexual relationship, our love and joy are rich and deep.

I wonder how much, if any, of our marital sex is truly pure, guided by 1 Corinthians 13 kind of love. If you are or were married, consider how much of your sex with your spouse has been patient, kind, without envy of others, included no boasting or dishonoring, was not self-seeking, was not easily angered, did not mention past wrongs, was protective, trusting, hopeful, and enduring. For many couples it's rare. Leading people to think about how little sexual activity in their marriage is truly Spirit-led and Christlike helps us level the ground for all of us. It removes the false notion that if I am heterosexual and married and I don't commit adultery or watch porn, I'm good.

Both singles and married people sin with lust and with various perversions. Lust, whether tied to pornography or romantic fantasy, is mental sin. Lust is more than temptation. Jesus was tempted, but he never lusted. Temptation is the attraction to sin. Lust is the mental engagement in sin. Temptation is the thought that a person is attractive. Lust is undressing that person in your mind or imagining sexual activity with them. Lust often encompasses coveting. We crave what is not ours (Matt. 5:28). What Jesus was describing is not simply being attracted to someone, but it is allowing that attraction to swell into an illicit desire to take or possess them.

Pornography is perhaps the most flagrant and obvious example of the kind of "looking to desire" that Jesus talked about. The viewer is the consumer, and the bodies viewed on a screen or printed page are products, and you are not seeing them as real human beings created in the image of God. Most adult men have watched pornography, as well as have many women. As Lisa Scheffler wrote, "Flip through a 'fashion' or 'men's' magazine and notice the way that the bodies of women (and increasingly men) are portrayed. Sometimes the models are faceless with only the most sexually stimulating parts of the body shown. This visual treatment emphasizes a person's sexuality over any other part, treating them as just a soulless collection of body parts. They are no longer a person, but a commodity to be desired and possessed."[5]

The Bible says, "Rather, clothe yourselves with the Lord Jesus Christ, and do not think about how to gratify the desires of the flesh" (Rom. 13:14). Pornography drives you to think about how to gratify distorted, sinful desires, so watching pornography is sin, and so is indulging in romantic fantasy about someone other than your spouse, no matter what kind of sexual fantasy that might be. The unrealistic, selfish, or distorted views of sex that are created by porn and erotica can ruin real intimacy in a marriage.

In short, marital sex celebrates our union, creates children, brings pleasure, and displays God's exclusive, loyal love. That's fine for married couples, but what about singles? Paul seems to say singleness is better than being married. Is it better?

Single Sexuality

"We've been praying for a husband for you since we first found out your mom was pregnant with you." Words said with a huge smile and deep love by many devoted Christian parents, and yet they betray an unbiblical view of marriage and singleness. What kind of prayers should we lead parents to pray for their children's relational futures?

As spiritual leaders, many of us in American churches have contributed to a truncated, distorted picture of singleness that has hurt millions of people and damaged the spread of the gospel. Our church bodies are weaker because often we have not honored those members who are single, but instead, we have sadly treated them as defective or, at best, second class.

Of course, this mind-set is usually not overt, but it comes through in casual questions in the lobby, such as, Are you dating anyone? It gets communicated in our programming, from singles ministries for "those people" who are not part of the mainstream of the church to all the seminars on building healthy marriages. Although singles make up roughly half the adults in America, an analysis of sermon content would likely reveal many more illustrations about married couples than singles.

In our student ministries, the purity movement creates campaigns that build up the wedding night to be a big deal. They also have the unintended consequence of giving no guidance to those who are single for a season or a lifetime. What message are we sending our teens about marriage and singleness? How can the church help singles steward their sexuality?

We have so romanticized and idolized sex that we have been duped into thinking it is essential for a good life. It is not. As we saw, in an overall biblical theology, sex is a good gift, but it is not essential for a good life. This means that singleness is not the great disaster that we have inadvertently made it out to be. It is not a crucial loss to give up having sex. And yet, by and large, American Christians have overblown the importance of sexuality, which has caused us to mislead our children, denigrate our singles, and make sex an idol. And it has eroded a biblical foundation on which to encourage LGBT+ people to flourish. Preston Sprinkle wrote, "Until the church can develop a better theology of singleness, it won't know what to do with celibate gay people in their midst. And this is a real crisis."[6]

Rethinking Our Theology

I invite us to rethink a biblical theology of singleness and its practical implications for our churches.[7] As a Protestant, I've made a significant shift in my thinking on singleness.[8] While you may have seen this truth long ago, it has been a new insight for me that has stretched my own thinking. My previous perspective, and much recent Christian teaching, has been that a few rare people have the unusual gift of lifelong singleness or celibacy, but most people should get married. Marriage is preferred over singleness. I have now come to a different conclusion: marriage and singleness are equally honorable, both good choices for how to live before God. Neither should be elevated above the other.

If we are honest, although we might not say it aloud, many of us suspect that adult singles are socially stunted since they apparently cannot find someone to marry. As parents, we are often disappointed if our children do not marry. Most people in our churches dream that their children will get married. Classically, moms envision the wedding festivities, and dads worry over how to pay for them. Parents might even have a savings account for their daughter's future wedding. As they picture her future, they eagerly look forward to grandchildren! Very few Christian parents have a vision of their adult son or daughter being single, except as an interim stage, a brief period to end as soon as possible. As Sprinkle puts it, Christians see singleness as "a period of life that you have to get through like standing in line for a ride at Disneyland. No one wants to be there, but we must grin and bear it so we can jump on a rocket and swirl around the Matterhorn."9

I think we have it wrong and are tragically leading our congregations off track. Let me briefly review biblical truths that have shifted my thinking. First, Jesus was single. He never married. He never had sex, and he lived a great life. He is the only perfect human being. On the face of it, single people have more in common with Jesus than do married people in the sense of being single. Singles model Jesus by following our single Savior.

Model Jesus

Jesus was fully human, so he was not asexual. He was fully male in every sense of the word, including hormones and all the body parts.

We must come to grips with this fundamental fact. Jesus was single, and he was not socially stunted. He could easily have found a woman to marry him, or God could have sent him a new "Eve." Todd Wilson does a great job helping us face the reality of Jesus' sexuality in his wonderful chapter on the topic in his *Mere Sexuality*.[10] Most of us can identify with Debra Hirsch when she wrote, "We have inadvertently cultivated a sexless Jesus."[11] Jesus' sexuality makes us uncomfortable. And on top of that, few of us have lingered over the reality of Jesus' singleness and, in particular, the goodness of his singleness. Todd Wilson wrote:

> The Son of God, though biologically sexed, lived a sex-free, fully contented life. Not an easy, pain-free existence, but a whole and deeply and richly human life. This is a remarkable fact—one that confronts all of us, whether we're same-sex-attracted or straight, married or single. It also confronts our secular culture and the evangelical church culture as well—I suspect in some uncomfortable ways. Frankly, as a happily married heterosexual, I find it's easy to forget (and tempting to resist the idea) that I don't need sex to be satisfied. Jesus didn't, and yet he was supremely satisfied in God. . . . While sexuality (our being biologically sexed as male and female) is central to what it means to be human, sexual activity is not. If we want to be fully human, we have to embrace our sexed bodies. But we don't have to engage in sexual activity to be fully human. The life of the Son of God makes that perfectly clear.[12]

I like to think we all agree that Jesus lived a good life, a fulfilled life, one that we are all to follow, and he was single. Maybe singles can have a great life without sexual activity!

Being an adult single is sometimes for a season of time, for those who delay marriage, or for after divorce or the death of a spouse. Other people spend their entire lives as single people as Jesus did. Not only did Jesus live single, but he affirmed singleness as good: "There are those who choose to live like eunuchs for the sake of the kingdom of heaven. The one who can accept this should accept it" (Matt. 19:12). Singleness can be a great choice for the sake of the kingdom.

Many single people, however, struggle with loneliness and long for a partner to share life with. This desire for companionship is not wrong since it reflects God's own observation that it is not good for "man to be alone" (Gen. 2:18). One of our elders unexpectedly lost his wife of many years. An infection overcame her body, and she died less than thirty-six hours after arriving at the hospital. We walked together closely through his grief, and he has shared his inner thoughts. As one of the godliest people I know, he discovered satisfaction in God alone, and yet after some time passed, he once again desired to experience the companionship of a wife. That desire stopped short of desperation, however, and readily submitted itself to the wiser will of God, who is the strength of his heart (Ps. 73:25–26). His heart is for the mission of Christ over a marriage. Sometime later God provided him with a wonderful new wife who had also lost her husband and who also is content in Christ. One of the reasons their new marriage is full of joy is that they are both commited to Christ above each other.

Could it be that many in our culture, including Christians, have glorified marriage over the mission of God? It is not surprising that for some singles the goal of finding a spouse is more important than connecting with Jesus or advancing the gospel and making disciples. This obsession with marriage (or sex) also reflects a poor theology of where we are headed. In theological terms, it presents a distorted eschatology. Biblically, not only does singleness model Jesus, but it also fits our destiny to live today as we will live in eternity one day.

Destiny

As we observed, Jesus taught there will not be sex in eternity (Matt. 22:30). Sex will be surpassed by our ultimate union with the triune God when we fully participate in the divine nature (2 Peter 1:4). As we look ahead we do not anticipate a sex-filled eternity with many virgins, nor do we expect to fill planets with children. Rather, we eagerly expect that we will be fully united with Christ in the physical presence of almighty God, utterly satisfied in him.

Between the ascension and the return of Jesus Christ, all believers live in the already-not-yet tension—the tension that Jesus has already won the victory over evil, and yet he has not fully eradicated evil from our world. The King has already come and initiated his kingdom through his church, but he has not yet established his physical kingdom rule on earth. Already we are redeemed, adopted by the Father, united in Christ, filled with the Holy Spirit, and living as citizens of heaven. But we do not yet possess our new bodies, and we still struggle with indwelling sin.

More and more, our aim should be to set our minds on things above, living today as exiles in the world in light of our current citizenship in heaven. Today singles are in a better position to be able to live in our common destiny by focusing on their union with Christ and anticipating their full fellowship in the life of the Trinity. Living in light of our eternal destiny gives fire to our mission today, to which singles can give their undistracted devotion.

Mission

Paul wrote to the unmarried that it is good for them to stay unmarried as he did (1 Cor. 7). This would allow them to offer undistracted devotion to God. Those who marry would face many troubles, and Paul wanted to spare them. While Paul referred to being gifted as single, he did not restrict singleness to only those with a special gift. Many have misread the text on this point, as I have.

Rather, Paul commended singleness as the better choice for many people, not just a few rare, gifted people. He addressed unmarried men and women without reference to any special gifting. Paul wrote:

I would like you to be free from concern. An unmarried man is concerned about the Lord's affairs—how he can please the Lord. But a married man is concerned about the affairs of this world—how he can please his wife—and his interests are divided. . . . I am saying this for your own good, not to restrict you, but that you may live in a right way in undivided devotion to the Lord. (1 Cor. 7:32–35)

Paul's statement does not sound like most contemporary Christian teachings that overexalt marriage as the highest human ideal. I'm not saying that marriage is undesirable—it is a very good thing. But singleness is also great when you live in obedience to God.

Ed Shaw summarized Paul's point by observing that "being single makes the Christian life easier."[13] We need to share healthy models with singles. Shaw shared a few:

Many of the most significant and inspiring steps forward in world evangelization were made by single Christians. . . . David Brainerd's ministry to Native Americans would be one famous example; Gladys Aylward's work in China would be another.[14] . . . Many of us have also benefited from contemporary examples of the gospel power of celibacy: the single woman who devotedly ran the Sunday school through which we first met Jesus, the books of that bachelor who could write so much because he had no wife or kids, the prayers of that maiden aunt who was, as a result of her singleness, able to devote so much time to praying for your conversion and those of many others.[15]

In fact, there has been a huge shift in the focus of God's plan with the coming of Jesus Christ. From the Old Testament to the New Testament, we see the shift from the physical tribe of Israel to the spiritual body of Christ. The focus is more on baptism into Christ than on marriage to a spouse.

Christ does have a bride, a new Eve. It is the church. The church replaces the tribe as the fundamental community. God's family is no longer tied to genealogical lineage but to salvation in Jesus Christ entered by spiritual rebirth. Our primary allegiance is to Jesus over our loyalty to our family. Singles often get this truth more readily and deeply than married people.

Finally, let me share one more biblical truth and benefit of singleness.

God's Oneness and Inclusive Love

Our God is singular in deity. We worship one God, alone and incomparable in his Godness. There is no other (Deut. 6:4). While married people show the loyal, exclusive love of God, single people display the open, inclusive love of God. Singles are not restricted to an exclusive intimate relationship with only one person, so they are free to form multiple close friendships over time.[16] The Bible says: "For God so loved the world that he gave his one and only Son, that whoever believes in him shall not perish but have eternal life" (John 3:16).

Singles can more easily show this universal love of God that offers eternal life to *all* people who believe in Jesus. According to theologian Stanley Grenz in his book *Sexual Ethics*, singleness expresses "the divine reality of the One who loves, namely the universal, non-exclusive, and expanding nature of divine love."[17] Remember, when Jesus described the greatest love, he did not point to a married couple, but to friends showing sacrificial love: "Greater love has no one than this: to lay down one's life for one's friends" (John 15:13).

Further, single people often better appreciate the church as the body of Christ, a community of love in which God dwells by his Spirit. With the coming of the Spirit, the church is the central social unit, the true family, in which we can build the closest relationships. We have so far to go, especially in America, to understand what it means to truly form a biblical community. Singles can help us grow in this area. While married couples can also engage deeply in building loving churches, we need single men and women of profound spiritual depth who will represent Jesus to a dying world and show us how to love one another in true biblical community.

Although marriage is a major biblical theme expressing the big story of God's reunion with his people, our God incarnated himself as a single man. The ultimate union to which marriage points is the believer's union with Christ, the groom with his bride, the church. At that point there will be no more human marriage, since it will have been eclipsed by the greater marriage of God with us, his people.

Bottom line: today marriage and singleness are equally honorable, good choices for how to live before God. Neither should be elevated above the other. In the history of the church, at times singleness was exalted so much that the priest had to be single. Today, in many Protestant churches, we have swung the pendulum the other way so churches only want to hire a married pastor. But the truth is that our human sexuality as male and female can find good and beautiful expression equally in singleness or marriage when we live to honor God.

Practical Implications

These truths about singleness have huge implications for practical ministry in our churches.

For our children's ministries and parenting courses: What vision will we give parents for their children's future? Could we lead them to pray not only for a possible future spouse but also for a devoted single life of peace and joy in Christ?

For our student ministries, let's reevaluate how we teach our teens about sex. While the purity movement has had many good results, we must be careful not to overplay sex as if it were the big moment to wait for. In addition to using 1 Corinthians 6 to teach teens to say no before they are married, perhaps we can use 1 Corinthians 7 to give our students a vision for singleness.

For our singles ministries, we need to consider what we are communicating about singleness and if a separate singles ministry is even a good idea for our church rather than embracing singles in all the existing ministries of the church.

For our adult ministries, education, discipleship, equipping, or whatever you call it, evaluate what courses, seminars, workshops, and conferences you sponsor in terms of single people. How much of your programming is primarily aimed at married couples? Or parents? And what about single parents?

For our sermons we need to think more carefully about what we are communicating, and not communicating, about singleness in our illustrations, outlines, and stories. Because I am married, I have a single person evaluate my sermon manuscripts and give me feedback. Sometimes I'm amazed at what I missed and embarrassed about what I inadvertently implied that I did not really want to say.

In our counseling and pastoral conversations, what advice do we give a person who is divorced or widowed? Do we try to play matchmaker? In our churches, we often subtly convey that emotionally and socially healthy people get married. Where does that leave Jesus?

In our hiring of staff and appointing of lay leaders over groups and ministries, we must ask how we view singleness. Are we reluctant to hire a single person, or have them lead a small group, or teach children? Why?

In the previous section when we looked at marital sexual sin, we observed the simple point that married people and single people are both guilty of lust and perversion. A common sexual sin among single people is found in an older term, *fornication*—sexual activity between two people who are not married to each other. The author of Proverbs 7 described a young man with no sense who hooks up with a woman who seduces him with her smooth talk. The Bible says: "All at once he followed her like an ox going to the slaughter. . . . little knowing it will cost him his life. . . . Her house is a highway to the grave, leading down to the chambers of death" (Prov. 7:22–27). The entire chapter presents a powerful warning.

A frequent question singles ask is, "How far is too far?" What "is" sex, anyway? When you start trying to define *is*, you are already in a bad place. Rather than seeing how close to the edge of the cliff you can get, why not take a big step back from the edge? I suggest you never cross three lines:

- The line of *respect* for the other person.
- The line of future *regret*. Will you regret this when you are married to a different person than the one you are with in this moment?
- And finally, the line of *passion*. Do not stir up desires that you cannot righteously fulfill.[18]

"But among you there must not be even a hint of sexual immorality" (Eph. 5:3). Apply this command to what you do on a dance floor, to what images you send on your phone, and to what kind of language you use when texting. Sexting carries with it more than a hint of sexual immorality!

What About Living Together?

Many people today live together before they get married. Cohabitation is increasingly common for senior adults, sometimes for financial reasons. And in light of all the divorce they have experienced in their families, single people often want to try living together before they make the lifelong marriage commitment.

So what's the big deal about living together? Recall that sex in marriage is designed to celebrate our union as one flesh for life and to display the loyal, exclusive love of God. These purposes cannot be fulfilled by two people having sex outside of marriage. The Bible says we should honor marriage: "Marriage should be honored by all, and the marriage bed kept pure, for God will judge the adulterer and all the sexually immoral" (Heb. 13:4).

Sex is designed for a permanent relationship. It symbolizes our lifelong commitment to each other. Speaking of couples living together unmarried and having sex, Christian ethicist Lewis Smedes put it succinctly: "It is wrong because unmarried people thereby engage in a life-uniting act without a life-uniting intent."[19] Living together sexually without being married is sin.

Having said that, I recognize that many people have lived together and are living together right now. As a spiritual leader, what counsel do you give? Often all the factors create quite a complicated situation. At our church, in short, with grace and in love, we encourage couples to get married, live separately, or end the relationship. Depending on the nature of the relationship, a couple may, or may not, be ready to get married. In any case, they need to stop having sex and seek wise counsel. We encourage them to take time to prayerfully consider their relationship before the Lord. As basic truth, obedience leads to blessing and sin leads to pain. We want blessing for our people.

Whether married or single, ultimate fulfillment and joy come in our relationship with Jesus. Our biggest hope in life should not be to get married or to have sex, but to be united with Christ, living in him and for him as his ambassadors on earth. Sex is good. God made it. But it has been distorted since the fall. In redemption, singleness is honored. We look forward to the new creation when sex will be surpassed, when our union with the one triune God exceeds the highest pleasures sexual union offers.

God gifted us with our sexuality as either male or female, so our calling is to honor God by being good stewards of our sexuality. If you are single, consider the blessings of singleness: to model Jesus, to live your destiny, to give yourself with undistracted devotion to

Jesus' mission, and to show the one and only God's open, inclusive love. Our life and greatest joy today are in our union with Jesus as we look forward to fully entering the fellowship of the Trinity when Jesus returns.

Discussion Questions

1. How do you think most people view the role of sex in marriage? According to this chapter, what are four biblical purposes of sex in marriage? Which of the four was most surprising or important to you?

2. How does marital sex relate to God himself? How does adultery violate or distort each of the four purposes of sex in marriage?

3. How can sex in a marriage relationship be marred by sin? At a practical level, how might a married couple live out a 1 Corinthians 13 kind of love in their sexual relationship?

4. How have you, or many Christians, viewed singleness as expressed in casual conversations, thoughts, and practices?

5. What are implications of the fact that God incarnated himself as a single human person? How might singles in their singleness uniquely reflect the reality of God himself?

6. How does singleness relate to our destiny? What value might singles provide for Christ's mission, and what unique insights might singles have into the body of Christ, the local church?

7. What could be some practical implications of this view of singleness for your life, for the ministries of your church?

CHAPTER 4

SAME-SEX SEXUALITY

Leading People to Read the Bible Humbly

Intense, deep emotions simmer behind closed doors and explode in public forums over same-sex issues. With their volatile feelings, people have divided denominations, fractured families, and fueled ugly political battles. In the midst of the debates, too often we lose track of real people. We are dealing with men and women, boys and girls, all created in God's image with hurts and dreams, names and faces. People we are to love. I think of my friends, such as Kent and Kellie and Judy.

Christians have a bad reputation in this arena, and sadly, in many cases it is well deserved. We do not have a good track record of showing love and pursuing justice for LGBT+ people who have commonly suffered ridicule, condemnation, rejection, exclusion, discrimination, and even violence.

In Philadelphia, a gay couple were on their way to get pizza when a group of men and women brutally beat them as they yelled homophobic slurs. One victim had to have his jaw wired shut for two months.[1] Christians should be the first to stand up for justice against this kind of abuse.

Since you picked up this book, you're probably aware of the American church's terrible reputation for being anti-gay. And you may have experienced the fallout of that reputation when you invited a gay friend to your church, and they looked at you as if you had invited them to be tortured. Why would they go where they imagine they would not be wanted? I identify with Preston Sprinkle, who said, "But I don't sleep as well as I used to. I frequently wake up way before my alarm, haunted by the pain that Christians have caused gay people."[2]

As a caring pastor, who wants to bring the love of Christ to people, you are looking for ways to effectively show God's amazing grace to LGBT+ people. And you may struggle, as I do, with how to lead your congregation to create a place of grace—a loving home for all kinds of people. This challenge increases when there are people in your church who fear a "gay agenda" as well as movement toward progressive or open-and-affirming (approving) theologies even within evangelical churches. Many in your congregation will expect you to stand for truth vigorously, with a Martin Luther–like, countercultural, "Here I stand; I can do no other" stance. Of course you, as well, want to hold to and teach biblical truth, but you do not want to be harsh, hateful, or graceless. We must strive for a level playing field rather than stack hard truths only against LGBT+ people.

And you doubtless want to reach LGBT+ people with the gospel of Jesus Christ, yet it feels impossible when the culture depicts us as in a war against each other. There is hope, according to Andrew Marin's extensive study, the first of its kind, which presents the surprising finding that 86 percent of LGBT+ people were raised in a faith community from ages zero to eighteen. This means that "an overwhelming percentage of the LGBT community spent their youth being taught, spiritually formed, and discipled in conservative religious circles. This fact flies in the face of the dominant cultural narrative, which casts the parties to this conversation as opposing forces. . . . In reality, the culture war has always been a civil war: us versus us."[3]

And yet, according to Marin, the sad truth is that "our data reports that 54 percent of our LGBT participants left their religious community after the age of 18. This is exactly double the amount of the general American population who leave their religious communities as adults."[4] So they were part of a church or other religious group to start with, but for a variety of reasons they departed from their religious community most likely in some way connected to identifying as LGBT+.

But another surprising finding is that according to Marin's research, for the vast majority (85 percent), the reason they left was not over theological disagreement about what is sinful.[5] This fact indicates that some would be willing to return to their faith community, even while still disagreeing on this issue. That assumption is supported by data indicating that while, according to the Barna Group, only 9 percent of Americans are open to returning to faith after making a decision to leave their faith community, Marin's data reveals that "LGBTs are open to returning at a rate 65 percent higher than the average American."[6] There is hope for reconciliation because there is openness to return not just to Christ but to Christ's church. Church leaders can take heart that LGBT+ people are not by and large closed to the church.

Repentance

In previous decades when the AIDS crisis was at its peak, few Christians responded with care and compassion to those suffering, or to their loved ones. Instead many were hateful, unkind, or, at a minimum, passive and uninvolved. And, in the decades that have followed, few churches have advocated justice for gay people who have been mistreated. According to one study, 91 percent of unchurched people said that "anti-homosexual" accurately describes Christianity.[7] Why are we not more commonly known for our love and compassion? As Christians, what should our response be to our past treatment of gay people?

My response is to apologize. I apologize to all LGBT+ people for not standing with you when you were unjustly treated and even abused and for not showing more compassion when you were sick and dying. In my own church, I have led us to repent and pledge to show grace to you.

As a spiritual leader, consider how you might personally repent and repent on behalf of those you represent. How does your church or group need to apologize for what has been done, and not done, in the past? As we come to the Bible, we come humbly acknowledging our sin personally and corporately.

Approaching the Biblical Text with Humility

You may not agree with all I say in this chapter or in the rest of the book. That's fine. We need to give each other room to disagree and space to grow in matters where the gospel of Jesus Christ is not at stake. Consider how you could lead your church to see that not every issue is at the same level of importance.

Our view of same-sex issues is not at the same level as our convictions about the deity of Christ. When we believe in a wrong Christ, we believe in a false gospel that does not save us (Gal. 1). On the other hand, we can disagree today about how to approach same-sex matters and still serve together forever in God's new creation. My hope is to open a conversation so that, more and more, we gain the heart and mind of Christ on sexuality. I find that tension is reduced when we give people space to agree to disagree, space to be in the process of thinking through what we believe. We need to model to our congregation that we, too, are growing in our understanding. Note: in a future chapter we will cover the important difference between ensuring agreement among the leaders of a particular local church and allowing variance among the people attending a local church.

Like many of you, I have gay family members. Years ago, my brother told our family that he is gay. My brother gave me the freedom to share his story. We are sixteen months apart in age and grew up sharing the same room until I was twelve. He is now married to his partner. While we disagree about some things, I love my brother, and we enjoy a good relationship. We joyfully share holidays together with him and his partner.

It would be naive for any of us to attempt to study God's Word on this topic as if we had no personal stake in the matter or no feelings or experiences to color our vision. Whether you see yourself as gay, straight, or something else, it's much better for us to become aware of our own perspectives, prejudices, and the effects of our personal experiences. We dare not give more authority or credence to our personal experiences and feelings, however, than we give to God's Word. Humbly, we come to the Bible not to confirm our positions but to submit our thinking to Christ, open to the Spirit bringing conviction and transformation.

Evangelical Christians in particular so want to be "right" about everything. As a spiritual leader, you likely think you know what the Bible says about same-sex issues. But I invite you to relook at the biblical texts with the spirit of a learner. When I stand before God in the new creation one day, I expect to be surprised at where I was wrong but thought I was right! My guess is that we will all be surprised when we get to heaven. I doubt that every bit of my theology is just as God sees it. Humility calls us to admit we could be mistaken and need to keep growing in our own understanding. If you are like me, you do not believe today everything you thought ten or twenty years ago. While my primary convictions remain firm, I am growing in my understanding of the nuances of sexuality, and what I write in this book remains "on the way," as I continue to seek the Lord in his Word and listen to the insights of others. We want to lead our churches to be lifelong learners in a spirit of humility as we search to know God and his ways.

Answering the Questions

When people ask us what the Bible says about homosexuality, it's wise to consider why they are asking the question. What underlying issues drive their questions? Your discernment impacts what you share and how much you share.

Are they eager to hear you denounce "homosexuals" as sinners? In view of the perceived culture wars, some people want to know that their pastor stands on the "right" side of the issue and will not compromise with the world. For some this has become a litmus test of orthodoxy. I've received emails in which this question was the deciding factor on whether a couple would join our church. They wanted to know where I stand. Do you affirm that you agree with them or do you challenge their thinking? That's where pastoral wisdom comes to bear. The issue is not only about what the Bible says, but it's also about how much you share and in what contexts. In general, I avoid addressing this topic by email. It's too easily misunderstood and misquoted. Instead I invite that person to a face-to-face conversation if they are local, or if not, to a phone call or video call. Of course, at times email is that person's preferred communication channel and the only way to reply.

Often a person's questions are deeply personal, so you want to know some of their story. Is this a parent wrestling with how to love their child who has "come out," so they are desperate to know what the Bible says? Is this woman struggling with her own sexual identity, eager to please Jesus and also be honest with what she feels? Sometimes the question is from a person who does not know what the Bible says and is confused because of conflicting things they have heard. Or they may have recently encountered an article or podcast that challenged their thinking. Other times the question comes from a combative person who is sure of what they believe and wants to debate or convince you. Increasingly, I am fielding questions from Christ-followers who are not straight but want to honor God and be part of the church. They want to know if their spiritual leader sees any place for them, so their question of what the Bible says about this topic is quite nuanced, and often they have studied the issue, maybe more than you have.

As a spiritual leader, you will find it's easy to lose credibility quickly when you are ill informed. Test yourself: How many passages in the Bible mention homosexuality specifically? Is lesbianism addressed in the Bible? Where? Which author in the New Testament wrote about homosexuality? Are there clear examples of a gay or lesbian couple in the Bible? Does Jesus ever specifically mention homosexuality? Does the Bible speak directly to same-sex marriages? Is homosexuality ever portrayed in a positive light in the Bible?

For Christians, Sprinkle put a sharp point on "the question" many are asking, and on which Christians disagree:

> The question is not about whether gay sex outside marriage is wrong. It's not about whether soliciting a same-sex prostitute or sleeping around with several partners is wrong. All genuine Christians believe these are sin. The question is whether two men or two women can date, fall in love, remain sexually pure before their wedding day, and commit to a life-long, consensual, Christ-centered, self-giving, monogamous union.[8]

What makes this question difficult is that no specific biblical passage speaks to it directly, but the Bible's overall teaching on marriage gives us guidance.

The Seven Direct Passages

All the Bible speaks to all humans, so the whole Bible speaks to LGBT+ people just as it speaks to straight people. Of course, most people want to zero in on the passages that speak directly to same-sex matters. I am going to be very brief here, adding a few caveats, and encourage you to read others who address these passages more fully.[9] We must be careful not to say more than the Bible says. Sprinkle's *People to Be Loved* is currently my top book recommendation for my church members on this topic.

Only seven biblical passages directly mention same-sex sexual behavior. But before we get to those, it all starts with creation. Creation theology lays a foundation for understanding sexuality. Here we are reviewing what we have already briefly covered. God made humanity in his image as male and female. He charged them to be fruitful and multiply. The man and the woman were to unite as one flesh. In talking about marriage, Jesus reaffirmed this creation theology:

> "Haven't you read," he replied, "that at the beginning the Creator 'made them male and female,' and said, 'For this reason a man will leave his father and mother and be united to his wife, and the two will become one flesh'? So they are no longer two, but one flesh. Therefore what God has joined together, let no one separate." (Matt. 19:4–6)

Jesus affirmed marriage as one man and one woman united for life. Revisionist scholars have pointed out what has been recognized by other Hebrew scholars, that in Genesis the phrase "one flesh" refers primarily to kinship bonds, two people forming a new family, not explicitly a male-female sexual union.[10] As pastors, we lose credibility when we refuse to acknowledge a valid point made by someone we disagree with. We want to model listening and honest dialogue.

"Did Jesus ever speak directly to homosexuality?" Grant the point. No, he did not. However, his appeal to Genesis confirms his affirmation of heterosexual monogamy. Additionally, his use of the Greek word *porniea* may encompass same-sex intimacy:[11] "It has been said,

'Anyone who divorces his wife must give her a certificate of divorce.' But I tell you that anyone who divorces his wife, except for sexual immorality [*porniea*], makes her the victim of adultery, and anyone who marries a divorced woman commits adultery" (Matt. 5:31–32).

Throughout the rest of the Bible, references to marriage assume heterosexual unions between one man and one woman. Marital warnings, commands, and blessings all assume a man and a woman. Parables, illustrations, and metaphors having to do with marriage, such as God's relationship with Israel and Christ's relationship with his church, are exclusively in heterosexual terms. Creation displays two biological sexes, male and female, who are to unite in marriage to fill the earth with children. And they are but two of several pairs in creation, including the heaven and the earth. As N. T. Wright shows, the Bible begins and ends with the heaven and earth, and with marriage, which pictures God's plan at the beginning and at the end. He said, "The biblical view of marriage is part of the larger whole of new creation, and it symbolizes and points to that divine plan."[12] It's not just in a few scattered verses here and there, but the whole divine narrative teaches that marriage is between one man and one woman for life, and sexual relations are reserved for marriage.

In the Old Testament, four passages directly address same-sex issues: two stories—one in Genesis 19 and a parallel one in Judges 19—and two laws in Leviticus. The first story is the account of Sodom where Abraham's nephew Lot was living. God sent angels who appeared as men. That night the men of the city called to Lot, "Where are the men who came to you tonight? Bring them out to us so that we can have sex with them" (Gen. 19:5). Despicably, Lot then offered them his daughters instead. The angels saved Lot, and the Lord destroyed the city. While the immediate threat was gang rape to men and women, the core issue was sexual immorality, as we learn from Jude.[13] "Sodom and Gomorrah and the surrounding towns gave themselves up to sexual immorality and perversion" (Jude v. 7).[14] A very similar story appears in Judges 19 where wicked men wanted to have sex with a visiting guest. Clearly same-sex sexually violent acts are condemned by God. Almost no LGBT+ people see themselves as being like the men of Sodom, and they would also condemn sexual violence. From *only* these two stories of sexual violence, it's important not to draw the conclusion too quickly that homosexuality itself is sinful, otherwise your conclusion is easily countered by those who disagree. From these two stories, let's move to the two laws.

The Old Testament law says, "Do not have sexual relations with a man as one does with a woman; that is detestable" (Lev. 18:22). The same law is repeated in Leviticus 20:13. How do we know those laws apply today when other Old Testament laws, such as not eating pork, do not?[15] In short, this law applied not just to Israel but to other nations as well. Second, God calls the act "detestable," one of the few acts to be described with that strong Hebrew word. Third, the restriction is affirmed in the New Testament (Rom. 1; 1 Cor. 6:9; 1 Tim. 1:9–10).[16] So creation depicts humanity as male and female uniting in marriage, the Old Testament law is opposed to same-sex sexual behavior, and two Old Testament stories condemn violent same-sex acts.

Three passages in the New Testament mention same-sex sexual activity. The main text is Romans 1. Paul wrote:

> Therefore God gave them over in the sinful desires of their hearts to sexual impurity for the degrading of their bodies with one another. They exchanged the truth about God for a lie, and worshiped and served created things rather than the Creator—who is forever praised. Amen. Because of this, God gave them over to shameful lusts. Even their women exchanged natural sexual relations for unnatural ones. In the same way the men also abandoned natural relations with women and were inflamed with lust for one another. Men committed shameful acts with other men, and received in themselves the due penalty for their error. (vv. 24–27)

In context, Paul was giving an illustration of humanity turning from the Creator to the creation. The lustful, unnatural sex of men with men and women with women is itself a consequence of sin. Paul's use of the term *unnatural* echoes the creation order in Genesis.[17] In the next chapter (Rom. 2), Paul flipped the table by including in God's condemnation those who self-righteously judge people, including judging gays and lesbians. I agree with Sprinkle, who wrote, "There is absolutely no room for moral pride here. It's an offense both to Paul and to the cross of Christ to look down your spiritual nose at the homosexual acts in Romans 1 and ignore your own greed, slander, envy, covetousness, and judgmentalism, which are also mentioned in Romans 1."[18] Paul argued that all are sinners in need of God's grace. We must read these opening few chapters of Romans in light of the whole book, which is a celebration of God's amazing grace in Jesus, available to all of us.

The remaining two passages in the New Testament put same-sex sexual behavior in lists of sins. One is found in 1 Corinthians 6 and the other in 1 Timothy 1. Paul wrote:

> Do not be deceived: Neither the sexually immoral nor idolaters nor adulterers nor men who have sex with men nor thieves nor the greedy nor drunkards nor slanderers nor swindlers will inherit the kingdom of God. And that is what some of you were. But you were washed, you were sanctified, you were justified in the name of the Lord Jesus Christ and by the Spirit of our God. (1 Cor. 6:9–11)

While there is still some debate, according to biblical scholars who worked on the NIV translation, "The words *men who have sex with men* translate two Greek words that refer to the passive and active participants in homosexual acts."[19] This sin is paralleled with adultery, greed, and slander. And yet, the focus in verse 11 is that by the power of the Holy Spirit in Jesus Christ, all of these people were washed, sanctified, and justified.

Notice which sins are paralleled:

> We also know that the law is made not for the righteous but for lawbreakers and rebels, the ungodly and sinful, the unholy and irreligious, for those who kill their fathers or mothers, for murderers, for the sexually immoral, for those practicing homosexuality, for slave traders and liars and perjurers—and for whatever else is contrary to the sound doctrine. (1 Tim. 1:9–10)

Quite a few sins are listed here, from murder to lying.

In short, seven passages mention same-sex sexual behavior specifically, four in the Old Testament and three in the New Testament. Lesbianism is only addressed in Romans 1. Paul is the only author who speaks directly about homosexual behavior in the New Testament. There are no clear examples of a homosexual couple in the Bible. The Bible does not record Jesus specifically mentioning homosexual intimacy. The Bible never speaks directly to same-sex marriage or orientation. Same-gender sexual intimacy is never portrayed in a positive light in the Bible. It is also relevant to note that until quite recently, Christian and Jewish teaching over the centuries has universally condemned same-sex behavior.

Let's come back to the question Sprinkle posed. What about a same-sex marriage that is Christ-centered, monogamous, and lifelong? While the Bible does not speak to it directly, the implications from several truths seems clear. Same-sex behavior is never portrayed positively and is condemned in the Levitical law and in Romans 1, echoed in the lists in 1 Corinthians and 1 Timothy. Sex is reserved only for marriage, and marriage is reserved only for one man and one woman for life. There is no biblical warrant for a same-sex marriage.

But many questions remain. Is it biblically wrong to have a same-sex attraction? A same-sex orientation? Is homosexuality itself a sin? These questions lead to quite a few practical, pastoral questions that we will get to later.

Discussion Questions

1. In your view, what is the church's reputation with LGBT+ people? Why do you think that is?
2. How do you evaluate Andrew Marin's data about LGBT+ people and the church? What implications do you draw?
3. Do you think it is appropriate for Christian leaders, churches, or organizations to repent of how LGBT+ people have been treated in the past? If not, why not? And if so, how could that look in your context?
4. What do you think it involves to approach the Bible humbly?
5. When people have asked you about homosexuality, what have been some deeper issues or questions that you suspected might lie beneath the surface?
6. What are the seven passages that speak directly to same-sex behavior? And how would you briefly summarize them?
7. What does the Bible say, and not say, on this topic, directly? What foundational biblical teaching gives guidance on this topic? What questions remain unanswered, in your view?

CHAPTER 5

SAME-SEX SEXUALITY

Leading People to Understand Being "Gay"

Can you be a Christian and be gay? Is it appropriate to refer to yourself as a "gay Christian"?

To answer these questions, we will explore what it means to be gay and what it means to be a Christian. A Christian is a person who has trusted in Jesus Christ and been regenerated by the Holy Spirit. But it's much more difficult and controversial to define what it means to be gay.

In our churches and in our culture, people understand "gayness" differently. These differences significantly undermine our ability to communicate with one another clearly. A better grasp of issues around what it means to be gay will help you lead your people better, both those who are straight and those who are not.

What Is Being Gay?

Currently there is no consensus on gayness, either among researchers in medicine and psychology, or among those who identify as gay. The term "gay" has shifted massively from its sixteenth-century meaning of "merry," to meaning something close to "a person who is romantically attracted to someone of his or her own gender." It's helpful to distinguish five common ways the term *gay* is currently used: gender roles, sexual behavior, identity, attraction, and orientation. Below is a quick summary, after which we will work through each one with implications for ministry at each point.

> *Gender Roles:* Gay has been used to describe social gender roles, sometimes in an insulting way to slander more feminine men.
>
> *Sexual Behavior:* The word *gay* can imply sexual behavior between two people of the same gender.
>
> *Identity:* Gay can define a person's identity, his or her self-perception, and the expression of who he or she is.
>
> *Attraction:* Gay can refer to the fact that a person is romantically or erotically attracted to persons of his or her own gender and not the opposite gender.
>
> *Orientation:* This might be the most controversial category because for some it is inherently sinful and sexual, while others see it as much more than sexual and can indeed be holy. It refers to how a person persistently sees persons of their own gender and conversely sees the opposite gender.

Gender Roles: Expanding Masculinity and Femininity

Is it unchristian for a guy to like knitting or for a girl to like watching football? Of course not. There is a wide spectrum of masculinity and femininity that need not provoke a moral value judgment. My son, Jimmy, now married to Emily, trained as a classical ballet dancer through high school. He danced because he loved it and music moved him, but other students were quick to question if he was straight or gay. You can imagine what he faced in a conservative suburb.

In this way, *gay* tends to be used as a slam against such things as the clothes straight teenagers would not wear: "That's so gay." Basically, almost anything they do not like that could be in the least bit viewed as feminine can be dismissed with that negative comment.

These days our society is so sexualized that we far too quickly label people as gay or fear that our children might be gay because of the activities they enjoy, the clothes they prefer, the hairstyles they like to wear, or even the way they carry themselves or gesture. When your daughter rejects dolls to play with a toy truck, depending on your point of view, you may worry or be pleasantly surprised. In middle school, when your son is not interested in sports and prefers theater, you might wonder if he is gay. We need a much larger range of how to be a healthy male or female without sexualizing and labeling our children, or ourselves, because they or we are a tender male or a tough female.

It is not unchristian to express your gender in ways that are outside the cultural norm, for men to be ballet dancers and women to rope cattle. This breadth of gender expression, however, does not mean that our created biological identities as male and female are meaningless. God did not create us as generic persons, spouses, or parents. Rather, we are men and women, husbands and wives, moms and dads. And yet while gender matters, we must resist rigid, fixed, and often narrow gender stereotypes that exclude nonconforming people and confuse biological males and females with cultural caricatures.

For instance, in churches it is common for the men's ministry to champion chest-beating, sports-crazed, muscle-bound he-men as the models of masculinity, and for the women's ministry to sponsor tea parties where a prize is given for the most creative table decoration and a workshop is offered on flower arranging. These are not wrong until we begin to impose them as supposedly biblical models of masculinity and femininity. Tender men have said they never doubted their masculinity until they started going to a church.

In our children's and student ministries we can inadvertently reentrench these cultural norms as if they are biblical. At our church, we have an event for the boys called "Big Bad Burly" where we shoot paintballs at a campout. Recently a twentysomething woman told me that when she was in our student ministry, that's what she would have wanted to do, but those activities were not offered at the girls retreat. I'm not saying all student events should be coed, but we have to be more sensitive to gender stereotyping that communicates you are not a man if you like decorating, or that you are not a girl if you like boxing. If you teach or preach at your church, think back over your illustrations and stories about men and women. To what extent are you reenforcing gender caricatures that leave nonconforming people out? Imagine how you could use your influence to help your church envision an expanded picture of masculinity and femininity.

Even worse damage is done to individuals when we ostracize them because they are more effeminate men or more masculine women, suspecting them of homosexual tendencies. These cultural expressions often have nothing to do with sexual attraction, identity, or behavior.

I'll address identity and attraction a bit later, but first, let's consider same-sex romantic and sexual intimacy. Can you be Christian and engage in sexual intimacy with someone of your same sex? This question raises a deeper question: For any of us, does our salvation depend on our sexual behavior?

Sexual Behavior: Degrees of Sin and Forgiveness

Many gay people have been told, "You are going to hell because you are gay." Sadly, a lesbian friend of mine in our church was told that recently. That statement she was told is false. Hell would be the just consequence for all of us who have sinned in multiple ways against the Creator of the universe were it not for God's mercy extended to us through Christ. Regardless of sexual activity, a person will go to hell if they reject the love of God in Jesus Christ. Salvation does not depend on our sexual behavior. It depends only on what Jesus did for us and our response to Christ in faith.

Biblically, same-sex sexual activity is sinful, as we covered in a previous chapter. Unlike sexual attraction or even orientation, every voluntary act of sexual behavior is clearly a choice. And yet, while same-sex sexual activity is *a* sin, it is not *the* worst possible sin. Go back to the relevant New Testament passages—Romans 1, 1 Corinthians 6, and 1 Timothy 1—to see same-sex sexual behavior listed along with many other sins with no hierarchy of "badness." As leaders, we have to guard against our people characterizing same-sex sexual activity as *the* sin above all sins, the one abomination.

The worst sin is to reject Jesus, because that determines your eternal destiny. It's interesting to scan through the Gospels to see what sins Jesus spoke against with the strongest words. Ironically, religious hypocrisy is high on the list (Matt. 23).

Can you engage in same-sex sexual behavior and be a Christian? Let's ask a related question: Can you sin and be a Christian? I sure hope so! Or we are all in trouble. All Christians continue to sin. When we sin, we should repent and freshly receive God's gracious forgiveness in Christ.

Some argue from 1 Corinthians 6:9 that Paul's phrase "will not inherit the kingdom of God" means that same-sex sexual behavior is a salvation (gospel) issue and that those who engage in same-sex sexual activity will not be in Christ's final kingdom. However, such a position requires you to say the same for the other sins in the list, including greed, swindling, sexual immorality, and drunkenness.

With many other scholars, I concur that Paul was talking about the kind of unrepentant behavior patterns that should by no means characterize those who will inherit the kingdom of God through Jesus Christ.[1] Without getting into deeper theological debates about how much transformation a person must exhibit to demonstrate that they are saved, at the least, a person engaging in self-evident, continual unrepentant sin without an effort to change calls into question the reality of that person's salvation.

When people identify themselves as gay, it's common to assume they mean they engage in sexual activity with people of their same gender. However, that is not always the case, which makes it important to ask people what they mean when they identify themselves as gay, especially if you are speaking to Christians. This is crucial for parents whose children "come out" to them. As a mom or a dad, you want to ask lots of caring questions to ascertain what your child is really telling you in that moment.

Identity: Is It Appropriate to Describe Yourself as a "Gay Christian"?

Is it unchristian to identify oneself as gay? It depends on what you mean by the term *gay*. For some Christians, it simply means you are a person who is more attracted to your own gender than to the opposite gender. You struggle with unwanted same-sex sexual desires. For other Christians, it means that your life is largely defined by your sexuality or you are sexually active with someone of your same sex. As Christians, our fundamental identity should be found not in our sexuality but in Christ.

But on secondary levels we identify ourselves in many ways. I'm a husband, father, grandfather, and racquetball player. I struggle with prideful ambition, and racially I'm white. My job is to be a pastor. None of those are core to my identity. It is dangerous, and can even lead to idolatry, to define yourself fundamentally by your race, marital status, occupation, or temptations.

Rosaria Butterfield provided a graphic analogy: "Making an identity out of temptation is like putting on the opposing team's jersey at a ball game and then taking to the field: it is confusing, deceptive, and dangerous."[2] We are called to represent Christ, not our temptation pattern. We are to flee temptation and resist the Devil. In our battle against sin, defining ourselves by our sin struggle diminishes our spiritual strength to fight it.

In her chapter "Self-Representation: What Does It Mean to Be Gay?" Butterfield argues strongly against anyone describing themselves as a "gay Christian." As she points out, the word *gay* carries a power and history that needs to be identified. It declares a political advocacy and sexual affirmation. In common usage, it is difficult to extract it from sexual practice. And why would you want to identify yourself with your sin pattern?

And yet I appreciate, in her chapter "Conflict: When Sisters Disagree," Butterfield quoting extensively from her friend Rebecca, who disagrees with Rosaria, arguing that not using *gay* is fraudulent and deceptive, as if we are not telling the truth about ourselves.[3] I believe we can walk together, agreeing to disagree as we all learn and grow in this area.[4]

As Butterfield acknowledged, there are other Christians who argue that it is appropriate and important to describe themselves as gay Christians. Tim Otto is in this camp. When he endorsed my previous book on this topic,[5] he agreed to do so with the stipulation that I identify him as a gay pastor, which I readily agreed to do.

Gay author and worship leader Gregory Coles agreed that we're more than our sexuality, but he then shared, "There are times I need a word to name my sexuality, and I need a different word to name yours. Without those words, we're glossing over the details that make our stories and challenges unique."[6]

In a similar vein, with detail and a caveat, Nate Collins pointed out that a person might identify as gay for a variety of reasons. In speaking of himself, he wrote, "For example, I have identified as a gay man in several kinds of circumstances, sometimes simply to inform someone that I wasn't straight, and other times to indicate a desire to stand in solidarity with gay people as a marginalized population. But a person can also identify as gay in a sinful, humanistic sense, especially if it is accompanied by an inner belief in the false doctrine of the intrinsic goodness of humanity."[7]

Sadly, in most places it feels like there is a war with two sides, gay and Christian, and people have to choose which side they are on. So, other people refer to themselves as gay to protest against the false disjunction of gay and Christians, to say that you can't be both. Thus they use the adjective *gay* as a way of providing space for others to be Christian and also be LGBT+. Of course, a danger is that the adjective may communicate something other than what the person means to say. While we may dispute the wisdom of using the term *gay*, it is gracious to call people by the terms they use to describe themselves. This is not an issue over which Christians should divide.[8]

In the end, I agree with Sprinkle when he wrote, "If someone uses the term 'gay' simply to mean that they are same-sex attracted, then I think it's fine in itself. It's simply a true statement about how they experience the world. I don't think it is necessarily wrong to describe yourself as 'gay,' if you are using the term not to speak of your core identity but your unique experience as a same-sex attracted person."[9] As a spiritual leader in your church, it is worthwhile to think through how you would feel about a member or a small group leader or staff member describing herself or himself as gay.

In our church, I encourage people that while today we guard

against identity theft through using a frustrating array of ever-changing passwords, there's a more important potential identity theft. Don't let anyone steal your spiritual identity. Having a sexual attraction does not convey your core identity. Your romantic desires do not define you. As Christ-followers, married or single, regardless of sexual desires, we are not called to affirm ourselves, but to deny ourselves. When you choose to follow Jesus, you leave behind other gods, idols, and allegiances. For every Christian, your fundamental identity should be that you are a follower of Jesus Christ. Then we can express many other secondary identities. And we are fine with leaders in our church identifying themselves as gay Christians if they are living faithful to Christ and recognize that gay is a secondary identity marker, not their fundamental identity.

Attraction: Desire, Temptation, and Lust

As is the case with most sin, it's enlightening to distinguish the temptation from the act. By the term *gay* some people mean to communicate that they experience same-sex attraction, SSA, but that they may not act on that attraction. The phrase "same-sex attraction" has become common in some Christian circles. However, because SSA has origins in the ex-gay movement that strongly advocated for reparation therapy, which tried to make gay people straight, some people reject that phrase. They often opt instead to simply say they are gay.

Jesus was tempted in every way as we are, which means he faced sexual temptations (Heb. 4:15). He was tempted, but he never lusted. All people face strong desires to do things they should not do. Temptation is not sin, but lust is. Most of us know the difference most of the time. When you move from appreciating the beauty of the other person to undressing them in your mind, you have crossed from temptation to lust.

Is same-sex attraction more like temptation or lust, or could it be either one? Let me give you a heads-up that there are challenging issues in this section and the next that are on the cutting edge of fresh theological thinking on this issue, where good scholars are wrestling, as I am too.

God never tempts us. All temptation comes from the world, the flesh, and the Devil, and if successful pulls us into sin (James 1:13–15). Thus, its intended end is sinful, so temptation is not something to be celebrated or to be a defining mark of our core identity.[10] Today, it is increasingly common among Christians to make a strong distinction between same-sex behavior and same-sex attraction.

Most biblical scholars agree that the Bible teaches same-sex sexual behavior is against God's revealed will, apart from a growing minority who see it as potentially holy in a same-sex marriage. In sensitivity to our brothers and sisters who struggle with persistent same-sex attraction, however, we are quick to equally affirm that temptation is not sin, thus there is nothing wrong with being same-sex attracted. So, you find Christians describing themselves not as gay, but as same-sex attracted, or if they say they are gay, they are quick to define that they mean they are romantically attracted to their own gender and yet are not living in sinful sexual behavior.

Biblical scholar Denny Burk raised the question of whether the desire for sexual activity with a person of the same sex is a morally benign desire. He said, "In the terms Jesus teaches us, it is always sinful to desire something that God forbids."[11] Butterfield agreed. She wrote, "To say 'temptation' is not a sin, therefore my temptation pattern is morally neutral or even 'sanctifiable' is misguided and dangerous."[12] Even when a sinful desire arises like a hiccup that feels natural and unchosen, we must take responsibility for it and resist it.

In opposition to Burk and Butterfield, scholars such as Sprinkle and Collins argue that James 1 clearly distinguishes between desire and sin. "Sin doesn't arrive on the scene until desire 'conceives.'"[13] In other words, a mere attraction or desire is not necessarily itself sinful.

Sprinkle argues that persistent attraction, or an orientation to one's same sex, is not something that needs to be confessed as sin, by which he means a morally culpable concrete act of disobedience, not just a product of the fall like being born blind.[14] He wrote, "Same-sex orientation is a general disposition, regardless of whether someone is acting on it or even thinking about."[15] As a comparison, a person may be heterosexual whether they are waking or sleeping. If a homosexual orientation were a morally culpable sin, presumably a same-sex attracted person would need to be repenting all night long.[16] He concluded, "If being same-sex oriented is sinful, then what would repentance look like? Every second of every day confessing the sin of your very existence and waiting for God to make you straight? That's not realistic, biblical, or pastoral."[17]

Going further, we need to delve into what is being desired. Obviously, not all desire is sinful. According to the American Psychological Association, same-sex attraction refers to "an enduring pattern of emotional, romantic, and/or sexual attractions to" someone of the same sex and includes other nonsexual relational bonds, such as "affection between partners, shared goals and values, mutual support, and ongoing commitment."[18] Gay Christians describe their attractions as including nonsexual relational bonds that are not sinful. Not all same-sex attraction is itself sexual or erotic. In fact, in my conversations, few gay people describe themselves as regularly thinking about having sex.

Could a person experience desire for same-sex intimacy that is pure and chaste? Collins offers an in-depth exploration of these issues as he wrestles with the concepts of desire, attraction, and beauty, on which I will rely and build.

We have biblical examples of intimate relationships between two men, such as David and Jonathan, and two women, such as Ruth and Naomi. So it would seem that there is potential to experience same-gender, non-erotic intimacy that is holy and honoring to God. This direction of thinking leads us to ask, to what is a self-described gay person attracted? In our hypersexualized culture, have we overread their desires as mostly sexual or essentially sexual when they often might be for close friendship, companionship, intimacy, sharing life? This is not to naively assume that *eros* is not crouching in the shadows, looking for the opportunity to draw us into sin. But this is true in opposite-sex relationships as well.

After lengthy reflection on these questions, Collins pushed the issue to the edge: "So, here's the million-dollar question that we've been preparing to ask: Is it possible for a gay man to passionately admire another man—or even another gay man, for that matter—without sinning? I think the answer to this question has to be yes, it is certainly possible."[19] I find his point challenging and potentially dangerous, and yet when I apply it to my admiration for a woman who is not my wife, it makes sense. Can we not appreciate beauty without lusting or coveting?

However we evaluate the morality of same-sex attraction, without question a Christian can be same-sex attracted and be following Christ, even as they face continuing sexual temptations. Our maturity in Christ is not measured by the diminishing power of our temptations but by the strength of our resistance and the clarity of our repentance. Although he did not suffer from original sin as we do, Jesus' sinlessness did not reduce the force of temptation he experienced. As we grow to become more like our Savior, we trust that our minds will be more transformed to be like his, but we have no guarantee that our temptations will reduce in intensity. The fact that a Christian is persistently tempted to a certain sin does not mark them as immature in Christ. As spiritual leaders we can offer gay men and women hope that while living with same-sex attractions, they can grow to maturity in Christ.

Orientation: What Is an "Orientation"? And Is It Sinful?

How does persistent same-sex attraction relate to sexual orientation? The widely acclaimed secular neuroscientist Simon LeVay wrote that "sexual orientation . . . is the trait that predisposes us to experience sexual attraction to people of the same sex as ourselves (homosexual, gay, or lesbian), to persons of the other sex (heterosexual or straight), or to both sexes (bisexual)."[20] A same-sex orientation describes strong, persistent attraction. Some people experience quite a bit of fluidity in their sexual attractions, but others describe a strong and persistent attraction only to their own gender, with no romantic or erotic attractions to the opposite gender.

Causality

It's common for people in our churches to ask, Where does the orientation come from? Are you born gay? Or do you choose to be gay? Traditionally, Christians have said being gay is a choice. However, our biblical theology of sin tells us that we are all born into sin. Each of us is born with tendencies toward various sins, but not all to the same degree. I'm more tempted to selfishness than my wife is. Sometimes I wish she were a little more selfish to make me feel better! But she is more tempted to fear. And she thinks I could use a bit more fear in my life. Likely, the causality of any sinful tendency, including same-sex lust, is a combination of genetics and environment and choice.

Apart from sexual behavior, is same-sex attraction or orientation itself sinful? On the flip side, we can ask, is heterosexuality itself holy? Both carry sinful tendencies to have sex with people with whom we should not, because we are not married to them.

Categories

Something may be amiss in the categories themselves. In his provocatively titled article in *First Things*, "Against Heterosexuality," Michael Hannon argues that the categories of homosexual and heterosexual are mere recent, fragile social constructs that are actually harmful. For a person struggling against same-sex desires, they intensify the battle by falsely rooting the desires in identity, undermining the freedom that Christ offers those who find their identity in him. For heterosexuals, it takes them off the hook as if they did not have sexual distortions built into their desires. He summarizes, "If homosexuality binds us to sin, heterosexuality blinds us to sin."[21]

Hannon builds on the work of Hanne Blank in *Straight: The Surprisingly Short History of Heterosexuality*.[22] Blank looks to Jonathan Katz's argument in his book *The Invention of Heterosexuality* that heterosexual orientation is a recent social construction.[23] Both observed that in 1869 the German-Hungarian journalist and author Karl-Maria Kertbeny coined the term *homosexual*, and in 1886 the German medical doctor Richard von Krafft-Ebing adopted the terminology in his influential work *Psychopathia Sexualis*. In a sense, it was impossible to identify as heterosexual or homosexual, as a kind of human being, before 1886.

Writing from outside Christian traditions, both Blank and Katz undermine the very concept of sexual orientation. Butterfield agrees, arguing that the concept of sexual orientation "creates fictional identities that rob people of their true one: male and female image bearers. Sexual orientation is a word that extends the definition of sexuality beyond its biblical confines."[24] Our differing sexual desires do not place us in different categories of humanity.

Denny Burk concurs with much of the analysis of these thinkers and the conclusion that Butterfield drew when she wrote, "There is no ontological category of sexual orientation. . . . At its best, sexual orientation is a vestige of our flesh. . . . And while you must repent of sexual sin, you cannot repent of sexual orientation, since it is an artificial category based on a faulty premise."[25] It may be wise for Christians to reject the entire concept of sexual orientation as a non-biblical category that can be harmful.

And yet, it's important to ask whether it is possible to distinguish "gayness" from the temptation to sexual behavior with a person of the same sex. Many, if not most, gay people describe being gay as much more than sexual behavior and the desire to engage in it.[26] The same could be said for most heterosexual people. Can gayness or heterosexuality be distinguished from the immediate sexual attraction for the other sex or the same sex? This is an ongoing and, as yet, unresolved conversation among Christian scholars.[27] The experience of being gay for many people seems to involve expressions of personality, interests, and feelings beyond or in addition to sexual and romantic desires.

Wesley Hill suggested that we might be able to make this distinction between gayness and immediate sexual attraction, and thus sanctify being gay. He wrote,

> Insofar as a homosexual orientation can represent a broader, deeper drive for non-genital, same-sex closeness, it is *not* objectively disordered and may instead be a sign of God's gracious reordering of one's erotic life in Christ. Deep friendship between persons of the same sex that includes fidelity, permanence, and intimacy is something the Christian tradition has always honored, and it is something that those Christians who experience a homosexual orientation may be uniquely poised to recognize, value, and help recover in today's Church.[28]

In his book *Spiritual Friendship*, as he unpacks the notion of friendship itself, Hill points to the possibility of such committed same-sex relationships.

While the beauty and goodness of non-erotic, same-sex committed friendships seems undeniable, Butterfield questioned whether that phenomena is best enveloped in the category homosexual (gay). She offered instead the notion of homosociality. "The concept of *homosociality* describes and defines social bonds between persons of the same sex."[29] Butterfield describes homosociality as "an abiding and deep comfort afforded in keeping company with your own gender, and finding within your own gender your most important and cherished friendships."[30] This is not sinful and should be encouraged in our church communities. Hill's work on friendship helps us in this regard.

But Collins saw Butterfield's solution as an overcorrection that does not recognize "the nonsexual elements of gay experience as potentially helpful ways of reimagining the givenness of gayness."[31] He argued that "in using the term homosociality, Butterfield is engaging in a brilliant bit of deconstruction, but at a cost. Like many queer theorists, Butterfield demonstrates an unwillingness to address the overlap between homosociality and same-gender sexual desire within the hearts and minds of gay people. But while queer theorists resist this overlap because they think it's meaningless, Butterfield seems to resist it because she believes that gay always equals sin."[32]

After an extensive analysis, however, Collins still concludes that the concept of sexual orientation is only of limited use for evangelical Christians. His main point is that "using sexual orientation as a category of personhood requires us to view relationality through the lens of sexuality instead of the other way around. Human persons are first and foremost relational beings, not sexual beings."[33] And yet he believes there is some real difference in orientation to life between straight and nonstraight people.

Perhaps same-sex orientation is more than sexual. According to Sprinkle, "Same-sex orientation includes a desire for conversational intimacy, same-sex physical touch, emotional bonds, companionship, doing life together, and expressing mutual affection toward members of the same sex. And if all of this sounds 'gay' to you, then David and Jonathan really were gay, since I am alluding to 1–2 Samuel."[34]

In fact, what if what we now call a same-sex orientation is not fundamentally about sex itself, but sex is merely an aspect of it? Collins takes these questions in a fresh direction that may be beyond where you are willing to think right now. He wonders if the difference between being gay or straight amounts to how we see beauty, so he suggests that we consider talking about "aesthetic orientation" rather than sexual orientation.[35] He wrote,

> If we are to speak of an aesthetic orientation and use it to differentiate between gay and straight, we would say that both gay men and straight women are, for example, less aware (in general) of the beauty of feminine personhood than straight men or lesbian women. These general patterns that we discern in the way people experience the beauty of others are now the basis for distinguishing between straight and nonstraight orientations, rather than an impulse toward sexual activity.[36]

This direction of thinking leads to provocative questions, such as what would a gay orientation have looked like before the fall or if the fall never happened? And correspondingly, will people maintain a gay orientation in heaven, fully sanctified, of course? These are impossible hypothetical questions to answer, but they helpfully push our thinking forward in evaluating the morality of a gay orientation today.[37] Regardless of how you evaluate Collins's suggestions, when we put sexuality at the center of personhood, or as a primary discriminator of kinds of humans, then terms such as *homosexual* and *heterosexual* can become identity markers sorting humanity into fundamentally different kinds of sexual beings, which I think distorts our ministries.[38]

Whatever you think about these last ideas as a spiritual leader, I hope bringing you into this discussion of orientation opens your eyes to embrace believers who continue to see themselves as oriented to be gay, even as they do not act on it in terms of sexual behavior or lust and repent when they do. It is possible to see orientation as more than sexual—and even other than sexual.

Let's come back to the question, can you be gay and Christian? In terms of *gender roles*, it's fine to be a more feminine man or a more masculine woman.

Same-sex sexual behavior is wrong. And yet you can sin and still be a Christian. We should confess, repent, and choose to honor God with our bodies, but because we sin does not mean we are not Christians, which is important because we all sin with our bodies. This same truth applies to repeated sin of any kind. Hill quoted Holmes, who said, "[T]he church is able to truly welcome all people only because it refuses to affirm anyone's identity or behaviour."[39]

In terms of *same-sex identity*, while it may be a fact that you struggle with unwanted same-sex attractions, your primary identity should be in Christ, even if you choose to use "gay" as a secondary descriptor for yourself.

In terms of *sexual attraction*, temptations are not neutral because they draw us to sin, but there is nothing immature about being tempted in an erotic same-sex way, or in any other way. You can persistently wrestle against same-sex erotic attractions or straight erotic attractions and be the most mature Christian in the church. And some same-sex attractions are not erotic at all.

In terms of *orientation*, it is possible to have a persistent pattern of temptation and be faithful to Christ. Also, it may be that a gay orientation is more of a way of seeing beauty than at its core a sexual inclination or distortion.

We all struggle with morally malignant desires to sin. Those who entertain sinful sexual lusts toward the opposite gender are equally guilty and responsible before God as those who entertain same-sex sexual lusts. All human sexual desires post-fall need to be transformed by the power of the Spirit in Christ.[40] All humans stand on equal ground as sinners corrupted by original sin. All believers share equal inheritance in the blood of Jesus who forgives us all our sexual sin, physical and mental. All who are indwelt by the Spirit share the same posture of repentance as we are regularly convicted of sin, sexual and otherwise.

As Christians, our identities, our lives, and our futures are in Jesus. God offers to meet our needs and more. King David cried out: "Whom have I in heaven but you? And earth has nothing I desire besides you" (Ps. 73:25). Not in our sexuality or in anything else, but in Christ we find our life. He is our Savior who comforts our sorrows and calms our fears. He is our foundation through the worst storms. He is our all. One day soon he is coming back to fully heal us all.

In the in-between time, while we wait for his return, we must all ask how we live faithful to Christ while dealing with our sinful sexual desires.

Discussion Questions

1. Before reading this chapter, when you heard the word *gay*, what did it mean to you? How does your previous understanding correlate to the five ways the term *gay* has been currently used as described in this chapter?

2. How are gender roles expressed in your church? What pictures of masculinity and femininity are communicated in your ministries and teaching?

3. In your opinion, can a person engage in homosexual sexual intimacy and still go to heaven?

4. How would you summarize reasons for and against persons referring to themselves as gay Christians?

5. Can you distinguish temptation from mental sin, and if so, how?

6. What are the cause(s) of same-sex desires as discussed in this chapter?

7. How do you evaluate the category of an orientation as it applies to sexuality? What does it mean?

8. How do you answer the question, can you be gay and Christian?

CHAPTER 6

SAME-SEX SEXUALITY

Leading People to Holy Ways of Living

No, you can't" is not an attractive way to present a vision for a great life in Christ. And yet, that's what LGBT+ people tend to hear first and loudest from churches. "No, you can't have sex." And, "No, you can't get married." Where is the vision of a robust, flourishing, abundant life in Christ?

For those of you who consider yourself gay or lesbian, let me quickly say that I cannot know what it feels like to walk in your shoes, but I am trying to understand. Several wonderful gay men and lesbians have helped me see through their eyes, and I acknowledge that your choices are difficult. Following Christ as a person with same-sex desires requires a level of self-denial that may be beyond what many others have faced. I wonder if that leads you to a deeper faith walk with Christ.

The apostle Paul suffered what he called a "thorn in the flesh" for which he prayed many times to be taken away, but it never was. We have no idea what the thorn was. Paul wrote,

> But he [God] said to me, "My grace is sufficient for you, for my power is made perfect in weakness." Therefore I will boast all the more gladly about my weaknesses, so that Christ's power may rest on me. That is why, for Christ's sake, I delight in weaknesses, in

insults, in hardships, in persecutions, in difficulties. For when I am
weak, then I am strong. (2 Cor. 12:9–10)

As a gay person, you likely face insults, unique hardships, persecutions, and difficulties, but as with Paul, whatever his thorn in the
flesh was, you can experience a deeper measure of God's grace and
power because when you are weak, he is strong. It's not surprising
to me that Ed Shaw wrote, "Some of the most godly people that I
have ever known are those who've also experienced same-sex attraction."[1] Shaw openly shared his own same-sex attraction, and how God
has shaped him, when he wrote, "Nothing has given me more child-
like dependence on God than my same-sex attraction—and, after
all, that's what being a Christian is about, according to Jesus (Mark
10:15)."[2] Just the pain of living with persistent desires that counter
God's good Word is difficult enough, but LGBT+ people also unjustly
face rejection, at times sadly from Christian people. This is wrong and
should stop, no matter where the mistreatment comes from.

How can the church be a place where gay men and lesbians, and
other sexual minorities, flourish in the abundant life that Christ
promises all of us? As spiritual leaders, we need to cast that vision
and point to examples to follow. What kind of abundant life and holy
living does God offer to LGBT+ people in our churches?

As we covered in the first chapter, we have no sexual rights before
God to fulfill our desires however we please. We discovered that while
sex is a good gift, it is not essential to a good life. Every believer deals
with unfulfilled and unfulfillable desires. Sexually, no married couple
has all their desires fulfilled. Living with unfulfilled desires is not the
exception of human experience; it is the norm.[3] So for those united
to Christ, called by the Father, and empowered by the Spirit, as an
LGBT+ person you have several God-honoring ways to live, starting
with celibacy.

Celibacy: A Choice of Devotion to Christ

Because of the cultural emphasis on fulfilling our every desire for personal happiness, and because of several theological missteps, celibacy for many people seems impossible and horrible. Which is why Ed Shaw's book *Same-Sex Attraction and the Church: The Surprising Plausibility of the Celibate Life* is so important. As a same-sex attracted pastor, Shaw speaks with authenticity and power as he casts a fresh vision for a flourishing life of celibacy, but that vision requires local churches to make some changes in both thinking and practices.

I appreciate how Shaw put the issue right out there: people think that if you can't get married and have sex, you will not be happy. But is happiness really the biblical goal for our lives on this earth? Certainly, God promises us joy, complete joy, but what will bring us true joy? Shaw correctly questions himself, as he comments, "Well, I am not convinced that doing what I think would make me happy would actually make me happy."[4] It's so easy to deceive ourselves. The Devil often makes the "fruit" look so tasty, and we think it will make us happy.

What if it were the case, the reality, that true joy comes from denying our sinful sexual desires? God's Word assures that obedience leads to blessing and violating God's Word leads to the opposite. Sexual fidelity to a spouse brings more happiness than a fling with that pretty young thing, as exciting as it may seem. And so with being gay, Shaw recognizes this truth: "When I want to live life as a gay man, to embrace the whole modern identity and lifestyle, God's Word assures me that it will not make me happy—even though denying my sexual feelings the affirmation and expression I so want sounds cruel and unloving, it is actually what I would choose myself if I knew what was best for me."[5] Of course our desires for a life partner are more than sexual whether we are gay or straight. Later I will address other approaches to meeting our needs for intimacy and companionship.

We need to shift our theology to reenvision singleness. As we've established, after Jesus and the Spirit came, the Bible narrative begins to honor singleness in a way that it was not honored before Christ's coming. Being single is not a curse but a blessing, equal to but different from the blessing of being married.

Celibate singleness is a great choice for many people, including those who are same-sex attracted. If sufficiently spiritually mature and gifted, such a person can give leadership in the local church, including serving as an elder or pastor, because, as we have already seen, there is nothing immature about being tempted. While habitual serious sin precludes spiritual leadership, temptation does not. In conservative churches men and women already in serving and leadership roles are coming out with their same-sex sexual past and present temptations. As church leaders, we need to be ready to stand up for repentant believers, especially when some in our churches will want them fired, suspended, or removed from their positions. It's costly to stand for grace and redemption, particularly in this area.

Being single and being married are equally good, God-honoring choices. The church of Jesus Christ as his body, the family of the Father, and the temple of the Spirit is the primary place where we are to form our closest relationships, show love, and experience community. Even the great discourse on love in 1 Corinthians 13, often read at weddings, does not appear in the context of teaching on marriage but in the context of teaching on the church.

This great love can be experienced by celibate singles. Writing as a gay, single, and celibate, Greg Coles asked great questions. "What if, in the end, celibacy is all about love? What if the gift of celibacy is a gift of loving well, loving differently, loving in ways that are outside the purview of the married life?"[6] It is possible to experience a kind of love that thrills you, and yet not have sexual intimacy. This 1 Corinthians 13 and John 15 kind of love arises among friends in the body of Christ, the family of the Father, where we embrace one another as brothers and sisters.

As spiritual leaders, let's lead our people away from seeing celibacy as a big fat *no*, and toward seeing it as a wonderful *yes* to love, relationships, and friends; to intimacy with the triune God; to serving others; to enjoying life's goodness. When we stop idolizing marriage as the sole place for true love and happiness, we can make space for the place of love and joy in the family of God, the body of Christ, the church. This kind of vision can save couples from massive disappointment when marriage does not meet their unreal expectations, and can give singles a vision to participate in the wonderful life that God has for them.

Singleness can be a way of living in which many people grow more Christlike than they would if married. After all, God's primary plan for us is not marriage but maturity in Christ. And yet, a Christ-follower's life as married or as single requires sacrifices. Much of the modern evangelical church offers a soft prosperity theology, that God wants us to be happy, so if you are suffering, it means something must be wrong. But that is not the way of Christ. As Shaw affirmed in the context of living single, "Of course, there will be suffering at times, but how could we expect otherwise in following the one who entered his glory via crucifixion and called on his disciples to travel the same road by denying themselves and taking up the cross?"[7]

And yet God does not just call us to suffer but also to victory in Christ. In Christ we have life now and forever, a life of peace and joy, regardless of our relational status. None of us, single or married, experiences the satisfaction of all our desires on this earth. This side of heaven we long for something more, for a union, a joy, we can't quite identify. We thirst and hunger for life that we taste in part with the bread and the cup at the table, but we await full satisfaction at the banquet to come when we are with our King. This time is a period of waiting, of longing.

Human sex here on earth points to the ultimate union we will experience with the triune God. Coles said, "Our longing for sex is a longing that will only ever find its true fulfillment in something beyond sex."[8] The call to celibacy recognizes and marks the truth that our deepest sexual desires express a longing for another world, another life, a kind of fulfillment we will know when we are face-to-face with our Savior.

Theologically, our eschatology can guide our sexuality. Shaw expressed this profound truth:

> In the new creation, the whole church will be married to Jesus (Revelation 21:2). There will be no single people in heaven—no lonely Valentine's Days—but instead one great eternal relationship of love that we will all be bound up in and celebrating together forever. Marriage to Jesus will be better than sex (Revelation 21:3–4). I hear that sex can be great. But if I die a virgin, I will not be missing out: the eternal consummation of my relationship with Jesus will be far better than the temporary consummation of any human relationships. The latter always leads to death and mourning and crying and pain; the former will bring nothing but lasting joy.[9]

Longing and waiting do not cancel out joy, but can actually stoke it. Think of waiting for a birthday or a vacation, for Christmas morning or a wedding. The anticipation itself fills us with joy when we know that what we are waiting for is wonderful, beyond imagining. Coles described it like this: "But a life of longing isn't a life without happiness. On the contrary, it's a life rich with detail, alive with wonder and beauty. It's when I am happiest that I long most. And someday, when I look into the face of my Savior, I will taste the fulfillment of an intimacy a thousand times sweeter than any pale earthly imitation."[10]

It's crucial that as spiritual leaders we affirm the goodness of both marriage and singleness, and that we portray sexuality in its proper place as good, but not the ultimate good. Both marriage and singleness present limitations and freedoms. Marriage offers the freedom of monogamous sexual union and the possibility of children. But singleness opens up freedoms that married people miss out on. Freedom from the anxiety of raising children, from the fear of divorce. Singleness offers the joy of deep friendships and opportunities to give time and money without consulting a spouse. We must actively resist the foolish idea that denying gay people a same-sex spouse denies them a fulfilled life.[11] However, we should never foolishly dismiss the fact that mistreatment of gay people disrupts their potential for a purposeful, fulfilled celibate life. The family of God is supposed to lower—not increase—the unique burdens of gay people.

This means that as the church we need to do a much better job of building biblical community, and it is single people who can lead the way. This includes same-sex attracted singles who may have a better understanding of friendship, and may know a depth of dependence on God that many married straight people never experience.[12] Wesley Hill extended a good challenge to church leaders when he said,

> Likewise, the discipline entailed by their choice of celibacy must be explored with acute attention and care; they must not simply be *told* to be celibate without also being offered psychological, moral, and spiritual direction, based on knowledge of the truest findings of psychological research as well as the rich reflections of the ascetic and spiritual traditions of Christian history. And finally, they must be encouraged—*we* must be encouraged, for I number myself among them—to view our particular existence as the "washed and

waiting," the same-sex attracted and celibate, not simply as a life of deprivation but as a life that is *directed* toward community, friendship, hospitality: in short, directed toward love.[13]

Practically speaking this means as spiritual shepherds we care for LGBT+ people as our brothers and sisters. As shepherds we will protect the sheep (LGBT+ people in this case) from mistreatment by others, whether that mistreatment takes the form of humor at their expense or being excluded. We will stand by them, stand up for them, and stand up to others on their behalf.

While gay singles' experiences are distinct from those of other singles, both carry the potential for building stronger biblical, loving communities. In our church communities, we could cast vision for different kinds of kinship partnerships in our church families.

Kinship Partnerships: Nonsexual Intimacy

American Christianity perpetuates the cultural myth of the nuclear family with mom, dad, 2.5 kids, a dog, and a well-maintained yard in the suburbs. When you hang around churches and listen to what is said in worship services, you might think those were the only kinds of kinship groups in the church. Or you might get the idea that the nuclear family is the ideal all other ways of sharing life together are measured against.

Let me suggest that you and your fellow leaders consider broader and more diverse versions of kinship. In our hypersexualized Western culture, we equate intimacy with sexuality, but there are ways to be intimate without being sexual, such as between a mom and her son. Relational intimacy is not necessarily sexual. Consider expanded kinship, intentional community, and celibate partnerships.

Imagine if families opened their homes to gay people to join the family unit. In much of the world throughout history, a household often included extended family as well as servants (employees). My point is simply that if our vision is merely a nuclear family, we have a truncated view of family and kinship. In many cultures, older relatives, from a grandma to an uncle, live with the family. In our life together, my wife and I have had a variety of people share our home for periods of time, including her brother and my sister's fiancé.

A different approach is intentional community. This is where a group of people, single or married, choose to live together in a common domestic space and share responsibilities, such as cooking, cleaning, and even finances. Some churches have built or bought spaces—private homes or apartment complexes—where this can happen.

Another form of kinship is committed friendship expressed in living together and sharing life. Many people who consider themselves not straight simply want a relationship that is deeply intimate but nonsexual, much like David and Jonathan. In our American imagination, that is hard to envision. If two men hold hands, we immediately suspect they are gay. It's our problem, and the church should hold up alternatives. Some people might call this kind of relationship a covenant partnership, or life partnership, to distinguish it both from marriage and from a simple friendship or roommate arrangement.

In previous centuries, the church has recognized two people of the same gender interacting in the public sphere as a social couple, without the relationship being sexual or erotic. In Alan Bray's award-winning history of friendship, he noted, "I visited Merton College chapel to see the great memorial brass that at the turn of the fourteenth century was placed above the tomb of John Bloxham and John Whytton, standing side by side under canopies."[14] In other words, the Roman Catholic Church recognized their relationship in a Christian burial. There have been couples who operated as an economic unit and socially related as a couple. Toward the end of his work, Bray commented, "It reduces the range of what we recognize today as being sexual to the narrow question of sexual intercourse, and it glosses over the historical disparity that, in the past, marriage has been one, as it is not in modern society, among several forms of what one might call voluntary kinship: kinship created not by blood but by ritual or a promise."[15]

Currently in the United States, unmarried life partners lack the legal rights of married couples, but they can enter into legal agreements, deeds, and wills with regard to their property and business. A life partner could be of the same or opposite gender.

In my church, Bob and Terry (two men) share a life together, but they are not romantic, yet they say "I love you" to each other, own a home together, and relate socially as a couple. But neither would identify as gay. Both have been married and divorced long ago. I've known them for more than thirty years, and they are leaders in our church with fruitful ministries, such as leading a small group, serving in a homeless shelter, and ministering to people in jail. Over the years I have had to defend them against unfair, untrue, and unkind accusations.

If we are going to provide relational support to gay people and offer a context in which they can thrive for Jesus, we need to be proactive about helping them envision and find forms of community in our churches. And we will need to help the rest of the people in our churches open their minds and arms to expanded versions of kinship that are blessed by God. This impacts our communication from the platform on Sunday in worship services, and how we talk about programs and ministries we offer.

Another holy way of living that some reject far too quickly is marriage between two people of the opposite sex where one or both partners identify as gay.

Marriage (Heterosexual): A Choice of Self-Denial for Christ

These relationships have been called mixed-orientation marriages. For some they work great, and for others they are a disaster. A fellow pastor friend of mine is married to a lesbian and has been for decades. She consciously chose to deny herself in terms of her sexual attractions by getting married and having children. While it is complicated, they have built a wonderful marriage and have led a church for years.

I appreciate Deb Hirsch's transparent honesty as she described her journey from a previous lesbian life, learning to love her husband, Alan. She admitted that, at first, even the thought of having sex with a man gave her "a sense of revulsion." She said it was more difficult to learn trust in order to experience true intimacy. She also shared the stories of a now-married man describing how being intimate with the opposite sex felt like walking around with his shoes on the wrong feet. Others say it's like learning to drive on the other side of the road. Over time some develop more romantic or sexual attractions for their spouse and others less.[16]

I have heard horror stories of gay people who get married to hide their gayness or to try to get rid of it. This rarely works and often explodes later, leading to divorce. A mixed-orientation marriage entered into with openness and honesty, however, can be healthy and joyful. As a gay man, Nate Collins lives in a mixed-orientation marriage. His work on the topic is helpful. He wrote, "In general, mixed-orientation marriages require the same kinds of qualities to thrive as do regular marriages, although the impact these qualities have on the marital relationship will be somewhat different because of the impact of the gay spouse's orientation on the relationship. First, honesty and transparency, particularly regarding the gay person's orientation, is critical to the success of a mixed-orientation marriage."[17] If entered into wisely, with spiritual counsel, a mixed-orientation marriage can be another healthy way to live that honors God.

Transformation: Nothing Is Impossible with God

Aside from marriage, another approach to holy living is transformation to a different orientation. I'm aware this is quite controversial, and in fact openly rejected by many today in reaction to the so-called reparation therapy movement.

Recently there has been a big and appropriate backlash against reparation therapy, the attempt to change a person's sexual attraction from homosexual to heterosexual. Sadly, many people were hurt by overly optimistic attempts to change a person's attractions. LGBT+ people make fun of Christians who think they can "pray the gay away." While there is a new widely held and accurate recognition that only a few people significantly change their sexual attractions, it appears that human sexual attraction occurs on a spectrum; for example, an individual person cannot simply be put in a box as heterosexual, homosexual, or bisexual as if those were distinct, permanent, fixed categories.[18]

There is quite a range in the strength and persistence of sexual attractions with a difference between fleeting thoughts and a persistent pattern—and a big difference between a little experimentation and a decades-long relationship. Teenagers often experience a range of sexual feelings as they are developing their adult identity. Just because you have certain feelings or attractions does not mean you are gay. There is a college phenomenon some call LUG, lesbian until graduation, referring to women who declare themselves lesbian and act that way in college and then after graduation get married to a man and have kids. Many people have noted greater fluidity in female sexual desires compared to greater fixity in males.

Biblically, we know that nothing is impossible for God (Matt. 19:26). He made the world and raised Jesus from the dead. While God does not promise to transform our sexual desires any more than he promises to heal every sick person, he certainly can do so. We must avoid a type of prosperity gospel teaching that promises more than God has actually promised in this life. As Deb Hirsch wryly commented, "Similarly I've never met a heterosexual who has been fully healed and still doesn't struggle in some way with his or her sexuality."[19] The gospel does not deliver us from one sexual desire to another but from sin to righteousness. And our struggle with sin continues until we see Jesus face-to-face.

I do not think we should write off transformation as impossible or always unhealthy.[20] While wholeness and sanctification do not necessarily include becoming straight to be more like Jesus, we do see some examples of transformation. Christian spoken-word poet Jackie Hill-Perry made a big splash with her announcement that God had changed her. While I do not know her inner feelings, she was a lesbian and is now married to a man. The bigger point is that the Bible does not command us to heterosexuality but to holiness.[21] The goal is to steward well your sexual desires before God, whatever they are.

Some people, however, experience a shift in the nature of their romantic or sexual desires. Sometimes this is the work of God; other times it just happens over time as a result of a variety of factors, not all of which we can probably understand. God's intent is for all of us to live holy lives no matter our orientation, attraction, or temptations.

We must see ourselves, gay and straight, in the larger context of what God is doing. In creation God made a good, beautiful world. Then in the fall humans wrecked it. Now in redemption God is fixing it. In the new creation God will fully restore it. Today we live in the in-between time, in a fallen world in the process of being restored. The Bible says we groan while we wait for the redemption of our bodies (Rom. 8:23). All Christians struggle with the demands of the gospel that counter our many powerful sinful impulses and desires. Gay Christians who are celibate can have much to teach all of us about how to live well in this difficult time between the resurrection and the return of Christ, including how to face hard questions every Christian wrestles with:

- How do we live well with unfulfilled desires?
- How do we battle constant temptation?
- How do we find our identity in Christ as broken people in the process of being restored?
- How do we deal with painful loneliness and relational tensions as we anticipate the day we will all unite in one loving community in fellowship with our triune God?

God lavishes his loving grace on all people of every sexual distortion, which is every post-puberty adult. The most important issue is not our sexuality but Christ's gospel. We can all find healing in Jesus Christ.

As church leaders, we have the opportunity to cast fresh vision for our gay and lesbian members to flourish for Christ in various ways, including celibacy, expanded kinship groups, marriage, or even transformation. We can hold up beautiful examples of celibate people, such as the British biblical scholar John Stott, and various kinds of healthy kinship groups beyond the nuclear family. We can talk about mixed-orientation marriages, and not dismiss transformation as impossible, nor uphold it as a promise from God.

Deep suffering brings great dependence on God. No matter your sexual desires and temptations, you have the opportunity to know great depths of God's love, forgiveness, grace, and power. You can be a wonderful gift to the church of Jesus Christ. None of us will be fully cured of sinful desires in this life. But in this life we can care for each other and bear each other's burdens. We can help each other up when we fall. We can defend each other when we are attacked. We can cry together, laugh together, and serve Jesus side by side. We can share the bread and the cup united together in celebrating the body and blood of Jesus as his one body.

And in that one body, how do we talk about these issues well?

Discussion Questions

1. What pictures of a fulfilled life in Christ does your church offer to LGBT+ people?
2. What does our theology of singleness have to do with how we think about celibacy? How would you evaluate the choice of celibacy for yourself? For others?
3. In what ways could a more robust church family help single, celibate people experience community and fellowship? In what practical ways could your church improve in this area?
4. What forms of expanded kinship partnerships have you encountered? What kinds of kinship could you imagine encouraging in your church? How might this impact your ministries and communication?
5. How do you evaluate the dangers and benefits of a mixed-orientation marriage?
6. Why do you think there has been such a backlash against reparation therapy? How do you evaluate the possibility of transformation? And how would you communicate this option with proper nuance in your church?
7. How could LGBT+ Christian men and women benefit your church if they were involved?

CHAPTER 7

JESUS' CONVERSATIONS WITH SEXUAL SINNERS

Leading People to Communicate Like Jesus

One Sunday in December during the season of Advent, I felt led by the Spirit to invite any LGBT+ people listening to come talk with me and tell me their stories. On my heart was how difficult the holidays are for many LGBT+ people, whether they have come out to their families or not. Almost invariably, not all the family welcomes them fully to the Christmas celebration. I shared that I wanted to shower them with the Father's unconditional love.

Some took me up on my offer, and I had several fruitful multihour conversations, all of which were healthy but also included elements of pain. Too many stories had this plotline: "I grew up involved in church and tried to follow Jesus. Then as a teenager I experienced unwanted same-sex attractions that I tried to get rid of. They created unspeakable pain, confusion, and shame. When I tried to talk about how I was feeling, I was made to feel even more ashamed and was told to tell no one. I was prayed over, but I felt shunned and unwelcomed. This led to isolation and depression, even suicidal thoughts, until finally I left the church to find love and acceptance somewhere else."

Church leaders, we simply must invest more thoughtfully into

LGBT+ lives so that in the coming generation we will hear of more stories filled with grace and overflowing with love. Can you imagine that the sinners who were drawing near to Jesus ever left him depressed and wanting to kill themselves? The despised people of Jesus' day were drawn to him like a magnet, so much so that the Jewish religious people (even core leaders) were upset.

As Christ-followers, we, too, want to be spiritual magnets who draw people to the light and love of Jesus, who can give them eternal life. And yet gay and lesbian people avoid churches like the plague. They often assume they will be hated and viewed as disgusting. Even if they come, they may try to act like they are straight so that no one notices them and thus won't judge them. As Bill Henson says in his Posture Shift workshops: "A gospel that excludes or rejects has no power to reach already banished and mistreated persons. We must offer greater acceptance and inclusion in order to foster spiritual identity formation in LGBT+ people—as with any people."

My wife and I invite gay friends to our church, assuring them they will be accepted. We invite them to sit with us and pledge to protect them from the odd person who might say something off-color. But some still will not come.

In fact, the church's track record on responding to gay people is so dismal that millennials are leaving the church based on how the church has mistreated gay people. The gospel is at stake! Sprinkle said, "It's not too much truth but too little love that's driving gay and straight people away from the bride of Christ."[1] If we do not love and embrace young gay Christians, then when they embrace a gay identity, we need to accept that some of the fault might be ours. To what extent have our attitudes, words, and actions pushed young gay Christians over the edge and away from the church? How can we lead our churches to be places where we can safely talk about these kinds of issues? As a church leader, ask yourself practical questions about the atmosphere of your church. In your church, how do these conversations go, if they go at all?

- Can parents openly talk about their gay children without shame? Or do we avoid ever sharing that our son is gay or our daughter is a lesbian?
- Can people express their fears over the cultural trend toward greater acceptance of gay people, which they see as the advancement of an aggressive gay agenda?

In our church, recently, a mom and dad sought my counsel because their daughter announced she was engaged to another woman.

A young man confessed that he just broke up with his boyfriend and wants to follow Christ.

A woman asked if she could tell people at the church that she is a lesbian and wonders if she is welcome.

Several teenagers have confessed romantic feelings that made them worry they are gay or bisexual.

A gay teen has experienced teasing in youth group and worries that reporting it will yield retribution—or even greater isolation and mistreatment

Could your church be a safe place for a thirteen-year-old girl to confess to an adult leader her attractions to other girls? Or for the boy who wonders about his gender identity? If we cannot become a safe place, we inadvertently push people out to somewhere else where they do feel safe to share.

Of all places our churches should be a safe refuge because we believe in the amazing, unconditional grace of God in Jesus Christ. We confess that we are all sinners desperately in need of that grace. No one can out-sin the grace of God. We believe that the truth of God will set us free. We know obedience leads to blessing, always.

My heart rejoices with same-sex attracted men such as Greg Coles and Wesley Hill who have courageously chosen to be celibate for Christ even as they continue to experience romantic attraction to men. Would they be accepted in your church without qualification or hesitation? How do we walk well with celibate gay[2] men and women, involving them fully in the family of God in our local churches?

We must provide space and grace for those who are devoted to following Jesus and at the same time are same-sex attracted. It grieves me that at this moment in our culture, the sides have been drawn so that often people feel forced to choose between being gay or being a Christian, as if they must choose sides in a war.

Christians must rise above the cultural war to care for real people. We need to hold the hands of those struggling with inner temptations and confusions. We need to dry the tears of those who have been ridiculed for not fitting cultural gender norms. We dare not be among those who continue to tell gay jokes at the expense of teenagers who are navigating very difficult sexual-identity issues. We must not be among those who make our children feel so ashamed that they would never dare share their deeply conflicted feelings.

The church is called to be the place of grace in this sinful world. There is no shadow for shame to hide beneath the cross of Jesus. The arms of God are the safest place there is. The Father sent his Son to die for each one of us while we were still sinners. If we are going to represent Christ to people, then we must be willing to pour love on people who may still be sinning. Who are we kidding? We are *all* still sinning. Will we self-righteously judge those whose temptations differ from ours? Who will cast the first stone? We should be all grace and all truth.

Jesus Christ is our Savior and our model. As his followers, we pray to the Father to form us by the Spirit to grow more and more in the likeness of Jesus. So we look to him to guide us, including in the arena of sexuality. Jesus had several conversations with people that involved sexual issues. How he handled the topic and, more importantly, how he cared for each person, gives us a great example to follow. You can point your people to Jesus' example for how to talk about these sensitive issues.

Partying with the Wrong People

Consider how Jesus talked to tax collectors. They were despised and avoided by religious people. And yet Jesus went to parties at their homes and had dinner with them. He did not affirm their sin but their humanity and shared the Father's love for them.

After services on Sunday, a woman in our church came to ask me a question. She said she is in a Bible study with a neighbor who describes herself as a lesbian. (Inside I was celebrating.) Then she asked me if she should continue since she did not want to communicate that she approved of being lesbian! I held myself back emotionally. My goodness, I would be thrilled if more people in my church had relationships with their neighbors, much less be in a Bible study! And with all the hatred and conflict between gays and Christians, what a wonder, blessing, and joy to be studying the Bible together. Jesus did not worry about whether religious people thought he might be affirming a tax collector's "chosen lifestyle"! He enjoyed dinner with Zacchaeus and the party at Matthew's house. We have to show our people Jesus and how to follow him. Association does not equal affirmation. May we and the people of our churches also be accused like Jesus of being a friend to sinners. Yes, please get into Bible studies and form relationships with gay and lesbian people.

A mom called me in sobs over her daughter who had married a woman and is now having a child with her partner. The mom confessed she had not responded with love when she first found out. After hearing me encourage her to show unconditional love and grace, she asked, "But where is the line?" In other words, at what point would her love possibly communicate approval? My counsel was that there is no line. Jesus did not worry that his unconditional love might confuse people into thinking that he approved of sin, and neither should we. I prayed that this mom would love her daughter extravagantly. She asked what I thought of asking her daughter to meet her halfway. My response was to suggest she not do that. Jesus does not meet us half-way. He went all the way from heaven to earth to join our humanity. He went all the way to the cross while we were still sinners, and so should we go all the way in loving others.

How did Jesus talk to people in sexual sin? In three stories Jesus talked with a woman of a different race living with a man after having been married five times; a woman caught in the act of having sex with a man; and a prostitute. His model gives us examples we can follow and use to guide people in our churches.

Woman Living with a Man

In John 4, Jesus met a woman at a well at about noon in the heat of the day. His disciples had gone into town, so Jesus was alone with her. Since she came alone at an odd time, he could easily suspect that something was wrong, and of course, he already knew her story but engaged her with grace. Consider reading the whole story again as if the Samaritan woman were a lesbian. Here are highlights of how Jesus loved her.

> The Samaritan woman said to him, "You are a Jew and I am a Samaritan woman. How can you ask me for a drink?" (For Jews do not associate with Samaritans.) (v. 9)

She was of a different race and a woman, both of which would cause a typical religious Jewish man of that day to avoid a conversation, but Jesus pursued her.

> Jesus answered her, "If you knew the gift of God and who it is that asks you for a drink, you would have asked him and he would have given you living water." . . .

The woman said to him, "Sir, give me this water so that I won't get thirsty and have to keep coming here to draw water." (vv. 10, 15)

First Jesus offered her "living water," the gospel of God's love in Christ that satisfies our every thirst. Then he moved to speaking truth about her situation.

He told her, "Go, call your husband and come back."

"I have no husband," she replied.

Jesus said to her, "You are right when you say you have no husband. The fact is, you have had five husbands, and the man you now have is not your husband. What you have just said is quite true." (vv. 16–18)

Jesus spoke truth about the woman's living situation in a matter-of-fact way. Before bringing up her living arrangement, he already had offered her living water that springs up to eternal life. He first looked at her as a woman made in the image of God. Then, aware of her spiritual thirst, he offered what would quench it before he acknowledged her sin.

The woman said, "I know that Messiah" (called Christ) "is coming. When he comes, he will explain everything to us."

Then Jesus declared, "I, the one speaking to you—I am he." (vv. 25–26)

Jesus did not try to convince her that living with a man unmarried is sinful. He did not demand that she kick the man out. He simply offered himself to her as the Savior of the world, the Messiah who could give her living water.

She took his offer, went back to her town, and brought back a crowd to see this amazing man, the Savior. In the Gospels, she's the first missionary (before she resolved her sexual sin of living with a man!). Could we, too, offer sexually sinning people living water? Jesus has entrusted his followers with his living water, his forgiveness, to give thirsty people water that will once and for all quench their deepest soul thirst, which no sex of any kind will ever satisfy.

Adulterous Woman

In John 8, Jesus came upon a woman about to be stoned by a crowd of men.[3] The teachers of the law brought her into the public street and said she was caught in the act of adultery. In an attempt to trap Jesus, they demanded from him what to do with her as they reminded him that Moses commanded she be stoned. Jesus' response provides a great model for us in talking with those guilty of sexual sin. His response was full of grace without diminishing truth. Jesus said two things to the woman, but I find many people only remember one or the other, and the order of the two is important.

> The teachers of the law and the Pharisees brought in a woman caught in adultery. They made her stand before the group and said to Jesus, "Teacher, this woman was caught in the act of adultery. In the Law Moses commanded us to stone such women. Now what do you say?" They were using this question as a trap, in order to have a basis for accusing him.
>
> But Jesus bent down and started to write on the ground with his finger. When they kept on questioning him, he straightened up and said to them, "Let any one of you who is without sin be the first to throw a stone at her." Again he stooped down and wrote on the ground.
>
> At this, those who heard began to go away one at a time, the

older ones first, until only Jesus was left, with the woman still standing there. Jesus straightened up and asked her, "Woman, where are they? Has no one condemned you?"

"No one, sir," she said.

"Then neither do I condemn you," Jesus declared. "Go now and leave your life of sin." (vv. 3–11)

Jesus defended this woman against those who wanted to condemn her. Could our churches see themselves as defenders of sinners? Jesus led the men to confess, to first look at themselves before throwing a stone. Then with the woman, Jesus led with grace. He first said "Neither do I condemn you." How could he say this when Jesus knew she was guilty, deserving condemnation? This is the heart of grace and the gospel. God forgives guilty people, and so should we. Then Jesus moved to truth: "Go now and leave your life of sin." He pointed her in the direction of wholeness and holiness built on the foundation of grace.

Could we be people who drop our stones of judgment? I pray our churches will become more like Jesus, refusing to condemn sinning people, while also calling people to sin no more. Rather than picking up our physical or verbal stones, could we instead be people who are keenly aware of our own sin and drop our stones instead of hurling them as posts on Facebook? Like Jesus, could we stand up for sinners against their accusers? Like Jesus, let's gently and humbly resist condemning people, even those in open sin, as we call people to leave their sin behind.

Prostitute

In Luke 7, Jesus was at a party where a woman was washing his feet with her tears and her hair, pouring perfume on them. The gospel writer described her as a woman "who lived a sinful life." Most likely she was a prostitute. How would Jesus treat her?

> When the Pharisee who had invited him saw this, he said to himself, "If this man were a prophet, he would know who is touching him and what kind of woman she is—that she is a sinner."
>
> Jesus answered him, "Simon, I have something to tell you."
>
> "Tell me, teacher," he said.
>
> "Two people owed money to a certain moneylender. One owed him five hundred denarii, and the other fifty. Neither of them had the money to pay him back, so he forgave the debts of both. Now which of them will love him more?"
>
> Simon replied, "I suppose the one who had the bigger debt forgiven."
>
> "You have judged correctly," Jesus said.
>
> Then he turned toward the woman and said to Simon, "Do you see this woman? I came into your house. You did not give me any water for my feet, but she wet my feet with her tears and wiped them with her hair. You did not give me a kiss, but this woman, from the time I entered, has not stopped kissing my feet. You did not put oil on my head, but she has poured perfume on my feet. Therefore, I tell you, her many sins have been forgiven—as her great love has shown. But whoever has been forgiven little loves little."
>
> Then Jesus said to her, "Your sins are forgiven."
>
> The other guests began to say among themselves, "Who is this who even forgives sins?"
>
> Jesus said to the woman, "Your faith has saved you; go in peace." (vv. 39–50)

Of course, Jesus knew the woman had "many sins." Interestingly the Bible does not tell us if she was currently engaged in prostitution or not. And he did not quote the law to her or tell her to stop it. Jesus let her touch him. In our churches and in our homes, will we let people "touch" us? Or serve us? Sometimes we Christians see our identity as those who serve people in need. Sometimes what is needed is allowing people in need to serve us.

Could we be people who rejoice more over prostitutes who come to Jesus than religious people who condemn prostitutes? We can orient our hearts more toward forgiveness than condemnation. When Jesus approached a woman with many sins, the story he told was not of terrible judgment but of lavish forgiveness. Lavish forgiveness yields love that pours out perfume on Jesus' feet, wets them with our tears, and washes them with our hair.

Could you imagine a day when churches are known as places of grace? Jesus did not say we will know his disciples by their moral stance on social issues. He said we will know his disciples by their love (John 13:35). God wants his churches to be places where struggling people find hope and healing. People rejected as sinners by other religious people flocked to Jesus. What if gay people were drawn to your church as a place of grace and truth where they would be welcomed and loved and given truth that sets them free? Where we say, "In Jesus your sins are forgiven" and "Your faith has saved you; go in peace"?

Jesus came bringing grace and truth, and they were not in conflict (John 1:16–17). Glenn Stanton wrote, "Truth without grace is abusive and grace without truth is mere sentimentalism. The two cannot exist without each other."[4] Too many Christians have strong convictions but embarrass Christ by how they relate to people. Other Christians are wonderfully civil but have no convictions. We must be people of 100 percent truth and 100 percent grace, neither watering down one or the other. We do not balance grace and truth, but bring both in full measure. Jesus' conversations model how to do this well. His compelling model is matched by principles in the Gospels and the Epistles, which we turn to next.

Discussion Questions

1. Generally speaking, do LGBT+ people in your church feel free to be open about their sexuality, at least with a pastor or a leader in the church? Do parents feel safe to talk about their children who have come out of the closet? Why or why not?

2. Are gay jokes and disparaging comments tolerated in your church? By you personally? How can you change this if it is a problem?

3. What principles of communication with LGBT+ people do you glean from Jesus in John 4?

4. Which of Jesus' two statements to the woman in John 8 comes to your mind first and fastest? How can we communicate both messages in our church conversations?

5. In reading the story in Luke 7, how is your church more like the Pharisee, and how is it more like Jesus? How could you lead your church or ministry to become more like Jesus?

6. How can your church both show grace and stand for truth, each in full measure?

CHAPTER 8

HOT POTATOES, LOGS, AND STONES

Leading Conversations with Our Posture

We've all had conversations we regret and spoken words we wish with all our hearts we could delete. And as church leaders we have cringed at the things church members and staff have said or posted on social media.

Sometimes it seems that no matter what you say, it is taken the wrong way. People are upset, offended, or hurt. While we cannot take responsibility for what another person does with our words, we must take full responsibility for what we say and how we say it.

How can we lead our people to have healthy conversations about sexuality in a Christlike, God-honoring way? No matter who you are talking with, there are things you do not do. In almost every case, we do not condemn, assume, ignore, exclude, or attack people. We do not shun them or shame them, nor do we lob Bible verses like grenades. It is usually quite unhelpful to say, "Don't you know God says, 'Don't do that'?"

As Christians we should walk beside one another. And when we fall, as brothers and sisters, we pick one another up. We do not shoot our wounded; we bind their wounds. Fyodor Dostoyevsky said, "Love can never be an offense to Christ."[1] No matter who you are talking with—a parent of a gay child, teenagers unsure of their identity, a married gay couple, a man and woman living together, or a person with convictions hostile to yours—in addition to Jesus' model, which gives us a great example to follow, the New Testament gives us three postures we can assume. The first is how I look at myself, a posture of kneeling, of confession.

Kneeling: A Posture of Confession

How I Look at Myself—Take the Log Out

Jesus backed up his command "Do not judge" (Matt. 7:1–5) with a colorful image from his carpentry shop. Imagine a person with a log stuck in his eye. The Greek word (*dokos*) translated as *plank* refers to a massive beam used to support a roof. Jesus said, "Why do you look at the speck of sawdust in your brother's eye and pay no attention to the plank in your own eye?" (v. 3).

This passage has sometimes been read as saying we should not judge others, meaning that we should never correct another person. A closer look, however, confirms that it does not forbid loving correction. Rather, it forbids *premature and improper* correction. Before you talk to others about their faults, Jesus wants you to examine yourself. We should not blindly rush to judge others while we turn a blind eye to our own failings. Many of us have a terrible tendency to exaggerate the faults of others and minimize the gravity of our own.

We need to ask ourselves: What do I need to confess? What are my prejudices and motives—fear, anger, disgust, and judgments, especially toward gay people or people opposed to my point of view? We can only judge others after we have judged ourselves. Have you seen your own sin and experienced the amazing grace of God? That experience has the power to deliver you from a critical, judgmental attitude.

Paul warned us to watch ourselves so that we are not tempted. This could be temptation into the same sin, or given what comes next, he could be talking about temptation to pride, thinking we are better than others. He wrote, "Brothers and sisters, if someone is caught in a sin, you who live by the Spirit should restore that person gently. But watch yourselves, or you also may be tempted" (Gal. 6:1–4). We are not to compare our sin to their sin, or our burdens to their burdens. After we get the log out of our eye, we can move from a posture of confession to a posture of care, which is how we treat the other person with arms extended.

Arms Extended: A Posture of Loving Care

How I Treat the Other Person

Read these next verses in the context of conversations about sexuality, especially heated same-sex issues. Peter said, "Above all, love each other deeply, because love covers over a multitude of sins" (1 Peter 4:8). Too often our first move is to expose sin, to gossip, to share the juicy news with others, but love covers even a multitude of sins.

And Paul told us what love looks like. Let this description of love guide your conversations with anyone on sexually sensitive issues:

> Love is patient, love is kind. It does not envy, it does not boast, it is not proud. It does not dishonor others, it is not self-seeking, it is not easily angered, it keeps no record of wrongs. Love does not delight in evil but rejoices with the truth. It always protects, always trusts, always hopes, always perseveres. (1 Cor. 13:4–7)

This is a high standard. Our conversations on these issues should be loving. So be patient and kind. Do not speak pridefully from above but humbly from beside. Do not be rude and self-seeking in how you speak. No matter what the person says, do not react in anger. After a conversation, let it go; don't keep a record of wrongs. Take no delight in others' failings, but rejoice that truth is being told. Protect your friends. Trust them, expect the best, believe the best, and hope the best. We should love each individual as much or more than any other person in their life loves them because they are our brothers and sisters.

If a person comes "out of the closet" to you, thank them for honoring you with sharing something so intimate, so difficult to share. Thank them for trusting you with it. It's much more loving to say, "I'd like to hear more about your life," than to say, "That's not right." This is a time for empathy. Sean McDowell rightly said, "We are not only supposed to like others; we are supposed to love others as we love ourselves. We shouldn't just tolerate other people; God commands us to care for them and to actively promote their good."[2] Here are three simple ways we can show love:

Listen First

Countless men and women have been told by church people not to tell anyone about their sexual sin, which only confirms their sense of shame. We need to do just the opposite. We need to open the conversation. Churches should be safe places to talk about your struggles. If a person shares with you that they have same-sex attractions or experiences, do not rush to label them. Love listens. Ask more about what's happening in their life. Seek to understand with empathy and compassion.

No matter who you are talking with, don't assume you know what's really going on with them, or know their full opinion and why they hold it, before you listen for a long time. Sadly, I agree with Stanton's observation, "Too often, this issue unfortunately seems to be an exchange of ideas and accusations built only on stereotypical extremes and emotionalism, rather than rational thinking, genuine listening, and appreciation of the fundamental disagreements over things that are actually true to either side."[3]

We need to consider who we are talking with. If a person is not yet a Christian and they do not believe in Jesus as their Savior, then that is the issue. The Bible says: "What business is it of mine to judge those outside the church?" (1 Cor. 5:12). We are not sin police. Our role is to show and share the good news that the Son of God gave his life to save our lives.

To minister well to other people, it helps to first put ourselves in their shoes. This increases our compassion and empathy. If you are not gay, imagine that you are. What would it feel like as you grow up to gradually realize that you are not attracted to the opposite gender but to your own? If you were raised in church and were a Christian, how would it trouble you? Imagine asking with great intensity how to reconcile your same-sex attractions with your Christian faith. Hear yourself crying out to God to change you, asking why God would allow you to feel this way.[4]

James wrote, "My dear brothers and sisters, take note of this: Everyone should be quick to listen, slow to speak and slow to become angry" (James 1:19). The old saying is true: God gave us one mouth and two ears, so we should listen twice as much as we talk. Take an interest in other people's lives. Find out why they view the world the way they do. Find out about hobbies, favorite music, and other things they are passionate about. There is more to each of us than our sexuality and opinions about it. Love listens first. Then love gives authentic help.

Help Authentically

Paul said we are to "carry each other's burdens" (Gal. 6:2). The word for *burden* means "a heavy weight or stone" someone is required to carry for a long distance. A burden can be a temptation or the actions that will be required to deal with the sin that has been exposed. We all have burdens, and God does not intend for us to carry them by ourselves. It is our joy to support each other in dealing with tough struggles. God told us that we are not to love just with words, but with actions and truth (1 John 3).

What could it look like to carry someone's sexual burden? So much depends on who they are and what's going on at the moment. It may look like going with a teenager to talk with their parents about what they are feeling about their sexuality. It could look like talking at length through the emotional burden of feeling different from the people around you. You could meet with a friend for accountability, support, and prayer. You could incorporate a single gay friend into your family for holidays and special events. You could go with them to confront someone who verbally slandered them. You could go with them to a counselor and help them find quality resources for the issues they are facing.

A Christian author who is gay said this on how to show love: "Do you love me? Don't talk about it. Show me. You know why LGBT people have such a bad impression of Christians? . . . Because of the Christians we know who stand idly by, thinking that if they're not actively *hating* us, that counts as loving us. That's not love."[5] Here are practical ideas she shared that challenge me:

> Stick up for me, even when I'm not around, such as when people make gay jokes or speak derisively about LGBT people. Protect children from LGBT bullying in schools. . . . Instead of asking me to join you in settings where *you're* most comfortable, look for opportunities to join me in settings where *I'm* most comfortable. Maybe I have a favorite coffee house, or I love to hike a local trail . . . And hey, maybe you could get to know my friends instead of expecting me to fit in with yours. You said you love me, right? Okay, then. Show me.[6]

Love helps authentically. We can associate with people without endorsing them. Jesus hung out with prostitutes and was accused of being a friend of sinners. It would be great if we earned the same accusation—"friends of sinners."

Speak Truth Gently

Regarding sexual issues, what truth would be important to share? Once again, you must consider each person and pray. Perhaps the truth that we are all made in the image of God and have value is what is needed to share first. Perhaps the gospel is the most important truth to share, the unconditional grace of God who forgives all sin and who makes us as white as snow (Isa. 1:18). Perhaps it is examining passages that show same-sex behavior as sinful. Paul said, "Instead, speaking the truth in love, we will grow to become in every respect the mature body of him who is the head, that is, Christ" (Eph. 4:15). Maybe it is reading the Psalms and discussing various characteristics of God through King David's writings.

Truth and grace are not in conflict but are united in love. Sometimes Christians hesitate to share that gay sex is sinful. While context and timing are crucial, God's truth is good for us. We want blessings in our friends' lives.

Even though gay men or lesbian women may believe with all their hearts that it is best for them to be in a sexual union with someone of their own gender, it is not. Often God's Word conflicts with our deep-set desires. What feels so right to us is not always right. Butterfield observed that "Adam's fall rendered my deep and primal feelings untrustworthy and untrue."[7]

We need to be more skeptical of our desires than of God's revealed will. Men and women have told me that their marriage is a sham, empty, not really a marriage. They are just roommates or worse. And now they have met someone else—their soul mate who really makes them happy. They ask, Doesn't God want me to be happy?

One woman whose dad is gay, shared with me, "I was so scared to tell my dad that I disagreed with him. I was afraid I would lose the relationship that I treasured. My biggest regret is waiting so long to be honest about my beliefs. God gave me strength not only to stand up for what I believed to be true, but also to pursue the relationship relentlessly. . . . And I never gave up on showing my dad Jesus's unconditional love." That's the heart of Jesus, full of grace and truth.

Students feeling same-sex attractions need to know they have done nothing wrong to merely have these feelings. They need to know they are loved and accepted.

We all follow cultural scripts that tell a story of how we should behave. There is a gay script that says, "Be who you are and you will be happy." What is the Christian script for same-sex attracted people? In many cases, it is merely, "Don't feel that way and don't tell anyone" or, "Well, God loves the sinner but hates the sin." We are almost telling people if they feel same-sex attraction, they do not belong here in the church, but they belong over there in the gay community.[8] Even more sadly, we often presume an LGBT+ person is living in sexual sin simply because they shared their sexual orientation with us. We jump to presumptive judgment rather than redemptive acceptance. This mistake fails to honor God—and it can deeply hurt people.

We need a much stronger script, a much more compelling vision. You can be a vibrant Christian who wrestles with same-sex attractions. The truth is that Jesus calls all of us to deny ourselves and follow him, to take up our cross, to lose our lives. Following Jesus should cost us everything, and if it does not, maybe we are not really following Jesus.

Jesus Christ offers you joy, fulfillment, and freedom from guilt and shame. The church offers you a loving community of people to do life with, to share your triumphs with, to cry with you over your tragedies, and to laugh with you over life's silliness. Jesus offers a mission worth giving your life for and a community worth investing your life in.

What if you are talking with a person who wants to follow Christ but has fallen into sexual sin, specifically with someone of their own sex? Galatians 6:1 applies: "Brothers and sisters, if someone is caught in a sin, you who live by the Spirit should restore that person gently."

The opening words, "brothers and sisters," remind us that we are in the same spiritual family. To restore means to bring something back to its original condition. It was used in regard to restoring torn fishing nets and healing fractured or dislocated bones. Our heart is to come alongside friends and help them recover, to restore them to fellowship with Christ, to call them to repentance and holiness. This usually involves speaking the truth in love, keeping in mind the active characteristics of love listed in 1 Corinthians 13.

Love involves listening first, helping authentically, and speaking the truth gently. In addition to the postures of confession and care, let me add a third: a posture of sitting attentively to share the gospel, which is how to advance Christ's gospel by sharing it in word and deed.

Sitting Attentively: A Posture of Sharing

How I Advance Christ's Kingdom

Advancing the gospel of Jesus should guide all that we say and do. The apostle Paul declared: "To the weak I became weak, to win the weak. I have become all things to all people so that by all possible means I might save some" (1 Cor. 9:22).

In regard to same-sex issues, this posture can help answer practical questions, such as: Do I buy a wedding gift for my same-sex family member or friend? Should I let my lesbian mom stay in our home overnight with her partner? Ask yourself what choice best advances the gospel of Jesus Christ.

What if you are talking with someone who is not same-sex attracted but they aggressively support same-sex marriage? Listen to Paul:

> Be wise in the way you act toward outsiders; make the most of every opportunity. Let your conversation be always full of grace, seasoned with salt, so that you may know how to answer everyone. (Col. 4:5–6)

Ask yourself the difficult question: How could I become all things to non-Christian gay people or heterosexual same-sex advocates in order to by all possible means, save some? In all your interactions, consider what you do for the sake of the gospel. The question is not what makes you comfortable or makes the other person happy, but what advances the gospel of Jesus.

People's eternal destinies are far more important than their opinions on sexuality. Jesus came for all of us, every one of us, while we were still sinners (Rom. 5:8). He came for you, no matter what your sexual history, attraction, or current experiences. Jesus' offer of salvation is not contingent on us cleaning up our lives or changing our views on sexuality. Rather, our salvation is based on what Jesus did for us. He offers to heal, to give living water so we never need thirst again.

What about same-sex attracted people in the church? We are churches for sinners. None of us are perfect people. Can greedy people be involved in the church? Can people who are tempted with adultery be in the church? If you are gay, lesbian, or same-sex attracted, you should be welcome in any gospel-centered church. All people are welcome and yet none are fully affirmed because we are all sinners in the process of being transformed by the grace of God. We only affirm Jesus, not any other human, because none of us are without sin. At our church we say, "We welcome all and affirm none."

We can walk well with people struggling with same-sex issues by taking three postures: confess, care, and share. Remember kneeling, standing with arms extended, and sitting attentively. I pray for our churches to be places of grace and truth—to be families where everyone is accepted even when we disagree. I pray we become places where we are each pursuing Christ, aware we are all in process, that none of us have arrived. We need to grant each other redemptive space to grow and become places of gracious spaciousness.[9] We are to become places where we speak the truth that sets us free, calling one another to be all in, holding nothing back as we follow Jesus with all our hearts, minds, and souls.

In our local churches, we are people—sinful people, hurting people, helping other people of all kinds to find and follow Jesus Christ who saves us all. We are all about Jesus, not about sexuality. We will follow his Word even when we don't fully understand it, even when it counters our deepest desires.

Discussion Questions

1. How do we tend to exaggerate the faults of others and minimize the gravity of our own? What do we need to confess before we address issues in the life of an LGBT+ person?
2. What could be a Christlike, loving response to a person who comes out of the closet to you?
3. Empathy is so powerful. If you are not gay, imagine that you are. What would it feel like as you grow up to gradually realize that you are not attracted to the opposite sex but to your own gender? If you were raised in church and were a Christian, how would it trouble you? What might you fear?

4. How can we practically love people who share their sexual temptations and sins with us, including bearing their burdens?
5. What is your church's "script" for an LGBT+ person who comes to your fellowship?
6. How might the mission of sharing the gospel impact how you relate to and talk with and about LGBT+ people?

CHAPTER 9

NOT IN MY CHURCH

Leading Those Who Struggle
Accepting LGBT+ People

One Sunday, in the context of a sermon related to the topic of this book, I opened my arms wide and warmly welcomed LGBT+ people to our church and encouraged them to bring their friends. My heart was to help my LGBT+ friends in our church know they are really wanted and that their friends—who likely think church people don't want them around—are welcome as well.

That next week a leader in our church came to me with concerns. He said, "You welcomed them. That's good, but I mean you *really* welcomed them! What if they come?" He knew in his mind that it was right to welcome all people, but his own discomfort prevented him from genuinely welcoming LGBT+ people from his heart. He went on to press me with this question: "What if I am checking my little grandson into the children's ministry, and a gay couple comes to check in their child? What do I say to my grandson?" It's important to acknowledge his concerns and his fears.

Empathize with People Who Struggle

We need as much grace for church people who struggle with gay people as we do for gay people who struggle with the church. Patience and love, empathy and a listening ear are what we bring to each person. We live in a rapidly changing world that has created emotional whiplash for many longtime church members.

In my office, a man from our church angrily expressed his frustration. "These gay issues are pushed at me at work with diversity training. My kids face it at school. And it's thrown in my face on the TV. I just wish the church could be a gay-free zone." I felt his frustration and fatigue. The arguing, the vitriol, and the scrutiny of the language police wear us all down. And yet this man knew what he was saying was not right; he just did not know what to do with his difficult feelings.

Another gentleman in our church wanted to be sure that I knew there was a gay agenda. Some folks in our churches are deeply invested in the culture wars. Sadly, fears are stoked by politically conservative Christian radio, blogs, and newsletters. Years of consuming a steady diet of this kind of rhetoric will shape your thoughts. We can get imprisoned in a subculture of culture-war discourse, and the walls are getting higher. Infotainment websites, political programming, and cable news generate views and clicks by confirming our biases. Your newsfeed becomes filled with what you already believe to be true about the virtues of your own position and the evils of the other side.

Living in your own carefully crafted media bubble only reinforces your perception of the world. This happens to gay people too. I wish for a week people could enter another person's world of informational input. One person's newsfeed confronts them with the latest attack on religious freedom while the other's announces the latest injustice to gay people who have once again been denied their rights. It's essential that we try to walk in each other's shoes and to hear the other person as a person.

To empathize with those who are uncomfortable with gay people, we can help them identify the root of their discomfort. Ask questions to put the fears on the table. Many people fear the "slippery slope," also known as the "camel's nose under the tent." When they hear you express compassion for gay people and see you give them a warm welcome to your church, they assume you are weakening your convictions. Because of recent shifts in our culture, their fears are not completely unfounded. Even fifteen years ago, few people would have imagined the rapid acceptance of gay marriage, much less the legal protection it enjoys. Also, some prominent evangelical leaders, scholars, and churches are moving away from a traditional position on gay marriage.

Assure Your Church That You Will Not Compromise Biblical Truth

One way to address these fears is to assure the person that you will not compromise biblical truth. They need to hear that, and see in your eyes that you mean it. As often as gay people have been told that Christians hate them, conservative Christians have been warned that churches will slide into liberalism.

Once when I was preaching a series through the book of Romans, two leaders in our church came to confront me together. They said they had listened to the recording of my sermon on Romans 1 multiple times (by now they probably knew my sermon better than I did), and not once did I say homosexuality was a sin, nor did I ever tell the congregation to quit homosexual relations. Honestly, I could not remember exactly what I said in the sermon, so I just assumed they were accurate. I assured them I did believe that Romans condemned sexual activity between two people of the same gender as well as gossip, envy, and pride. Since they were clearly unsatisfied (it was years ago before I was wise enough to know I should have stopped there), I went on to point out that Paul said it is "unnatural" (not explicitly "sinful"), which is the language I used in my sermon. At the end of the day, these men left our church because they felt I was "soft" on sin—or at least on this sin.

In our church families, how can we lead well those who have fears and discomfort with gay people and who struggle with issues around the topic? Broadly we want to lead them to grace while holding to truth.

Start with showing grace to the person with the concern, if you have an opportunity to talk with them. Listen deeply. We do not know what that person has experienced. The varied experiences of people run a huge gamut. You may discover people who confesses that they, too, have wrestled with romantic feelings for their same gender and feel so ashamed that they have become loudly anti-gay to fight against themselves. And yet another may have lost his or her job because they were perceived as being politically incorrect after some intense sensitivity training. Sometimes a workplace will pressure employees to engage in diversity or sensitivity celebrations that push a Christian to the edge of their convictions.

If they have felt pressure to compromise their convictions in their work, school, or family, they want to be assured that their church will stand strong. They fear that the church, too, will lose its moral bearings. Often this fear extends to a fear of the "other." In this case the "other" is the monster of the gay agenda, a faceless and sinister invader that threatens to attack the church and our culture. An us-versus-them narrative is created. Both sides use strong, emotional language associated with combat and violence to bolster support, raise money, and encourage political action. Talk of the "battle for our faith" and "losing the culture war" stoke both fear and anger. To combat this mentality, it's important to humanize and personalize. Remind people that the ground is level at the foot of the cross.

Remind Them That the Ground Is Level at the Foot of the Cross

It's so easy to demonize the "other"—the one you see as your opponent on the side you are fighting against. Gay people can be characterized—or rather caricatured—as abominations, the worst of sinners. Knowing that people in your church have this distortion in their minds, you can help them by reminding them we are all sinners.

This might seem easy at first, but when a person's perspectives are deeply engrained, it takes time. Pastorally, how you respond depends entirely on your relationship and trust with a given person. In a bond of great trust, you can raise the issue of the purity of a person's own sexuality. Almost no adult person would truthfully declare that he or she is without sexual sin. Short of that you can talk about sin in general.

But often a person in this frame of mind is determined to convey how homosexuality is a despicable sin, perhaps the worst imaginable. If a person knows their Bible, it can help to show them lists of those sins characterized as the worst, such as in Proverbs 6:16–19, which explains that the Lord hates haughty eyes, lying, murder, wicked schemes, evil, false witness, and a person who stirs up conflict in a community. Or consider the sins against which Jesus was the strongest: selling in the temple and hypocrisy. You could show them the seven woes from Jesus in Matthew 23.

Jesus' Sermon on the Mount convicts all of us. Nearly every postpuberty human has struggled with lust, worry, or materialism. We are all sinners in need of the grace of God. The ground truly is level at the foot of the cross. As Collins put it, "In the moral exam of life, straight people don't get partial credit simply for being straight. Every one of us, gay and straight alike, experiences intrinsically disordered sexual desires."[1]

Leading a heterosexual person to see that their sexual desires are also disordered can be helpful. An unstated assumption by many is that since I'm heterosexual I am normal, and in fact my sexual desires are not sinful. However, in a nice turn of a phrase, Collins pointed out that "the biblical pattern of sexuality is not heterosexuality but uni-heterosexuality—sexual orientation toward one opposite-sex person who is one's spouse."[2] Neither heterosexuality nor homosexuality itself is the point, but rather how a person is acting on desires and temptations of all kinds. Whatever various flavors our temptations come in, we are each responsible to respond to them in a God-honoring way. Being heterosexual does not give one a sexual pass from sin. That inclination to be carried away by sexual desire for a friend is just as twisted and perverted whether that friend is an opposite-sex friend or a same-gender friend.[3]

Sometimes a person suddenly opens his or her eyes. That happened in one conversation with a man in our church who was really wrestling with his discomfort over gay people. He had been warning me of a gay agenda and telling me how we were too welcoming and so on. Somehow the conversation turned to addictions. He began to share his multiple-year addiction to chewing tobacco and how it was one of the hardest addictions of all to break, and that unlike alcohol and drugs and even smoking, there are very few support groups. He found an online support group and was very emotional and happy to tell me God has set him free from this terrible habit that had become for him a sinful addiction.

I looked at him and said, "We would have welcomed you in the years before you quit." In his eyes I could see he got it. And he started weeping. All of a sudden the Spirit of God showed him how he was judging others for their sin. Let's teach people to empathize with people whom they struggle to embrace.

Most straight people have no idea of the anguish and pain that many gay people have lived through. Some of the pain is because of their treatment by churches; some of it because of homophobia in the general culture. Many gay people literally fear for their own safety. They have been beaten up at school or on the streets. They have been called horrible names and verbally assaulted in public. As a church leader you can help your people develop compassion by exposing them to the suffering of gay people. Often I find that people on the religious right are so immersed in media reinforcing how *they* are supposedly being attacked, that it's hard for them to see the reality for others.

The following data from Collins can help people see the truth of what gay people face that straight people do not.

> Hate crime statistics are notoriously difficult to track, but data from the FBI website supports the claim that LGBT people are per capita the second most frequently targeted population in North America, behind Jewish people. They are twice as likely per capita to be the target of a hate crime as African Americans, who come in third. In terms of violent hate crimes, LGBT people are at the top of the list and are three times as likely per capita to be targeted as either Muslims or African Americans (numbers two and three, respectively). For the sake of comparison, the hate crime rate against heterosexual people is statistically insignificant at around one in thirteen million (or 0.00000008 of the straight population in the US). A gay person is more than thirty-five times as likely to be the victim of a violent hate crime than a straight person is.[4]

You might look for current news stories of gay people being treated unjustly, especially in your local area. Christians should be the first to stand up for justice for anyone who is being mistreated—think good Samaritan. Could you encourage your church to pray for gay people who are being abused in one way or another?

The suffering of LGBT+ youth is frankly heartbreaking. So many teens, especially in religious communities, suffer from guilt and shame in secret. One of my friends, who is a pastor, found out after his daughter was an adult that as a teenager she struggled with lesbian feelings but was scared to share them. Without her parents knowing, she got a part-time job and paid for her own counseling to try to "fix" herself. Our churches must become safe places where teenage girls can share their sexual struggles.

When LGBT+ teenagers come out to their parents, sometimes the reaction is violent or at least harsh. As a result, too many of our LGBT+ teenagers become homeless and desperately need help. Could your church get involved in your city with helping homeless teens, no matter their sexual orientations?

According to the groundbreaking research by Andrew Marin, "LGBT youth are four times more likely to commit suicide than other teenagers—and that number more than doubles when they feel rejected by their family."[5] People's lives are at stake. By shaming gay people and speaking of them derisively, we make it difficult for teenagers to share their feelings as they are growing up. Churches need to become safe communities where we can share deep struggles. And we want to lead our families to be safe places for children to share openly with their parents without fear of rejection. Lives are at stake, physically and spiritually.

Recall Them to the Mission of Christ

People's eternal destiny is at stake. God so loved gay people that he sent his one and only Son to die for them, so they could spend eternity with him. We should love as God loves.

To break the us-them culture war mentality that has captured the minds of some Christians, I encourage you to consider Andrew

Marin's book *Us versus Us*, in which he reports the most extensive research done to date on the religious backgrounds of people in the LGBT+ community. One shocking discovery was that 86 percent of people in the LGBT+ community reported a significant level of church involvement at some point in their childhood or teenage years.[6] Most LGBT+ people have a religious background. They are us.

The tragic reality is that we have pushed gay people away from the church with our lack of love. My experience matches what Preston Sprinkle wrote:

> Having listened to countless testimonies and looking at startling statistics, I am disheartened to say that the Christian church has often played an unintended yet active role in pushing gay people away from Christ. . . .
>
> But here's the thing: most people who are attracted to the same sex don't end up leaving the church because they were told that same-sex behavior is wrong. They leave because they were dehumanized, ridiculed, and treated like an "other." . . .
>
> People will always gravitate to where they are loved. And if they don't find love in the church, they'll go elsewhere.[7]

Whether you share these truths with an individual in your church, with a leadership group, or with the whole church, you are helping the church face the ugly reality of being unloving to a certain group of people. That is a huge step in moving forward. If leaders in your church can apologize and repent of being unloving, that will be a powerful moment. This act can help the people in your church move further into grace and love for gay people. After all, repentance is the doorway to life.

Look for ways to introduce people to each other. If a straight person does not know any gay people, they are emotionally handicapped in their ability to love gay people. You can't love people in the abstract.

One of my pastor friends tells his staff, "If you do not have someone you know and love who is gay, then don't teach or talk about it, but you do need to talk about it, so find a friend and build a relationship." Without a name and face, it's hard to love. You may have a gay person at your church who is willing to share their story with a small group or with the whole church or with your church staff. That takes courage in a theologically conservative church, but it can provide a powerful moment for an entire faith community.

Today, even without the stories of real people in your church, you can share stories from Christians such as Greg Coles, Rosaria Butterfield, Christopher Yuan, and others who have shared their journeys. More and more resources are available, including short videos that could introduce people in your church to real flesh-and-blood people with very human, touching stories. Several ministries have arisen to help churches in this area. Check out Lead Them Home; The Center for Faith, Sexuality, & Gender; and Hole in My Heart, where you can find small-group resources and seminars you could bring to your church.

If you can get people in your church to move beyond their significant discomfort, lead them another step forward by talking about minorities' experiences. Perhaps some in your church have experienced being in the minority at some point in their lives. As a minority, you find it extremely difficult to believe you are truly wanted at the table when you have been consistently disinvited or uninvited. I have a Hispanic friend who leads strongly in a Hispanic environment, but in a gathering of white leaders, he has to fight his tendency to defer. So we make a special effort to encourage him to lead in that context. The experience of being in a minority shapes emotions and perceptions in ways that those in the "majority" of whatever category usually find difficult to imagine.

Because we Christians have a long and on-going history of being perceived as anti-gay, we have a lot to overcome. Many gay people presume that Christians hate them, see them as abominations, and wish they did not exist. Now you want to invite them to your church. Would you go where you are pretty confident you are not wanted?

Explaining the minority experience has helped people in our church understand why I put so much emphasis on grace and welcome. Many wonder why I don't first tell gay people their sexual activity is sinful. My response is that gay people are crystal clear on our church's teaching that gay sex is wrong. In fact they go much further and imagine that we think being gay is the worst sin imaginable and that we hate them. Therefore, we have to go to great lengths to share what they do not know: that we love them and welcome them just as they are, as Jesus does. We have to say over and over that we want them here in our church family.

People who are minorities are often constantly on their guard, feeling like they need to protect themselves at every moment. They live in a survival mode and feel singled out because they are different. In a majority straight church, we must make extra effort to express loving welcome to our LGBT+ friends. If enough churches move in this direction, we can create a new church history where Christians are known for healing, not hurting, LGBT+ people.

If we do not take this kind of leadership in our churches, we are exacerbating a major credibility problem for the church. We are hurting the gospel especially with the next generation. Millennials and those after them are keenly watching how churches love or don't love their LGBT+ friends. Whether they are gay or not, they are highly concerned that each person is treated justly. In fact, how a church cares for LGBT+ people is a litmus issue for some in these younger generations. The gospel's impact in our time is at stake.

I find that even after people go with me to this point in the conversation, they raise a common objection or a really sincere concern: Will our love miscommunicate an affirmation of same-sex unions or that we approve of gay sex? Here I encourage you to take people right to the life of Jesus, as we did in chapter 7. Association does not convey affirmation. Jesus ate with sinners and was attacked for doing so by religious people, but he never seemed too concerned about their noise, and neither should we. Our love for sinners should override the sniping of church members. Sometimes we need to address judgmentalism head-on as Jesus did. Remember his story of the Pharisee and the tax collector, someone the Jews saw as notoriously bad.

> To some who were confident of their own righteousness and looked down on everyone else, Jesus told this parable: "Two men went up to the temple to pray, one a Pharisee and the other a tax collector. The Pharisee stood by himself and prayed: 'God, I thank you that I am not like other people—robbers, evildoers, adulterers—or even like this tax collector. I fast twice a week and give a tenth of all I get.'
>
> "But the tax collector stood at a distance. He would not even look up to heaven, but beat his breast and said, 'God, have mercy on me, a sinner.'
>
> "I tell you that this man, rather than the other, went home justified before God. For all those who exalt themselves will be humbled, and those who humble themselves will be exalted." (Luke 18:9–14)

I love what Kyle Idleman wrote: "The church should not be known for outrage towards people outside of our community who need grace; we should be outraged by people inside our community who refuse to give grace."[8]

We can teach our people how to love as Jesus did, full of grace and mercy, not compromising truth or holiness. People were drawn to Jesus who felt rejected and excluded by the Jewish synagogues of the day. What if our churches were magnets for gay people? I'm compelled by the vision of our church becoming a place where gay people want to be, where they are drawn by our love. Collins put it this way: "Christians not only need to remove all cause for those outside the church to believe that they don't like gay people, but our churches need to become the havens of grace, love, and truth they are called to be. The gospel requires nothing less."[9] If the church is the body of Christ, should we not act like Christ?

Be patient with those who struggle with gay people but do not allow them to hold the church back from loving gay people. The gospel is at stake. Have the courage to stand for grace even if it costs you a few church members. Jesus stood up for the disenfranchised. We should too. It's called love and justice.

Discussion Questions

1. Put yourself in the shoes of a person very uncomfortable with this whole conversation and even the thought of LGBT+ people in their church. What might this person be thinking, feeling, fearing? What experiences might they have had that influenced them to this position?

2. How could you help such a person realize our common humanity and guilt before the holy God and that we are all sinners in need of grace? Think of specific people in your church. What might you say to them to help them gain this perspective?

3. What stories could you tell to help a person see and feel the pain that LGBT+ people have experienced in our culture and, more sadly, from churches and Christian people?

4. How could you help people in your church see how our approach toward LGBT+ people directly impacts Christ's mission? What might you say to cast a fresh vision for the mission of the gospel?

5. What are the implications of the truth that association does not convey affirmation? And how could this truth help people who are worried that we might compromise biblical truth?

6. In what situations might your church need to have the courage to stand for grace, and what might be the cost?v

CHAPTER 10

SEXUAL SIN AND HEALING

Leading Us as Sexual Sinners

All of us who are past puberty have sinned sexually, at least in our imaginations and lusts. We are all broken people. There are no sexually perfect people. I've not met an adult who said their sex life was perfect from puberty until now. We all—church leaders and church members, including me—live with sexual regret.

Our churches are filled with people riddled with sexual guilt. The #MeToo movement has exposed the vast amount of sexual abuse and harassment that women have suffered, largely from heterosexual men. It seems that the majority of women have suffered some form of physical or verbal sexual abuse at some point in their lives. Flip that statistic and consider how many men at some point abused a woman in one way or another. Those men are in your church suffering with secret shame and, in some cases, fear of being exposed.

Sexual sin and shame are no respecters of persons. Straight people, gay people, and everyone who identifies in any other way have sinned. Attempting to compare the severity of one kind of sexual sin with another rarely helps a person cope with their guilt. To think that my sin is worse or not as bad as another distracts me from honestly dealing with it before God.

For straight people, it's not uncommon to be disgusted with gay sexual sin, but have they ever turned it around? Listen to the feelings of a gay man: "I had seen the pornography my straight friends were captivated by. I had heard men talk about women as if they were competitions to be won, as if they were aerosol canisters to be used up and discarded. It made me sick. Those men were broken in ways I had never been, just as I was broken in places where they were whole."[1] We are all sexually distorted and broken, just in different ways, with desires perverted in different directions. Coles wondered if it's the case that "every sexual orientation after the fall is a disordered form of original sexuality as God had intended it to be."[2] He wrote, "Gay men see women wrong. Gay men see other men wrong. But then again, straight men see women wrong too. Straight men see other men wrong. Women of any orientation see women wrong, see men wrong. We are all guilty of exchanging healthy intimacy for ravenous sexuality or emotional distance."[3]

I am so thankful for the grace of God. My hope is that we can lead all kinds of people in our churches to move out of paralyzing sexual guilt into the freedom of God's amazing grace. My prayer is that many can find freedom from deeply embedded sinful habits.

Our society has deified desire. It says your body is your own, so you have the right to do anything you want with it as long as you don't harm another person. This big lie echoes the lie of the serpent in the garden. If you want to eat the fruit, do it (Gen. 2:8–3:19), as if we have the right to do whatever we choose.

Western culture has exalted desire as sovereign. The serpent seduced Eve to believe God was holding out on them and that eating the fruit would make them happy. Since then, humans have assumed we know better than God what is good for us, including sexually. How many times have you heard, "I know God says we should not, but I want to anyway, and this is what will really make me happy"? What if, rather than being skeptical of God's will, we were skeptical of our desires? Not all our sexual desires are good.

In our hook-up culture, we have trivialized sex and treated it as casual, as just another bodily appetite. Even churchgoing Christian people engage in sex in various forms, as if it has nothing to do with following Christ, as if it were not a big deal. But sexual sin is serious. And guilt over it traps us.

How can we as church leaders help our people understand the significance of sexual sin? In 1 Corinthians 6, Paul presented the spiritual consequences of sexual sin.[4] In a culture desperately confused about our bodies, we need a biblical theology of the body. What Paul had to say is not in any public school curriculum on sexuality. He did not warn against sexual immorality because it can cause STDs (sexually transmitted diseases). Rather, he gave us a biblical view of our bodies and their use in relation to the triune God. We do not just have bodies; we are embodied persons.

At a deep level, it is an understanding of the gospel in terms of our new identity that shapes our sexual behavior. If you are a communicator in your church, it's important to help people understand their Trinitarian bodily identity—their bodies' connection to each member of the Trinity. When they do, they will see sex differently. The Bible presents sexual union as much more than simply a biological function. It is an intimate communication involving whole persons, and for Christians, involving God himself—Father, Son, and Holy Spirit.

You can point believers to 1 Corinthians 6 to help them see their body's connection to the Father, the Son, and the Spirit, a Trinitarian theology of the body that should compel us to flee sexual sin to honor God with our bodies. Paul wrote:

> "I have the right to do anything," you say—but not everything is beneficial. "I have the right to do anything"—but I will not be mastered by anything. You say, "Food for the stomach and the stomach for food, and God will destroy them both." The body, however, is not meant for sexual immorality but for the Lord, and

the Lord for the body. By his power God raised the Lord from the dead, and he will raise us also. Do you not know that your bodies are members of Christ himself? Shall I then take the members of Christ and unite them with a prostitute? Never! Do you not know that he who unites himself with a prostitute is one with her in body? For it is said, "The two will become one flesh." But whoever is united with the Lord is one with him in spirit.

Flee from sexual immorality. All other sins a person commits are outside the body, but whoever sins sexually, sins against their own body. Do you not know that your bodies are temples of the Holy Spirit, who is in you, whom you have received from God? You are not your own; you were bought at a price. Therefore honor God with your bodies. (vv. 12–20)

Paul gave two clear commands: flee sexual sin and honor God with your body. What's powerful is the compelling rationale for why we should flee sexual sin: to honor God with our bodies. For a believer in Christ, your physical body is directly associated with each member of the divine Trinity.

Paul quoted a Corinthian slogan, "I have the right to do anything" (1 Cor. 6:12). Sounds a lot like what we hear today: "You can't tell me what to do with my body. God made me this way. It's not against the law. What people do in private is their own business."

Paul offered two counters to this slogan. First, the issue is not whether an action is lawful or right, but is it good? Is it beneficial? This is a much higher standard. It might not be illegal for you to watch that movie, but is it beneficial? Second, Paul said, "I will not be mastered by anything" (1 Cor. 6:12). Be warned that what you think you have the power to do may in turn take power over you. We call it addiction. You think you are in control of your sexual activity, and then it controls you.

Paul then gave us three huge theological truths, each tied to a member of the Trinity, each forming a massive foundation stone in the rationale for why sexual sin is so bad.

Resurrection: God the Father Will Raise Your Body

What You Do with Your Body Matters Forever

Physical resurrection means your body is eternal, so what you do with your body matters forever. Paul quoted a Corinthian slogan: "You say, 'Food for the stomach and the stomach for food, and God will destroy them both'" (1 Cor. 6:13). In other words, they were saying, "Just as we need to eat, so we need to have sex, and after all, God will destroy the physical, so it doesn't really matter. It's not a spiritual issue. No big deal."

Paul countered with a powerful truth. The body is for the Lord. And the Lord is for the body, proven by the fact that your body will be raised. Jesus is the Lord. So your body is for Jesus, and Jesus is for your body. He is telling us to live as who we are. What we do with our bodies should be for the Lord. We are to use our hands and feet, our muscles and minds for the Lord.

The rationale is the resurrection. Just as God raised Jesus bodily from the dead, so he will raise you (1 Cor. 6:14). Salvation includes our bodies, which are an intrinsic aspect of who we are. We do not just have bodies; we are bodies. Sexual sin violates our eternal bodies. Our bodies will not be destroyed, but resurrected, so there is continuity between my present body and my new body. Now let me quickly add that our bodies will be transformed into spiritual bodies. When we are with the Lord, he will heal our wounds and dry our tears. Since God will raise our bodies, we should flee sexual sin to honor God. The second Trinitarian rationale comes in the connection of our bodies to Jesus Christ.

Union: Christ Is United to Your Body

What You Do to Your Body, You Do to Christ

Paul asked rhetorically, "Do you not know that your bodies are members of Christ himself?" (1 Cor. 6:15). Paul was talking about physical limbs and organs. He said, "Shall I then take the members of Christ and unite them with a prostitute? Never!" (1 Cor. 6:15). Since your body is united with Christ, what you do with your body, you do with Jesus.

Notice the word *union* is used twice, in a sexual way and in a spiritual way. It is a bit shocking to see Paul parallel union with a prostitute through sex, and union with Christ in spirit. The Greek word for *unite* means to bind closely, to associate, and was even used to mean "glue together."[5] More than a physical coupling happens when a person has sex. A sexual act, whether between married partners or not, fuses the partners together into one flesh. There is no such thing as casual sex without lasting bonds and consequences.

Your body is united with Christ, so if you sexually unite with a prostitute (or with anyone to whom you are not married), you are taking Christ into that encounter. You do not want to take Christ into the proverbial back seat of the car, into that club, to that party, or into that hotel room. What you do with your body, you do with Jesus. Sexual sin violates Christ. Flee sexual sin to honor God with your body because Christ is united to your body. The third Trinitarian rationale comes from our body's connection to the Holy Spirit.

Presence: The Holy Spirit Lives in Your Body

Bodily Sins Are Against the Spirit

Since the Holy Spirit lives in your body, bodily sins are against the Spirit. Many people think that the Spirit indwells your soul or your spirit, but Paul explicitly says that your *body* is the temple of the Spirit (1 Cor. 6:19). So if you sin sexually, you are not only violating the Father and Jesus Christ, but you are also violating the Holy Spirit.

Notice that Paul does not say to *endure* temptation to sexual sin. We *endure* trials, but we *flee* from temptation. In other words, if someone is flirting with you, you do not sit there and try to endure—you walk away. Picture Joseph with Potiphar's wife, a story in which she tries to seduce Joseph multiple times. Finally, she grabs his coat (Gen. 39). Picture Joseph peeling off his coat and running out the door. When you are sexually tempted, picture "running Joseph." That's who you want to be. When you are tempted sexually, *run*. Leave the party. Flee. If the group is going to a club where you shouldn't go, drive away, flee. If you keep seeing him or her there, don't go back to that restaurant. Change gyms; even change jobs.

In our digital world, there are two tools you can use to flee: the mouse and the remote control. When the image pops up on your screen, don't stare and click the mouse. When the movie turns nasty, change the channel or fast-forward immediately. Flee sexual sin to honor God with your body because the Holy Spirit lives in your body.

Paul wraps up his argument with a powerful closing point: You are not your own. You were bought with a price, a high price, Jesus' blood. Sexual sin is against your own body, which ironically is not your own, but God's. This is the message of the gospel. Our salvation is not free; it comes at a great price, the cost of Jesus' own blood. Jesus Christ gave his life in our place to win our freedom. Now God offers us freedom through believing in Jesus Christ. Realize you are not your own. Your body is God's twice. He made it, and he bought it.

Our bodies are uniquely connected to the triune God. God the Father will raise our bodies, Jesus Christ is united to our bodies, and the Holy Spirit lives in our bodies. This is why sexual sin is so serious. Because our bodies are eternal, members of Christ, and temples of the Spirit, sexual sin is an eternal body violation, a violation of Christ, and a violation of the Holy Spirit. So flee sexual sin to honor the triune God. But here's the big problem. As we recognized at the start of this chapter, all of us have sinned sexually.

What Can I Do Since I Have Sinned?

Since we have sinned and we know sexual sin is serious, what are we to do? Like old fence wood, we are scarred, broken, and splintered. Not only have we messed up, but many of us have been wounded sexually by another person. Some have been abused. If you've ever tried to remove embedded rusty nails from old fence wood, you know how hard it is. Sexual sin can be like that. Destructive patterns are so embedded that they are hard to remove. That's why we need outside help. That's why we need a redeemer, a savior, a divine healer. And we need each other.

Rachel Gilson wrote about her lesbian temptations: "Our sexuality does not own us or define us. Jesus does. He understands our secret hurts and our hidden battles. He doesn't shake his head; he holds out his arms."[6]

In searching for how to lead people in our church out of the prison of sexual guilt and shame, I have developed the following modern liturgy.

A Liturgy for Sexual Healing

Please feel free to use or modify this liturgy in any way to fit your tradition and particular church context. It's designed to be followed in either a communal or private setting. As a leader, you can walk people through an experience with God in three movements: from confessing our sins, to receiving God's grace in the Lord's Supper, to praising God.

Introduction to Liturgy

The darkness of sexual sin makes the beautiful light of grace shine brightly. In our brokenness, guilt, shame, and sorrow, we come to the Healer. We lay our burdens and shame before the One who forgives, heals, and restores. Come as you are to the loving, gracious God, who has hope for the hopeless and open arms for all who have wandered.

Confess Our Sin

Healing often starts with confession. Proverbs says: "Whoever conceals their sins does not prosper, but the one who confesses and renounces them finds mercy" (28:13).

Secrecy destroys us. In the darkness, sin festers and grows. When you shine a light on sin, you take away its power. Concealing sin stunts your spiritual growth. But the one who confesses, prospers in Christ. Sadly, many waste away in self-denial, never facing their sin. It does no good to ignore or deny the truth about ourselves, as ugly as it might be. The Devil wants to keep us in the dark, hiding our sin where he imprisons us accused and guilty. Confession invites God's forgiveness: "If we confess our sins, he is faithful and just and will forgive us our sins and purify us from all unrighteousness" (1 John 1:9).

Confession brings freedom. Following his sexual sin and confession, King David penned these words:

> When I kept silent,
> > my bones wasted away
> > through my groaning all day long.
> For day and night
> > your hand was heavy on me;
> my strength was sapped
> > as in the heat of summer.

Then I acknowledged my sin to you
    and did not cover up my iniquity.
I said, "I will confess
    my transgressions to the LORD."
And you forgave
    the guilt of my sin. (Ps. 32:3–5)

We confess our sins and shame to the One who forgives, heals, and restores. You may need not only to resolve fresh sins, but also long-ago ones that you have never fully resolved with God. Those sins may include abusing another. Or it may be you need to confess judgment, prejudice, and hatred. Come as you are to the loving, gracious God who has open arms for all who have wandered. Listen to Peter in the first sermon after Christ came: "Repent, then, and turn to God, so that your sins may be wiped out, that times of refreshing may come from the Lord" (Acts 3:19). God promises to wipe away your sins through Jesus Christ. When you repent and turn to Jesus, you will find times of refreshing. That's what wounded, guilty people can experience. God can bring you sexual healing. Confess so that your sins will be wiped out by God's grace in Christ.

Scripture Reading

Read these words of Scripture aloud slowly, affirming their truth:

For the sake of your name, LORD,
    forgive my iniquity, though it is great. (Ps. 25:11)

Have mercy on me, O God,
    according to your unfailing love;
according to your great compassion
    blot out my transgressions.

Wash away all my iniquity
and cleanse me from my sin.

For I know my transgressions,
and my sin is always before me.
Against you, you only, have I sinned
and done what is evil in your sight;
so you are right in your verdict
and justified when you judge. (Ps. 51:1–4)

Physical Response

Posture is powerful. God calls us to present our bodies to him as living sacrifices (Rom. 12:1). Consider using bodily posture to express each of the three movements, from confessing your sins to receiving Christ's grace to praising God. A posture of kneeling helps express confession. [If they are physically able, invite them to get on their knees in a posture of confession.] On your knees, pray the following prayer of confession written by John Knox, who was a leader of the Scottish Reformation in the 1500s:

> Gracious God, our sins are too heavy to carry, too real to hide and too deep to undo. Forgive what our lips tremble to name, what our hearts can no longer bear, and what has become for us a consuming fire of judgment. Set us free from a past that we cannot change; open to us a future in which we can be changed; and grant us grace to grow more and more in your likeness and image through Jesus Christ, the light of the world. Amen.[7]

Continue with this prayer of thanks:

> *Dear God, thank you that you welcome broken and contrite hearts. We confess to you our sexual sin, and other sins, deeply*

sorry that we have grieved you, our Father and Savior. You made
our bodies and have redeemed them at a high price. Thank you
for your grace and forgiveness in Jesus. Amen.

Receive Jesus Christ's Amazing Grace

From confession, move to a posture of receiving. Confession positions us to receive Jesus Christ's amazing grace. Jesus symbolizes his grace in the Lord's Supper. [Get some bread or a cracker and wine or juice to partake of the Lord's Supper.] We receive God's grace in the act of eating the bread and drinking the cup. In the Old Testament, God promised to forgive our sins. Through the prophet Isaiah, God said:

> I, even I, am he who blots out
> > your transgressions, for my own sake,
> > and remembers your sins no more. (Isa. 43:25)

It is through the Messiah, Jesus Christ, that we find forgiveness. Paul wrote: "In him we have redemption through his blood, the forgiveness of sins, in accordance with the riches of God's grace" (Eph. 1:7).

Jesus bled for us as the ultimate and final sacrifice for sin. In the limitless riches of God's grace, he offers to forgive us, no matter what sins we have committed, and no matter how many times we have sinned. No matter what we have done sexually, God offers to forgive us. Many people find this truth hard to believe. Even after you confess, you keep beating yourself up for your sins. You live paralyzed by guilt. But think of what you are implying. Are you saying the blood of Jesus on the cross is not sufficient to cover your sin? In Jesus, God totally forgives you, washing you white as snow, remembering your sins no more (Isa. 1:18). You are free.

When we believe in Jesus, God forgives all our sins. The Bible says: "All the prophets testify about him that everyone who believes in him receives forgiveness of sins through his name" (Acts 10:43). We can all find healing in Jesus Christ.

As Christians, our identity, our life, and our future are in Jesus. He is our Savior who forgives our sins, covers our guilt, and removes our shame. We share the bread and the cup, united together to remember the body and blood of Jesus as his one body, regardless of our sexual attractions, temptations, or past sins.

Scripture Reading

We see encouragement in Scripture to bow humbly, raise hands joyfully, shout and sing loudly, clap hands, and even dance before the Lord. God wants our hearts, our minds, and *our bodies*. He wants all of us. [Invite people to stand and read God's Word aloud, proclaiming the truth of God's forgiveness found in Psalm 103. Read this beautiful truth with appreciation:]

> The LORD is compassionate and gracious,
>> slow to anger, abounding in love. . . .
> He does not treat us as our sins deserve
>> or repay us according to our iniquities.
> For as high as the heavens are above the earth,
>> so great is his love for those who fear him; as far as the east is
>> from the west,
>> so far has he removed our transgressions from us. (vv. 8,
>> 10–12)

Physical Response

Stand to receive the Lord's Supper. Matthew recorded what happened the night Jesus gave us this memorial that Christians have shared across the world for more than two thousand years:

Jesus took bread, and when he had given thanks, he broke it and gave it to his disciples, saying, "Take and eat; this is my body."

Then he took a cup, and when he had given thanks, he gave it to them, saying, "Drink from it, all of you. This is my blood of the covenant, which is poured out for many for the forgiveness of sins." (Matt. 26:26–28)

Assume a posture of reception, standing with your hands out, palms up, to receive the Lord's Supper, signifying that you are receiving the gracious gift of God's grace in Jesus Christ. God has forgiven you in Christ.

Pray and Partake

Pray: *"Lord Jesus Christ, we remember what you did in your amazing grace to provide for our forgiveness. Thank you, Lord, for your body given for us."*

Partake: *Eat.*

Pray: *"Thank you, Lord, for your blood poured out for us."*

Partake: *Drink.*

Pray: *"Dear Father, thank you for your amazing grace and love in sending your Son. Jesus, thank you for giving your body and blood for our forgiveness. We remember what you did and we celebrate your victory, our salvation. In Jesus' name, amen."*

Praise God for His Glorious Salvation in Jesus Christ

From confessing our sins and receiving God's grace, let us move to our third posture, a posture of praise to thank God for his glorious salvation in Jesus Christ. We have kneeled in confession and stood to receive the Lord's Supper. Soon we will raise hands in praise and worship. Paul said: "Do not offer any part of yourself to sin as an instrument of wickedness, but rather offer yourselves to God as those who have been brought from death to life; and offer every part of yourself to him as an instrument of righteousness" (Rom. 6:13).

We present our bodies to God as living sacrifices in an act of worship. We dedicate our bodies to God to use not as tools for sin but rather as tools for righteousness to do God's will. Use your body to serve God. We do this in community with others, not alone, but we unite together as one body of Christ.

Paul delighted in God's salvation in Jesus when he wrote:

> Therefore, if anyone is in Christ, the new creation has come: The old has gone, the new is here! . . . God made him who had no sin to be sin for us, so that in him we might become the righteousness of God. (2 Cor. 5:17, 21)

Paul quoted Psalm 32, declaring the wonderful blessing of the righteous God's remarkable forgiveness:

> Blessed are those
> > whose transgressions are forgiven,
> > whose sins are covered.
> Blessed is the one
> > whose sin the Lord will never count against them. (Rom. 4:7–8)

Zechariah, the father of John the Baptist, sang:

> Praise be to the Lord, the God of Israel, because he has come to his people and redeemed them. (Luke 1:68)

Today, as God's family, we are to declare God's praises. Peter told us:

But you are a chosen people, a royal priesthood, a holy nation, God's special possession, that you may declare the praises of him who called you out of darkness into his wonderful light. (1 Peter 2:9)

Scripture Reading

Stand once more and read these verses aloud with strength and volume. These are glorious truths, truths worth celebrating.

Praise be to the God and Father of our Lord Jesus Christ! In his great mercy he has given us new birth into a living hope through the resurrection of Jesus Christ from the dead. (1 Peter 1:3)
Then I heard every creature in heaven and on earth and under the earth and on the sea, and all that is in them, saying:

"To him who sits on the throne and to the Lamb
be praise and honor and glory and power,
for ever and ever!" (Rev. 5:13)

Physical Response

Stand, raise hands. Use your posture to express praise to God. You may not normally be a hand raiser, but in this moment, consider trying it. Raise your hands to declare your praise for God's glorious salvation in Jesus Christ, our King. Praise him from your heart with whatever words come to your mind.

Conclusion

By faith, let's pray that the Holy Spirit will give us willing hearts to offer our bodies back to God to use for his cause. He made our bodies and gave us the gift of sexuality. After we wrecked things back in the garden, Jesus came to give us his body. In another garden, he told the Father, "Not my will, but yours be done" (Luke 22:42). He has redeemed us, including our bodies, forgiving us in his amazing grace, so in grateful worship, we offer our bodies back to him as living sacrifices (Rom. 6:12–13; 12:1–2).

In salvation God brings Trinitarian healing. The Father has adopted us into his family, the Son has united with us as his body, and the Spirit dwells in our bodies as his new temple. Now as the body of Christ, we build loving communities of forgiven single and married people, straight and gay people, taking the next steps on the path to Christlikeness together. We look for the day soon when we will see our Lord face-to-face and experience a divine union to which sexual union can only faintly point. Our reality today, our joy, our life, is found in uniting in Christ as we represent Christ to each other and to a desperate world.

In terms of sexual sin, our people struggle in two major opposing directions: engaging in sexual sin too easily, and remaining caught in the grip of sexual guilt. To help them see the seriousness of sexuality, we can teach them about the body's connection to the triune God. And to free them from guilt and shame, we can walk them through a biblical liturgy of sexual healing, which will be needed over and over, to move from confessing to receiving God's amazing grace to praising him in thankful worship involving hearts, minds, and bodies.

Discussion Questions

1. What are various kinds of sexual guilt that we see in ourselves and in our church family?
2. How does sexual guilt paralyze Christians in their spiritual growth and in their ministries? Why is finding freedom in Christ from sexual sin so vital?

3. Reread 1 Corinthians 6:12–20. What two commands did Paul give? What three huge theological truths did Paul present in connection with each member of the Trinity that explain why sexual sin is so serious?

4. Take time to walk through the Liturgy for Sexual Healing, alone or with your group, and evaluate its content and applicability to your church.

CHAPTER 11

ALL IN THE FAMILY

Leading an Inclusive Church Community

How do we build a church family to welcome and nurture much more diverse groups than the typical American nuclear family with mom, dad, and 2.5 kids? Whom do we include in our family?

God offers us the promise of refuge; in the fullness of salvation, he will lead us to green pastures and quiet waters. He prepares a table for us even in the presence of our enemies, anoints us with the oil of healing, and pours out goodness and mercy on us with the promise of dwelling in his house forever. Could we do this in our churches as Christ's body, as "temples of the Spirit," as families of the Father? The Father has always called his people to welcome the stranger, to be people of radical hospitality. And the Lord God has always charged his people to stand up and step up for justice, especially for the oppressed, for those without a voice.

Can you imagine a church that provided a safe refuge for all people, including sexual and gender minorities, that provided a loving family of friends, an open table for hurting people, and a seat for justice? My heart is to help build that kind of biblical community in our church and to help you build it too. I long to see churches become inclusive families of gay and straight people who join voices together to sing God's praise, who kneel together to receive the Father's love as his children, and who stand together for love and justice.

Bill Henson, the founder of Lead Them Home, often shares his classic line "A gospel of exclusion has no power to reach already banished persons."[1] One of the three main goals of this ministry is to "enhance church inclusion." By this they do not mean anything goes nor that anyone serves anywhere, but rather that they accept people where they are, love them, and offer to walk with them to healing and maturity in Christ. They welcome them into their home and offer to be family to them.

People groups who have suffered decades of widely perceived mistreatment by churches are more difficult to reach for Jesus. Many LGBT+ people feel banished from churches in their own minds because of what they have personally experienced or heard about others' experiences, all reinforced by a cultural narrative that says Christians hate gay people. As missional church leaders, we have a steep challenge to genuinely show the love and grace of Christ to those who suspect that for all our nice words, we really don't want them involved in our churches.

Provide a Safe Refuge, a Place of Gracious Spaciousness: *Charis*

What if our churches were known as places of safe refuge? Historically, local churches have been safe places, echoing all the way back to cities of refuge set aside in the time of Israel in the Old Testament. Imagine "notorious" people, often excluded by religious people, seeking out your church because of your reputation as a safe place for any hurting person, regardless of who they are or what they have done. My heart is that churches could offer gracious space for all people, especially those who see themselves as sexual and gender minorities, who have long felt unwelcome in churches. Divine, amazing grace opens the way to building a safe refuge if we can offer grace for sin, for gradual growth, and for differences of belief. This space for differences of belief applies mostly to people in the church. Local church leaders need to be unified in their moral convictions.

Grace for Sin

In previous chapters, we've reminded ourselves that the ground is level at the foot of the cross. Those of us in the sexual majority can lead the way in confession of sin. Previously we asked if a person could engage in sinful same-gender sexual activity and still be a Christian. The answer is yes, because we are all still-sinning Christians, including for nearly all of us still-sexually-sinning people. None of us are perfect people this side of heaven. We all live grateful for God's forgiving grace in Christ. And so we should forgive as we have been forgiven. And at the same time, when we are aware of sin in our lives, we should repent of our sin. And we dare not approve of what God calls sin.

It's all too easy for church leaders to fall into a false, self-perceived sense that we are right and good. We are clean, or that's the image we feel we must portray to the people in the church. But we all know better. Many of us desire to lead our churches to be places where people recognize there are no perfect people, places full of broken people being remade by the power of God. That's healthy and grace-filled leadership.

When we look back into the Bible at the heroes, we find a list of quite sinful people whom God used in spite of themselves. I've heard Larry Osborne, senior pastor of North Coast Church and author of many books for pastors, help provide perspective by asking what we would think of this church leader: a guy who got in a business partnership with a known criminal and married his daughter. Then he built an expensive mansion for himself before the church did their building campaign for the worship center. And he engaged in some palm reading to help him make decisions, but he still prayed to God and sought him for wisdom. Imagine the blog posts, the social media blasts, and the comments from the Christian community. Then Larry takes us to 1 Kings 3, where we read about the king who led Israel to some of its greatest moments:

> Solomon made an alliance with Pharaoh king of Egypt and married his daughter. He brought her to the City of David until he finished building his palace and the temple of the Lord, and the wall around Jerusalem. The people, however, were still sacrificing at the high places, because a temple had not yet been built for the Name of the Lord. (1 Kings 3:1–2)

And yet we honor Solomon for his wisdom and his leadership.[2] God used him to build Israel's greatest temple (worship center) and largest "budget." Perhaps we need more grace for one another and for our sins as church leaders.

At Christ Fellowship we pray that grace marks us, and we try to live it out. As I'm writing this, I'm filled with gratitude to God for what happened last Saturday. Five years earlier, a leader in our church had left his wife for another woman. We confronted him at that time, implementing the full "Matthew 18 process." Sadly, he divorced his wife and left the state. About three years later, he repented. He came and apologized and asked if he could come back to the church. He pursued reconciliation. One Saturday afternoon in May, he remarried his wife, who had taken him back. I cried. It was beautiful.

Years ago a straight man who had been a pastor and writer of Christian books came to me asking if he could come to our worship services. The man had committed sexual crimes and spent many years in prison. His crimes were serious enough that they had been reported in the local newspapers back then. Long ago he had repented, and now he said he just wanted to serve Jesus with the years he had left. We welcomed him with appropriate restrictions. At first he served in ways that were behind the scenes. Later we had an administrative position open on our staff and he applied. In talking about it as elders, we knew that—given the opportunity—we would encourage a business person in our church to hire him for such a role. For us, grace required that we allow him to apply just like anyone else. We hired him in this part-time role. But we started to get questions from people who knew the story from years ago. One Sunday we held a restoration service, sharing his story of sin and redemption and included people from his past who had been involved in his previous church. We were confident that this service was beautiful from heaven's vantage point. However, around one hundred people left the church. Some were angry. Some were scared. We even had a staff member abruptly resign. Grace costs. We took a stand for grace and would do it again.

We want to be a church that accepts sinners, even ones who have committed heinous sins that are abhorrent to God and to our culture. Could we lead our church to embrace people who are currently sinning? In one sense this is a silly question because we are all currently sinning, and in desperate need of God's grace, including those of us who are the leaders of our churches. As sinning church leaders, we are no less in need of God's gracious forgiveness than the sinning people to whom we minister. It's not "us righteous people" and "those sinners," but all of us are sinners who are fleeing for refuge into the arms of the Father. This does not mean that we tolerate sin. The Bible calls us to admonish one another and bear each other's burdens when one of us is caught in sin. Love walks with people by showing grace that covers sin and speaking truth that confronts sin. My hope is that our church will have grace for people who are on the way, even though at this moment they are living in unrepentant sin, perhaps even unrecognized sin, and for those who are trying to grow in Christ.

Grace for Growth

You probably use some language about spiritual growth analogous to ours at Christ Fellowship. We encourage people to move up a path to Christlikeness from exploring, to starting, to growing, to maturing. None of us arrive until we see Jesus face-to-face. In theological terms, sanctification is a process. Although I became a Christian as a kid and went through every discipleship program available, as I look back now on my spiritual "maturity" in my twenties, I'm a bit embarrassed. From my vantage point now, I wonder how I could possibly have been any kind of godly husband, dad, and pastor. What business did I have raising kids as immature as I was, much less helping to lead a church? And yet, I hope that decades from now I will look back at where I am today with a similar feeling, because I hope to keep growing in Christlikeness.

Let's give people gracious space to grow in their maturity in Christ and in their understanding of biblical truth. Think about Peter in Acts 10–11. He was still hung up on what he thought was the right (restricted) biblical diet until God brought down a feast containing all manner of foods on a sheet in Peter's vision and gave his blessing to eat. Even more important, Peter was shunning people he needed to embrace, namely Gentiles, the uncircumcised pagans.

Do you ever wonder that what you believe today to be true, you will find out you had wrong when you see God? I'm pretty sure that not everything I believe is exactly how God sees it. I wish I could know today where I have it wrong, but we can't see what we are blind to. In historical hindsight, we can see that every generation of Christians has gained insight into biblical truth and has blundered in ways that sometimes seem astounding (supporting slavery or opposing women's suffrage or even advocating physical violence against those who differ theologically). A few centuries from now, how will Christians look back at twenty-first-century evangelicals? The whole "who is on the wrong side of history" argument is tricky because none of us can see the future and none of us have "the present" perfectly right, so it is healthy to recognize that we are all on the way to greater understanding. We all see "through a glass darkly." My guess is that you do not believe everything you thought twenty years ago, and that you have nuanced positions you once held as firm.

Wendy VanderWal-Gritter promotes what she calls in the title of her helpful book *Gracious Spaciousness*.[3] While she and I do not agree on everything, I appreciate the call that Wendy and her ministry are giving to churches to show gracious spaciousness. In some of her writing, she encourages gracious spaciousness based on our inability to know with certainty. Wendy wonders who has the right theology since reasonable Christians disagree, and she asks who could really know who is right since none of us humans can know as God knows.

In my opinion, we can ground gracious spaciousness in a more solid place than our human epistemic limitations (what we cannot know). Let's position gracious spaciousness not in opposition to rational theology but in a more robust, holistic theology that carries with it theoretical rigor informing loving practice. Rather than avoiding taking a position (as if that could be done), form well the position that you take. Truth held with conviction does not mitigate or undermine love. What detracts from love are self-righteousness, pride, fear, prejudice, and hatred. Truth and grace are not opposed nor to be held in balance, but both ought to be brought in full measure, as Jesus was full of *both* (John 1).

In regard to LGBT+ brothers and sisters, do we extend to them the same grace to grow spiritually that we give to straight brothers and sisters? Or do we have unrealistic expectations that they will be living righteously at a high level soon after their conversion? At times it seems that we expect LGBT+ new believers to attain a finely nuanced understanding of orthodoxy quite quickly. Every one of us as leaders, and everyone in our churches, is in the sometimes painfully slow process of growing to know the mind of Christ and display the fruit of the Spirit.

Let's talk about sexually related sins. In Africa, when a man comes to Christ who has multiple wives, and children with most of them, how do the church leaders respond? Consider in America how we minister to the person who has been married multiple times and is now living with someone who is unmarried. And of course, we must face the elephant in the room, that the majority of the men in our churches are involved in various kinds of pornography to one degree or another. Now then, consider the gay couple who comes to your church to seek God. And the teenager who "comes out of the closet." And the person coming to your church with a fully affirming position toward gay marriage. Consider how you could lead your church to show grace for growth for *all* of us as we are on the way to gaining more wisdom and righteousness in Christ by the Spirit. And to show grace for differences of opinion.

Grace for Differences

Christians too often fight over minor matters, personal preferences, and opinions. Should we balance grace and truth, so that we have grace for people who in our view don't have truth? That sounds right, but no, we don't balance grace and truth. Neither grace nor truth should be minimized or compromised in any way. They do not have to be compromised because they are not in conflict. Grace and truth are complementary. Truth explains grace, and grace tells the truth. In an analogous way, love and discipline are not opposites, but in fact discipline expresses love. Love disciplines. When your child needs discipline for lying, you do not say, "Son, I love you, *but* I am going to take away your Xbox." You say, "Son, I love you, *so* I am going to take away your Xbox." Love disciplines. Grace tells the truth.

Some theological issues are worth fighting for. When do we, like Martin Luther, say, "Here I stand," and when do we agree to disagree? Let me suggest we distinguish between P1 and G1 issues, Philippians

1 and Galatians 1. In both chapters there is conflict between people who identify themselves as Christians. Paul wrote to the Philippians,

> It is true that some preach Christ out of envy and rivalry, but others out of goodwill. The latter do so in love, knowing that I am put here for the defense of the gospel. The former preach Christ out of selfish ambition, not sincerely, supposing that they can stir up trouble for me while I am in chains. (Phil. 1:15–17)

Some people were preaching the gospel from bad motives. Likely, in their selfish ambition they were trying to get people from Paul's church to come to their church while Paul was in prison. I imagine they had reasons why their flavor was better than Paul's. How did Paul respond? "But what does it matter? The important thing is that in every way, whether from false motives or true, Christ is preached. And because of this I rejoice" (Phil. 1:18). Paul did not condemn them or try to shut them down. He did not critique them or tell people not to join their group. Paul said the important thing is that Christ is preached no matter what the motive or what the flavor. If Christ is preached, let's rejoice. It's like we are all on the USA Olympic hockey team. On the back of the jersey we have our college team name, but on the front we all have USA in big letters. Our Christian churches may have different names on the back, but we are all on the same team. We are all for Jesus Christ.

Now look at Galatians 1. How is G1 different from P1? Paul wrote to the Galatians,

> But even if we or an angel from heaven should preach a gospel other than the one we preached to you, let them be under God's curse! As we have already said, so now I say again: If anybody is preaching to you a gospel other than what you accepted, let them be under God's curse! (Gal. 1:8–9)

How is the situation different in Galatians 1 than in Philippians 1? In Philippians 1, the other people are preaching the true gospel of Christ, but in Galatians 1, the other people are preaching a different gospel. Paul used some of the harshest language in the entire New Testament. He fought for the truth of the gospel. Why? Because people's eternal destinies are at stake. If you sincerely believe a false gospel, you are not saved, even though you might wrongly think you are.

So when do you fight for the truth? When do you stand up and say, "So help me God, I will die for this truth"? When the gospel is at stake. When the issue is motive or minor matters, you rejoice that the gospel is preached, even if you would not personally go to that church or belong to that group. When the gospel is perverted, you condemn those who are throwing people into confusion. We must distinguish P1 issues from G1 issues. Is this a minor matter, a personality issue, or is the truth of the gospel at stake? If the truth of the gospel is at stake, we fight against those who pervert it because people's eternal destinies are at stake.

These days some groups in the American Christian church are using the word *gospel* for nearly everything—from marriage to songs. While it's commendable to bring the gospel of Jesus to bear on all of life, and it's true that the gospel has been truncated in recent American popular evangelicalism, such as in simplistic salvation tracts, it can be harmful to use *gospel* as a heavy adjective to turn P1 issues into G1 issues.

So, here's the question: Are our opinions about gay marriage "gospel" issues? Some say they are because of 1 Corinthians 6:9–11:

> Or do you not know that wrongdoers will not inherit the kingdom of God? Do not be deceived: Neither the sexually immoral nor idolaters nor adulterers nor men who have sex with men nor thieves nor the greedy nor drunkards nor slanderers nor swindlers

will inherit the kingdom of God. And that is what some of you were. But you were washed, you were sanctified, you were justified in the name of the Lord Jesus Christ and by the Spirit of our God.

However, this is a misreading of the text. Paul's point is not qualifications for the kingdom, but rather the kind of life that should characterize citizens of Christ's kingdom. God's kingdom will be a kingdom of righteousness, and believers who are inheritors should live righteous lives.[4]

What you believe about gay marriage will not determine or undermine your eternal destiny. I'm not saying that our theology of sexuality is unimportant or uncertain, but I am saying it's more of a P1 issue than a G1 issue, more an issue where Paul would rejoice that the gospel is being preached rather than an issue over which he would say let them be eternally condemned.

Others have wondered if the issue of gay marriage is more of a Romans 14 meat-offered-to-idols issue on which Christians can agree to disagree. This category refers to behaviors that some Christians see as sin but others do not. Examples could include masturbation, watching media with sex scenes, smoking, drinking, or gambling. Same-gender sex in marriage, however, does not seem to fit a Romans 14 toleration issue because, unlike meat offered to idols, which was not intrinsically sinful, same-gender sexual behavior is sinful. Put simply, what we eat is rarely a matter that becomes immoral; however, what each one of us does with our body sexually is either moral or immoral. For this reason, comparing sexual activity to eating traditions is biblically unwise. Now, of course Christians disagree on this. And each of us will stand before God for our view. This is not a matter over which we should be condemning each other, but rather listening to each other and seeking to grow in our understanding.

At Christ Fellowship we describe ourselves as theological centrists, meaning our focus is on where we agree with other Christians through the centuries on the central doctrines of our faith. We do not focus on our distinctives, on how we might differ from others. It grieves God to see Christian teachers and leaders attacking other Christians over minor differences. The Devil wants us fighting each other when we need to be fighting the Devil, not shooting each other. When Christians tear one another to pieces in front of a watching world, serious damage is done to the advancement of the gospel of Christ.

In simple terms, how will a tree ever grow to produce fruit if we keep stomping all over the seedling? Please, could we stop wounding each other with friendly fire? We can encourage unity without demanding uniformity by majoring on the majors and not on the minors. It's so easy to see every issue as a mountain and forget there are molehills. On these nuanced sexuality issues, it's wise for spiritual leaders not only to wrestle with what we believe but also to evaluate how major or minor a given position might be.

The leaders of our church are committed to guarding our unity, but that includes grace for differences. We deliberately set up a big tent with space for people to differ and to grow. I like what Henson said: "Biblically, love endures much, and it is capable of absorbing all kinds of belief gaps in everyday life. If love truly demanded unity in belief, all marriages would fail, and all churches and fellowship groups would fracture."[5] He added: "Love that cannot endure differences is ultimately the root of divorce, and the end of friendships, and the precursor to war."[6] We can lovingly agree to disagree. Marin poignantly made this point as he wrote: "Trust, reconciliation, and strength of conviction should not be contingent on agreement. . . . We don't have to agree in order to love each other well."[7]

And yet Sprinkle called out the question among Christian leaders: "Are affirming Christians heretics? Wolves in sheep's clothing? False prophets? Or is this a secondary issue that believers can disagree on—like keeping the Sabbath and baptism—and still join hands in worship? Does it come down to a simple disagreement on how to interpret a few passages? Or is it a gospel-issue that is a threat to orthodoxy?"[8] My view is that gay marriage is a Philippians 1 issue, even though it is not a Romans 14 issue, meaning it is a matter of sin even as in Philippians 1 Paul said the other group was involved in envy, rivalry, and selfish ambition, which are clearly against God's Word, yet Paul rejoiced that the gospel was being preached. In other words, the group was clearly involved in the three sins he listed, and yet Paul did not shut them down but rather affirmed their efforts to advance the gospel of Jesus Christ.

And furthermore, before we divide into camps and sign mutually condemning documents, could we realize there is nuance, that not all people who are "affirming" or "nonaffirming" have the exact same positions? I appreciate Sprinkle's conclusion for himself: "Maybe I will change my mind on this. But for now, I want to hold to my biblical convictions and not demonize or condemn everyone who disagrees with me about homosexuality."[9] This is the place where I'm leading our church. We are working and praying to be a safe refuge by providing a place of grace for sinners, for people to grow and for the grace to differ.

Provide a Family of Friends, a Place of Loving Inclusion: *Koinonia*

In addition to a safe refuge, our intent is to provide a family of friends, a place of loving inclusion where we live our *koinonia* (fellowship, partnership). As we covered in the early chapters, in the New Testament the church family is at least as important as the biological family. And yet we usually fail to live that out in our churches.

We have small groups, as you probably do in some form. And we intend for those groups to practice the "one another" commands, to live in biblical community, engaging in *koinonia*.[10] Sometimes it happens in the best groups, but too often it does not. My favorite stories are from the people who tell me that their life group is closer than their family. One couple chose not to move to be near their grandchildren in another state because they did not want to lose the relationships in their life group, which were closer than family.

In our churches it's important to ask how people who are not married with 2.5 kids and a dog fit into our small groups. Does a widowed family feel welcomed? What about a single man in his thirties? In the group discussion does the interaction assume a certain living arrangement, as if everyone is married with kids living at home or grown and moved away? We can help our groups broaden their vision to include grandparents raising their grandkids, multigenerations living together under the same roof, singles living with roommates, both male and female. Consider those who are gay, whether single, in a mixed-orientation marriage, or married to a same-gendered partner, and those who are living as life partners without a sexual dynamic. We probably know our church family is quite diverse, but does our ministry model and our weekly ministry recognize and embrace that, especially for those in the minority? Can we say not just from the pulpit but in our smaller groups, "We love you"? As Henson said, "This is your home. This is your family—no matter what."[11]

This kind of loving inclusion can get very practical. Marin posed a striking example: "What will churches do with the eighty-year-old gay man who has committed himself not only to the church but to celibacy as a theological conviction? He doesn't have children to support him or to serve as next of kin or as power of attorney for his medical care. He doesn't have descendants to listen to his stories or pictures of grandchildren to share with his peers. Who will be his advocate, his family, his community? It's a reality that theologically conservative churches need to start planning for if they are going to promote LGBT celibacy."[12] Will our church family include and support gay men and lesbians throughout their entire lives in real, practical ways?

A lesbian friend of mine in our church asked me if she could tell people in the church that she was lesbian. I said yes, hoping whomever she told would respond with love and grace. She was part of one of our life groups. One night she told her story and came out to the group. They loved her and embraced her. Later she told me that touch is her love language. Previously she had had very little experience in any church. With tender emotion in her eyes, she shared with me that the people of the group gathered around her and laid hands on her and prayed for her, and that it was a very powerful experience of love for her. That's what I hope happens over and over in our churches.

God calls his church to be a family, the predominant biblical metaphor for church. We are brothers and sisters adopted by the same Father, born again by the same Spirit, who share the same blood of Jesus Christ. Not only are we family, but we also are organically united as the one body of Christ, in which we each are a part of the body and have a vital role to play. No part of the body is more important than another (Rom. 12; 1 Cor. 12). This is obviously true for both straight and nonstraight brothers and sisters.

In his book *Spiritual Friendship*, Wesley Hill opens the eyes of his readers to the nature of friendship and stimulates church leaders to imagine qualities of relationships beyond that of an average small group. Hill inspired me to what could be in our church.[13] Pastor Ed Shaw joined Hill, writing: "If our churches put as much time and energy into promoting good friendships as they do good marriages, life would be much easier for people like me. And, interestingly, much better for everyone else too."[14] In addition to promoting good marriages, could we not also promote and protect loyal friendships (Prov. 17:17; 18:24; 27:5–6, 9–10). Jesus said the greatest love was for one to lay down his life for a friend.

LGBT+ people are not an issue to be solved but are people to be loved. In our churches can we stretch our imaginations to envision people forming friendships in which they can experience nongenital intimacy? Intimacy does not require romance and erotic activity. Love is the center of being like Christ as an individual and as a church. Sprinkle quoted a gay pastor, sharing a desperate plea that grabbed my heart: "'I wish that somehow, rather than ending up in the arms of that anonymous man, I could have found myself in the arms of the church . . . I wish in the church I had found myself loved.'" That last phrase should be branded on our hearts with glowing iron: "'I wish in the church I had found myself loved.'"[15] Your church and mine can be places of love, people of love, who wrap our arms around people, especially those who suspect the church does not love them.

Imagine if your church was known more for your love for LGBT+ people than for your stance against gay sex. I dream that gay people would know they are wanted in our churches, and that when they come they would be embraced. Too many gay people (including those who are celibate) come to churches only to hit barriers to full participation in the life of the church. This results in a sense that they lack spiritual worth or value, perhaps even that they are feared as being sexually dangerous to children or others.

How can we love people without investing time and proximity? We have to be together, pray together, worship together, serve together, rejoice together, and cry together. Some of this is as simple as including people in what you are doing already. Shaw wrote, "Acting like a church family doesn't necessarily add a whole host of new things to the to-do list; it just means involving your brothers and sisters in Christ in what you were planning on doing anyway. And you can take the initiative in doing this, whether you're married or single."[16] If you are having a party, whom will you invite and, unintentionally perhaps, not invite, whether it's the Super Bowl, July Fourth, or a birthday?

For all human beings, one expression of love is physical

affection—a hug, a pat on the back, a touch on the shoulder, even a warm handshake. Nate Collins pointed out the sad lack of affection for some: "Finally, the unavoidable truth is that many gay people in conservative Christian communities don't receive physical affection from others simply because their orientation makes other people uncomfortable."[17] Because most gay people have experienced rejection and avoidance, they are keenly sensitive to whether you genuinely embrace them or are hesitant to touch them. As is culturally appropriate in our churches, we should love one another with our culture's equivalent to "holy kisses." That means physical expressions of love—hugs for most of us in America and a kiss on the cheek for Latin cultures. Collins said that "gay people are uniquely impacted by the affection Christians show them."[18] Hugs do not compromise theology.

In wrapping up this call to provide a family of friends, a place of loving inclusion, I was freshly inspired by Marin's simple, powerful challenge to wild love:

> Love cannot be bought or sold or messaged as relevant. Love is wild and sometimes reckless in its attempts to be heard and felt. Love is genuine and unencumbered by expectations or cultural, political, or religious norms. Love is attendant to yearnings for peace, safety, and emotional, mental, physical, and spiritual security. Love knows no bounds of its work and influence. And most importantly, love is simple.[19]

Provide an Open Table, a Place of Hospitable Welcome: *Philoxenia*

In addition to providing a safe refuge and a family of friends, our churches can provide an open table. In the New Testament the Greek word for hospitality, *philoxenia*, means to welcome or love the stranger.

In the book of Hebrews, God tells us, "Do not forget to show hospitality to strangers, for by so doing some people have shown hospitality to angels without knowing it" (13:2). In the context of our churches, we can think of "strangers" as unsaved people or unchurched people, at least guests who are not today members of our church.

You know that God so loved the world that he sent his Son, and Jesus came to seek and to save the lost. Then he sends us, as the Father sent him, to carry on the same mission as his witnesses. We are to have his heart for the lost coin, the lost sheep, and the lost son (Luke 15). My hope is that the people of Christ Fellowship are looking into the distance like the father of the prodigal son, hoping to see him walking down the dusty road, to then get up and run to him with arms open wide, ready to throw a party for him. Could you imagine if unsaved LGBT+ people knew that's how we felt about them? What about teenagers who grew up in our church, came out of the closet in college, and have never come back? What about Christian gay people who have abandoned the church?

Most of our cities have communities that would welcome anyone who identifies as other than straight. Sprinkle made a sharp point when he said, "And if the world out-loves the church, then we have implicitly nudged our children away from the loving arms of Christ."[20] How do we embrace and love those among our family and friends who declare a sexual identity different from ours?

We have to see that love is not compromise, that kindness does not condone sin. Rather, love crosses boundaries. It embraces enemies. Jesus said, "If you love those who love you, what reward will you get? Are not even the tax collectors doing that? And if you greet only your own people, what are you doing more than others? Do not even pagans do that?" (Matt. 5:46–47). In fact, a loss of biblical love compromises the gospel as much as a loss of biblical truth.[21]

Our paradigm would change if we were to adopt a missional mindset toward the LGBT+ community, seeing them as a marginalized, lesser-reached people group in missional terms. As a good missionary you would want to get to know them, their history and experiences. You would learn that they are a historically oppressed minority who has undergone systematic victimization for decades, including castration for males. You would not be shocked by their sin, or their customs that differ from yours, nor surprised that they celebrate different events and days. You would want to connect with their fears and hopes and dreams so you could share the wonderful good news of Jesus that offers life, peace, and joy eternally. You would learn what it feels like to grow up as a sexual minority fearing rejection from your family and bullying from your peers. You would need to learn what words and images communicate clearly to them and which miscommunicate because of their backgrounds. Sadly, you would have to face that these wonderful people, made in God's image, will have to overcome horrible stereotypes of Christians that are embedded in their culture. You would realize the height of their barriers to entry into Christian faith, specifically the cost of leaving their communities where they may have deep relationships and the fear that becoming a Christian might damage those relationships. These are similar to the barriers a Muslim or Hindu convert could face in regions of India.

And yet loving, gracious hospitality can open doors as we invite people to share our tables. In her book *The Secret Thoughts of an Unlikely Convert*, Rosaria Butterfield tells her story of how God used the power of hospitality to open her eyes to God's love in Christ. According to the summary on the back of her book, "Rosaria, by the standards of many, was living a very good life. She had a tenured position at a large university in a field for which she cared deeply. She owned two homes with her partner, in which they provided hospitality to students and activists that were looking to make a difference in the world."[22]

Rosaria was an associate professor at Syracuse University in a lesbian relationship and was involved as an activist in the gay community.

In her late thirties, however, Rosaria encountered Pastor Ken Smith, who encouraged her to explore her questions and invited her to dinner at his house. Before she set foot in a church, Rosaria spent two years meeting with Ken and his wife, Floy. In the supernatural power of God's love that flowed through hospitality, Rosaria came to trust in Jesus Christ and experienced the transforming power of the Spirit. I hope and pray for more Rosaria stories that come as we break bread with "strangers" in our homes and in our churches.

Church is not only for believers but also for those still seeking to find God. In many churches there are discussions over who is the focus of worship services: believers, seekers, or God himself (the audience of One). The multiple-choice answer is all of the above. Paul singled out unsaved people when he wrote to the Corinthians, "But if an unbeliever or an inquirer comes in while everyone is prophesying, they are convicted of sin and are brought under judgment by all, as the secrets of their hearts are laid bare. So they will fall down and worship God, exclaiming, 'God is really among you!'" (1 Cor. 14:24–25).

Paul assumed that non-Christians, those who may be exploring faith, will be present in the worship services. Worship services are designed to engage people in an experience with the living God. We should aim for our services to be understandable to new people and unbelievers. We do not want anyone to feel like a foreigner. This includes sexual and gender minorities. We want them, as much as possible, to feel at home in our house and at our table where we have set a place for them as our honored guests. I know it is not in the Bible, but my wife always told our children, "Give your best to your guest."[23]

Throughout our church ministries we need to communicate a spirit of hospitality, an open table that welcomes people who do not yet believe. The previous pattern in local churches was believe, then belong, then serve. Today people often need to belong before they will believe, and it's not uncommon in our church for people to choose to serve, especially in helping our surrounding community, before they even belong to our church. In Acts 15 at the Jerusalem Council, Peter decreed, "It is my judgment, therefore, that we should not make it difficult for the Gentiles who are turning to God" (v. 19). Translated into the topic of this book, we should not make it difficult for sexual and gender minorities to turn to God, and we should encourage them to abstain from sexual immorality of any kind (v. 20).

To put this principle into practice, listen to what Sprinkle said: "We need to create and cultivate a safe and honest environment where people who experience same-sex attraction don't feel gross or ashamed; where they can talk openly about their struggles in their small group and the room is not filled with cold silence and terrified stares."[24] Think through your church ministries to determine if you have created unnecessary barriers for gay people. For instance, consider your men's and women's ministries, your small groups, who can serve where, and so forth. What messages are being sent to LGBT+ people?

I shared in chapter 7 about when I made an open offer before Christmas to talk with anyone who identified as LGBT+, knowing the holidays could be difficult. One of the women I talked with said she had never shared her entire story with anyone ever. She brought in multiple sheets of paper and talked nonstop for well over an hour. While she had participated in a women's Bible study, she had not regularly attended worship services. Her story touched my heart. After our talk she joined our medical safety team and serves nearly every Sunday. She is in a women's Bible study and serves with our students on Wednesday nights. She has found a place at the table as a member of the body and a member of the family. She's a friend who encourages me and prays for me. In a recent disruptive moment in a worship service, she brought a calm spirit and wise counsel to all of us handling it. All this from a woman who had previously felt unjustly rejected.

Provide a Seat for Justice, a Place to Stand for What's Right: *Dike* (Justice)

Churches form inclusive communities by providing a seat for justice, a place to stand for what's right and stand against what's wrong. Jesus came to bring justice—*dike* (the Greek word for justice). Just as historically the church, and before that Israel, was to be a place of safe refuge, so also God's people have always been called to exercise justice.

Against the backdrop of decades of perceived and actual mistreatment by the church, we Christians, of all people, should stand up for sexual minorities when they are mistreated. Listen to the clear words of Scripture:

> Speak up for those who cannot speak for themselves,
>> for the rights of all who are destitute. (Prov. 31:8)

> Defend the weak and the fatherless;
>> uphold the cause of the poor and the oppressed. (Ps. 82:3)

> Learn to do right; seek justice.
>> Defend the oppressed. (Isa. 1:17)

As you may have, too, I've encountered stories directly or indirectly that break my heart. According to the Williams Institute, 20 to 40 percent of homeless youth in America identify as LBGT+. Of these kids who live in shelters or on the streets, 59 percent have been sexually victimized and 60 percent have attempted suicide.[25] In general, LGBT+ teens are two to four times more likely to attempt suicide than their heterosexual peers, up to eight times more likely if they have experienced serious rejection in their lives, such as from family.[26] Two big risk factors are bullying and family rejection.[27] This is a tragedy, and churches should be the first to stand up for gay teens at risk for bullying and family rejection—as well as those who have already been disowned or kicked out of their homes and are living on the street. In a time when churches are viewed as intolerant and self-righteous, we must show the extravagant grace of God. What could your church do for homeless gay teens in your community?

In the area of justice, it helps to start with confession for the past. We can take responsibility and apologize. Our churches can take a humble posture and cultivate sorrowful hearts as we empathize with the mistreatment and marginalization of gay people by Christians and churches. Collins wrote, "We must recognize that acknowledging the shamefulness of these past actions is part of maintaining a clear conscience in this matter before a holy God who hates injustice."[28] Try to walk in the other person's shoes, to feel what it would be like to be mistreated, bullied, rejected, and even victimized. Remember, children are often the ones being mistreated!

Think about our children. Most of the people in our churches are unaware of what LGBT+ students face in schools. According to the GLSEN *National School Climate Survey* biennial report, which includes a sample of 10,528 secondary students from all fifty states and the District of Columbia:[29]

- *Most LGBTQ students have experienced harassment and discrimination at school.* Over 8 in 10 (85 percent) experienced verbal harassment based on a personal characteristic, and nearly two-thirds (66 percent) experienced LGBTQ-related discrimination at school. Due to feeling unsafe or uncomfortable, nearly a third (32 percent) of LGBTQ students missed at least one day of school in the last month, and over a third avoided bathrooms (39 percent) and locker rooms (38 percent).
- *Hostile school climates negatively affect LGBTQ students' educational outcomes and mental health.* LGBTQ students who experienced high levels of anti-LGBTQ victimization were

twice as likely to report they do not plan to pursue postsecond-
ary education. Also, LGBTQ students who experienced high
levels of anti-LGBTQ victimization and discrimination had
lower GPAs, lower self-esteem, and higher levels of depression.

• *The majority of LGBTQ students report hearing biased remarks
from school staff, and school staff often fail to intervene when they
hear these remarks at school.* Most LGBTQ students report that
they've heard homophobic remarks (56 percent) and negative
remarks about gender expression (64 percent) from school staff.
There was also a decrease in school staff's frequency of intervention in these types of remarks from 2013 to 2015.

My desire is to lead our church to stand up for those who are
harassed or bullied in any way. Certainly *inside* our own churches
there should be no tolerance for gay bashing, gay jokes, or put-downs.
Do you passively allow these kinds of false and damaging statements
in your church?

"If they weren't homosexuals, maybe they would not get beat up."

"Being homosexual is a mental illness."

"It's a choice. They could change if they want to."

"Pray the gay away."

I agree with Sprinkle and the strength of his charge to us. "We
need to put homophobia to death. . . . Affirming Christians can't be the
only ones concerned about homophobia in the church. Nonaffirming
Christians should be just as relentless—if not more—in confronting
the unchristian posture toward gay people that runs rampant."[30] As
elders, pastors, and teachers in our churches, let's increase the priority
of protecting anyone who is bullied or judged. Let's not tolerate any
kind of name-calling, especially against those who over the years have
not been protected by churches.

In our churches we can take the initiative and step up to advocate
for justice for all, including sexual minorities. They should not be

discriminated against in our communities. Can we not support civil protections for LGBT+ people while still holding to our biblical convictions? Actually, we would be standing for our biblical convictions for justice, without changing moral standards. Someone's sexual identity does not exempt us from defending their rights. As many churches unite with other groups in the private and public sector to improve education or housing, to run food banks, and to help people get their GEDs, could we not also unite with LGBT+ groups to address teen homelessness and teen suicide, both of which hit the LGBT+ community disproportionately?

My prayer is that there will be no more cases like that of Ben Woods. Ben was a churchgoing teenager. According to the *Charlotte Observer*,

> On a Wednesday evening in the summer of 2008, when Ben was 16, [his mom] said he went to church to help plan a mission trip. He returned home unexpectedly, his cheeks flushed, his breathing rapid. He looked as if he was about to cry.
>
> He told her the new youth leader had singled him out as gay in front of the others. He said the leader asked who felt comfortable being around him, and then said: *Do you understand that Ben is going to hell?* According to his mom, Ben never fully recovered. She said, "If you already have been ridiculed, and then your very being is deemed unworthy by your church and your God, it does change your soul, your psyche, your feeling of safety and belonging in the world."[31]

A few years later, at twenty-one years old, Ben tragically took his own life. It will take courage for church leaders in conservative areas of the country to stand up for "Bens." But we must.

Collins challenged me when I read his analogy to apartheid. He wrote, "It meant something to be a white Christian living in

South Africa during apartheid. There were good and bad ways to be both white and Christian during that era. Similarly, it means something to be a straight pastor in the South during LGBT Pride month, particularly to gays and lesbians who attend churches pastored by straight people."[32] This thought stretches me in good ways. It exposes how my own heart for justice needs to grow. What a challenge to lead our churches to stand for what's right for the oppressed, even along with those who traditionally oppose our moral stand in regard to gay sex. And yet would we not coordinate with those of other faiths, and no faith, to provide food for the hungry and homes for the homeless?

And if we have no authentic, healthy relationships in the LGBT+ community, how would they possibly know that we are seeking to transform our churches to be inclusive communities? Dream with me of your church being a safe refuge, a place of grace, where LGBT+ people think to turn first for help when life gets hard. Imagine your church being a family of loving friends where everyone is included. Imagine both churched and unchurched LGBT+ people being drawn to your open table of hospitality where they are warmly welcomed to your home as honored guests. Picture your church providing a seat for justice where oppressed people know they will be fiercely defended. By the grace of God and the power of the Spirit, our churches can become more and more these kinds of inclusive communities. People will be loved and lives can be transformed by the power of God flowing through his people, shining his light in the darkness.

Discussion Questions

1. Would you describe your church as a safe refuge for LGBT+ people? Why or why not?

2. What might it look like in your church to show more grace for sinning people? Can you think of specific people or situations where you did or could have shown the Father's amazing grace?

3. How have you grown in your walk with Christ? Where does your church struggle to give people grace to grow?

4. Over what minor matters, personal preferences, and opinions do people in your church tend to have conflict?

5. In your own words, how would you distinguish P1 from G1 issues? Give examples of each, especially if you can identify some in your own church and community.

6. How do you evaluate the *koinonia* in your church, and how could you improve it, at least in the ministries where you serve and especially in regard to LGBT+ people?

7. How do you evaluate your church's *philoxenia*? What steps could you, your ministry, or your church take to adopt a more missional approach to LGBT+ people and create a welcoming, hospitable climate in your church?

8. How would you rate your church's concern for justice? Which of the statistics about LGBT+ teens most distressed you? What are some simple, practical steps you or your church could take to stand for justice for LGBT+ people?

CHAPTER 12

SEXUAL QUESTIONS AND CHURCH MINISTRY

Leading in the Complexities

Based on what we have covered so far, how we can practically lead our churches to show grace and stand for truth in the messiness of real lives? In this chapter and the next, we will consider aspects of daily church ministry, starting with leading our elders and staff. From there we'll move to teaching and preaching, weddings, and employment.

We cannot ignore that these sexual questions, and how we care for people around them, are some of the most crucial issues facing the church in the twenty-first century. This is true for the unity of our churches and the light of our witness. Sprinkle said, "Whether we realize it or not, the evangelical church is on the verge of a catastrophic split. People on both sides of the debate need to think deeply about how they view those on the other side."[1] Without careful attention and nuanced, loving conversations, Christians could split denominations, networks, and local churches. The world is watching how believers in Christ treat sexual minorities, especially the millennial generation and Generation Z following them. As Christians, we have already severely damaged our witness to younger people with weak love and thin grace.

Love

For each of the specific topics we cover in these last two chapters, several principles are foundational. Love rises above every other virtue. Love's prominence is obvious even to a casual reader of the Bible, but ironically, its ubiquity can cause us to dismiss love as cliché or as assumed. But we dare not pass by love so quickly.

The two great commands are to love God and love our neighbor (Matt. 22:34–40). Jesus' new command is to love one another (John 13:34). The greatest witness to the world is our love for one another by which they will know we follow Jesus. Paul said love is the greatest virtue of all, that without it we are a clanging noise (1 Cor. 13). LGBT+ people are not an issue to be debated, as much as they are God's image bearers to be loved, as we all are.

Some conservative evangelical Christians are so wrapped around the doctrinal axle that they can miss love. It's vital to remember that sound doctrine and love go together; in fact, the paragraph above on love is a doctrinal claim. And yet somehow it's easy to allow a focus only on truth, taken to an extreme, to excuse a lack of love. The old line "I was just speaking the truth" does not wash away rude words, an ugly tone, or a lack of grace in the telling of that truth. Few marriage relationships thrive with regular truthful but graceless communication between a husband and wife.

In addition to watching our theology, we must pay attention to our tone. The same words spoken in different tones convey such different messages. Recently I was reminded once again of the difference between reading bare words on a screen contrasted with seeing those words spoken. In walking through the difficult season of releasing a beloved worship leader from our church, I sent him an email containing the text I had written to share with the church family on a Sunday morning. As they read those words, he and his wife did not feel love and grace, and so they reacted in anger and sent a tough reply. Hours later, when they saw almost the identical message delivered in person with a loving tone, tender eyes, and a face full of grace, they sent an email retraction, and told me on the phone, "Your tone was perfect and message was appropriate." In conversations on difficult and sensitive matters, our tone is as important as our theology. Our bearing matters as much as our message.

Bill Henson does a great job of helping us see that our posture matters as much as our position. We can retain our theological position while radically adjusting our posture.[2] Our posture can and should be formed by spiritual virtues. When we speak with humility, the same words sound so much better than when we speak those words with pride. Self-righteousness obstructs spiritual conversations. The fruit of the Spirit fills conversations with beauty and grace. If you wonder how Jesus could attract sinners while remaining utterly holy, consider his posture, his tone, how he was always full of the Spirit. Love, the 1 Corinthians 13 kind of love, disarms and invites. Like a magnet, love draws people in. When you are a person who cares and blesses and who speaks truth, you will attract people to your message of hope in Christ. Sexually sinning people were drawn to Jesus as a lost person is drawn to bright light in the darkness. He offered living water, eternal life, and forgiveness. We can offer the same in his name.

Some of the people in our church get confused about love, thinking that compassion might signal affirmation. It's a distortion of spiritual zeal to imagine that loving a person condones their sin. God loved us enough to send Jesus to die for us while we were still sinners. And the Father loves us now in Christ, even while we keep on sinning.

A related confusion is the notion that proximity implies approval.

The thought is that if I go to the party or the dinner or "their" home, I will be tacitly approving of someone who is doing something wrong. Think about that. We are all doing things wrong. We would have to avoid every other human and could not even live with ourselves if this were the case. Then think back over Jesus' ministry. He came to the world out of love, to be with us as one of us. Why was he accused of being a friend of sinners? Because he hung out with them. He ate dinner with them and joined them at their parties. Remember who Jesus offended and who he welcomed.

As church leaders we must lead our people to love and help them break through the sad confusion that showing love would be condoning sin, that compassion equals affirmation, or that proximity conveys approval. Essentially, we show people Jesus' example and encourage them to go be with lost, obviously sinning people, even to the degree that other "religious" people might worry about our actions, as our first-century counterparts worried about Jesus hanging out with the "wrong crowd." Around the world, missionaries seek to get close to unbelieving people acting in ungodly ways to bring them the gospel of Jesus Christ. Without proximity we have no influence.

Finally, as we consider specific issues, I encourage you not to spend hours writing careful policies and position papers. As trained communicators, pastors can get hung up on words. These sexual questions are so nuanced that capturing them in writing is incredibly difficult. And as I just described, words on a mere page often miscommunicate. They lack the majority aspects of communication: tone, face, eyes, body language. Even video conferencing lacks the dynamic of human togetherness in the same space. Love and grace and tender care are extremely difficult to convey on paper. To add one more reason to care for individuals over writing policies: people are unique; each individual story matters with all its turns and twists, its joys and sorrows. For all our good intentions, policies and papers are impersonal. Focus more on loving specific people than on writing policies, more on individual stories than on generic position papers.

Leading Your Elders and Staff

All of this spiritual direction should start with leading your leaders at your church—whatever you call them: elders, deacons, pastors, directors, or lay leaders. By a leader I mean those who have followers, a leader of people, including those who hold a position and those who carry influence without a formal position.

As you, or a few of the leaders in your church, start studying issues in this book, you can quickly get off pace with the rest of the leaders. You begin using vocabulary they have not encountered. You will be growing in your understanding and nuancing what you previously thought. If the other leaders are not learning together with you, you can easily find yourself in conflict, unintentionally.

To avoid this potentially disrupting disconnect, I encourage you to learn together. This can look like reading a book together as an elder team or staff team. You might bring in an outside speaker on the topic, such as Bill Henson or Preston Sprinkle or others who offer workshops for churches and church leaders, so that you grow together in your understanding and approach.

At our church we often gather as elders with our spouses on Sunday nights at one of our homes. Like a typical small group, we share a meal, pray for one another, and spend time studying. Over the years we have read books and worked through courses, such as those offered by Centers of Church Based Training (ccbt.org). We've found benefit in learning together as couples.

Then on Mondays, often, our pastoral staff will get together to study the same book or course the elders are studying. That way we create unity between the elder team and the pastor team. We are speaking the same language. For difficult or important topics, we have sometimes gotten the two groups together for a half-day meeting to wrestle through the issues to foster greater insights and unify our hearts and minds.

These kinds of times together also allow us to share our own journeys. When you all share your story and your family's story you get to know one another at a level you usually don't reach when you are only talking about church business. Ministry moves at the speed of trust, and you can build trust by learning together and sharing your lives together. When one person takes the risk to open up to a new depth of vulnerability, it opens the space for others to do the same. One night the wife of a pastor shared about the physical abuse she suffered in a previous marriage, including being tied up with duct tape. Our hearts ached for her, and others felt free to share more of their personal pain. Our leaders have shared about their LGBT+ children.

Your teams will go deeper in spiritual maturity as you wrestle together to find unity on how to lead your church well in this time of sexual questioning. For the sake of unity, Henson suggested the leaders of a given local church create a covenant statement on biblical marriage and sexual expression to be signed by core leaders. He provided a sample that you could adapt.[3] This is not quite the same as a position paper, and some churches will see it as best not to put their agreed-on position in writing with a covenant statement, but for others it will be helpful.

One important issue to cover with your leaders is language. Words are incredibly powerful—God spoke the world into existence. Jesus is the Logos, the Word. Words hurt and heal, destroy and restore. Whoever said "Sticks and stones will break my bones, but words will never hurt me" was utterly wrong. The sad truth is that Christians have wounded and excluded and crushed LGBT+ people by abrasive, ignorant, and downright mean words and phrases. The point here is not to yield to the god of political correctness but to be loving in our language. And the wording can seem subtle, but the difference can be dramatic. Sprinkle pointed out that his Jewish friends say there is a big difference between asking "Are you Jewish? And are you a Jew?"[4]

Without some training, your church leaders could unintentionally foster the impression that your church is unloving, unkind, and even hateful. We must try to put ourselves in the other person's shoes and hear our words as they might hear them—tough to do but crucial. More times than I want to count I have been too unaware of how a person might receive my words given their context and current situation, including this week, when words sent with no bad intent were received as harsh, cold, and uncaring, and that reception was shocking to me. Although when I sat with that person face-to-face to listen, I began to see how from his and his wife's vantage point, my communication could appear cold, even though the intent was to be caring.

Here are a few messages that might seem innocent enough. But listen through the ears of a celibate gay person trying to follow Jesus:

- "Married people always get their sex needs met."
- "Unmarried people are not living a full life."
- "Gay men may be a danger to children."
- "I know a gay guy who is now totally straight."
- "You can't be involved if you identify as gay."
- "Keep praying: God will heal if you believe enough."
- "I've noticed you are looking more masculine lately."

In his posture-shift training, Bill Henson does a great job helping church people rethink their words with a new sensitivity to how they are heard. See his chart below.

When we say . . .	They hear . . .
"Homosexual"	"Bigotry, judgment"
"Love the sinner, hate the sin."	"God hates you."
"Adam and Eve, *not* Adam and Steve."	"You are *so* stupid."
"You can change if you are willing."	"You are being *so* disobedient."
"You are choosing this lifestyle."	"You are *so* evil and reject God"
"I refuse to call you gay."	"I despise who you are."

Then Henson provides a translation of what straight church people might say and how LGBT+ people might talk about it far differently.

What we call . . .	They call . . .
behavior	relationship, family
immoral	intimacy, love, marriage
sin	identity, who I am
lifestyle choice	born gay
unbeliever	gay Christian
he (Benjamin)	she (Jaylee)

Give yourself a test on your sensitivity to language. Henson offers a chart of words and phrases you might use in talking with LGBT+ people. Which words or phrases might it be good to avoid and why? I started with his list, added a few and subtracted a few. And by the time you are reading this book, one or more of these words may have taken on a different sensitivity. The cultural tone of words changes over time. Consider the terms *African American, black, colored, people of color.* Which word or phrase is most appropriate has changed and will keep changing. If we love people, we will be sensitive to the words that matter to them. Take the test. Which words or phrases below might it be good to avoid and why?

lesbian	same-sex attraction (SSA)	alternative lifestyle
transgender	gender dysphoria	gay
same-gender loving	pansexual	a trans
homophobia	LGBTQIA+	homosexuality
questioning	transgenderism	queer
cisgender	love the sinner, hate the sin	straight
preferred lifestyle	the gays	lifestyle choice
LGBT+	heteronormativity	butch/dyke
homosexual	genderqueer	asexual
gay lifestyle	partner	gender fluid
the sexually broken	heterosexual	gay agenda

Note: information and format of preceding tables adapted from Bill Henson, *Posture Shift Implement Tool*, DVD, 48 and 88.

How do you think you did? Talk to a fellow church leader or a group of leaders about the exercise as it applies to your specific context. You might ask someone who identifies as LGBT+ to help you grow in understanding the most recent ways language is being heard.

Let's talk about a few of the phrases.[5] The phrase "gay lifestyle" can be off-putting. Think about it in reverse. If you are straight, do you have a "straight lifestyle"? What is that? This kind of phrase homogenizes gay people, as if they all share the same lifestyle. And it implies some sort of choice to live in a sinful, inappropriate way that dishonors God. It confuses identity, attraction, and behavior.

A similarly damaging phrase is "practicing homosexual." What about a "practicing heterosexual"? When you flip the phrase, it's easy to see how weird it sounds. Are you trying to get better at it, like practicing a golf swing?

Even the word *homosexual* is unhelpful. While it appears in some modern translations of the Bible (such as NIV and ESV in 1 Timothy 1:10), almost no LGBT+ persons would use this word of themselves. This does not mean we do not quote the Bible, but would you want someone to put you into a category you would not use yourself? This word is outdated and clinical, impersonal. Using it could make you sound like calling black people colored people.

Equally off-putting is the phrase "gay agenda." Once again, turn it around. What about a "straight agenda"? You might be thinking that I'm politically naive. Hold on for a minute. There are many people and groups with agendas of all kinds, but all gay people do not share the same agenda. There are radical people on the fringes of almost every issue. There are straight Christians with some crazy agendas that I do not support at all. Each of us would hate to be judged by the people on the fringes of the issues we care about and support, whether that is the environment or gun control or whatever. Love guards our tongues and measures our words.

Preaching and Teaching

Careful language choices are so important in our public teaching and preaching. Those of you who preach carry tremendous power to shape the culture of your church with years of weekly sermons. I well know that what you say from the pulpit gets heard in many different ways. We offend someone nearly every week. Mother's Day is treacherous with so many women who wish they were a mom or have lost a baby or lost their mom, those who don't want to be a mom or have step-children they adore or despise.

So in this area of gender and sexuality every word counts. One word to one side and you are a heretic, and one word to another side and you are a hate-monger. The delicacy and danger can persuade us to avoid the topic altogether, but that run to apparent safety actually injures the church. Then your people have no idea how to be faithful to Jesus in this area. You leave them unequipped and ill prepared to represent Jesus well to their families, neighbors, and friends in their workplace.

Let me share a few tips on how to teach and preach on sexuality. First, educate yourself. Invest the time, as you are in reading this book, to understand the issues better. This is a way you can lovingly serve your church body. Study the Scripture and make sure you know where you stand and why. Point people to the Word of God—not just what the Bible says on same-gender sex, but what the Bible says about grace, forgiveness, hospitality, and more.

If you serve a more conservative church or are in a conservative region of the country, you face the temptation to reinforce the cultural narrative of your people. You can use the sound bites that make them feel comfortable, but in doing so you run the danger of reinforcing homophobia. From our pulpits we need to kill homophobia. Jesus is not anti anyone or any group of people.

When you talk on these issues, realize deeply who is listening to you. Collins said we should consider what happens "when a pastor talks about the 'sin of homosexuality' from the pulpit without the slightest degree of awareness that someone listening in a pew right in front of him might be gay. Pastors have dehumanized gay souls in this way for decades without even knowing."[6] Especially if you are speaking to a larger audience, assume LGBT+ people are there and speak directly to them. And speak to their families. Sprinkle shared how he prepares to speak publicly: "If I ever mention homosexuality from the stage, I always ask myself: 'How would I hear this if I were a teen struggling with same-sex attraction, or a visitor who is a lesbian, or a parent of a gay son who just committed suicide?'"[7] In advance listen to the words you are about to say from each of these vantage points.

To increase love and kindness, you can correct the false idea of comparing sins, and thus judging some sin as abominable. Also you can help people empathize with the plight of LGBT+ people historically. Tell stories of what they have actually experienced and even a story of very recent abuse or mistreatment in the news. Help people get out of their own information bubble to hear others' stories and experiences. Share the story of a gay teen who committed suicide in your area. Humanize and personalize what some see as an "issue." Apologize on behalf of the body of Christ for past mistreatment by churches.

Consider stories such as the good Samaritan and who might have been lying on the road beaten and why. And the prodigal son, contrasting the father with the older brother. Are we excited to throw the party, or are we standing outside, resenting or unsure we should be celebrating? Help your church distinguish theology from tone, position from posture.

In his *Implement Tool*, Henson provides some good, practical advice on how to write a "posture shift" sermon, as he calls it.[8] He makes suggestions, such as to invite LGBT+ people who may be hurt by your message to your dinner table. In your message, explain words and phrases such as *gay lifestyle, lifestyle choice, sexual preference, alternative lifestyle, practicing homosexual,* and *love the sinner, hate the sin* that can deeply hurt or trigger LGBT+ people. Help people shift from seeing homosexuality as an issue out there to recognizing that we are talking about our children in our church. Offer a powerful call to see Christian LGBT+ people as our family, to move beyond us-them. Invite LGBT+ listeners, Christians or not, to lunch afterward to talk and seek their opinions. Listen to them. Only preach what you are willing to post online. These days it's best to assume you are being recorded, and that that recording will be shared publicly.

Motivate and inspire people to whom you teach and preach to love LGBT+ people. Help them understand dynamics I shared in the previous chapters, such as that presence and proximity do not imply affirmation. We can and should share life with people who may be far from God. Show them the examples of Jesus with Matthew and the woman at the well and Zacchaeus and others. As Henson said so well, "Love does not sacrifice the gospel: it fulfills it."[9]

Depending on your context, audience, and time, call people to action, to practical expressions of love and justice. Challenge your church to stand up against bullying and teasing of gay teens. Encourage them to reach out with love to LGBT+ friends and family. Equip parents to be prepared if their child or their child's friend comes out to them or asks probing questions. Tell stories of real people, or have them tell their own stories.

In our church I did a five-week sermon series on sexuality. In advance I met several times with our elders and staff to prepare them. Then we had a training session with our small-group leaders to equip them to guide discussion in their groups (we have a sermon-based small-group approach). The materials for that series are in an appendix at the back of this book. Feel free to use them and modify them for your context if they are helpful.

What About Weddings?

Sarah asked if we could meet privately. As one of the younger ladies on our church staff, she had never asked to meet with me, so I sensed it was important. It was. Her sister had just announced her engagement to her same-sex partner. Since Sarah was really close to her older sister, she was pretty sure her sister was going to invite her to be a bridesmaid. She asked me what she should do. How would you have advised her? What questions should she ask?

Questions such as hers have become more frequent since the US Supreme Court *Obergefell v. Hodges* same-sex marriage decision in 2015. And yet, Bible-believing Christians disagree on how to respond to an invitation to a same-sex wedding. Some say you should attend, and others say you certainly should not attend, and both quote Scripture.

I wrote a book on this question: *Same-Sex Weddings: Should I Attend?* subtitled *A Wise Way to Develop Your Own Response.* The small book is designed to help you, your family, and your team or group think through the issue biblically and practically. Rather than arguing for any one particular point of view, it helps you think through the issue yourself.[10] I provided several short articles from multiple points of view to compare and test against the main biblical passages that apply to these questions about weddings.

The attend-the-wedding-or-not question raises issues not only about same-gender sexual relationships but also about the nature of marriage and of weddings, which are not the same thing. Multiple biblical principles come into play. Framing this issue well requires looking through multiple windows. In working through the issue, look through the following windows and any others you can identify.

Morality: What is the faith of the person(s) involved? Are both people Christians? Is only one a Christian, neither, or are you not sure? Is it biblically acceptable for a Christian same-sex couple to marry? What about for a non-Christian same-sex couple?

Marriage: What is the nature of marriage biblically? Is it a sacred institution? Is it only between a man and woman for a lifetime, or could it be between any two people who truly love each other? Could the marriage be a civil union recognized by the government rather than a religious union sanctified by God?

Relationship: Is the person getting married a family member, a close friend, a business associate, your boss, a coworker, a major client, or are they merely an acquaintance? How long have you known them?

Motive: Look into your heart to prayerfully discern your motives. Are you driven more by your desire to show love? To draw your friend to Christ? To avoid approving what you see as sin? Anger? Revulsion? Are you simply uncomfortable? Do you feel pressured by societal norms? Perhaps you are pressured by your concern over what others might think if you attend or, conversely, if you refuse to attend.

Context of the ceremony: Is the wedding a religious sacrament before God or a secular, civil ceremony? Where will the wedding be held—in a church or in a neutral setting such as a courtroom or garden? Will the wedding be conducted by a pastor or by a nonreligious person such as a judge?

Cultural meaning: Given the kind of wedding and the nature of your relationship, what will your attendance convey? Are you endorsing the marriage or simply supporting the person? In general, what does attending a wedding communicate in your cultural context? How does it compare to a non-Christian attending a Christian baptism? How would you compare or contrast attending a same-sex wedding with the wedding of a couple who is getting married only because the woman is pregnant, or who is too young or who have only known each other a very short time? Does the size of the wedding matter, several hundred versus merely dozens of attendees?

Biblical principles: Which biblical principles should guide your decision? Are some principles more important than others? How do you weigh standing for righteousness over acting in love? How do you weigh endorsing an action you oppose against expressing hospitality to people you love? What does the gospel imply for how we should respond?

Courses of action: There are far more options and variables than simply attending or not attending the wedding. For instance, will you give a gift? Make a toast? Be in the wedding party? Go to the reception only? Offer a prayer of blessing during the wedding ceremony or at the reception? If you are qualified, would you perform the ceremony? As a father, would you walk your daughter down the aisle? What about sending a note of congratulations? Or asking how the couple enjoyed their honeymoon trip to Hawaii? Could you have a conversation in advance with your family member or friend who is getting married, empowering them to decide whether they really want you there or not, given that you disapprove of the wedding?

It's important to distinguish a theology of marriage from a theology of weddings. Christian ethicist Lewis Smedes wrote, "Marriage is an invention of God; weddings are inventions of cultures."[11] Those of us in church leadership must also face the questions of whether we perform a wedding and whether we allow a wedding to take place in our facility or on our property. These are questions for which I encourage your church leadership to get on the same page for the sake of unity and clarity.[12] I have decided not to perform a same-sex wedding because I believe that the Bible teaches marriage is only between a man and a woman. I would attend a same-sex wedding to be a witness for Jesus; however, and I strongly encourage parents to attend the weddings of their children.

Employment

Who can serve on your church staff or be a pastor? Who can be an elder or a governing board member?

Matters of sexuality relate to who you hire or appoint as church staff, as well as who you put on an elder team or governing board.

Henson said, "There is no hierarchy in terms of who God loves, but there absolutely is a biblical reality that ministry leaders are held to a higher standard than church or ministry members."[13] And as with weddings, it's important for the elders and pastors of a church to be unified in decisions about who is in leadership. Henson added, "A *single biblical ethic* on marriage and sexuality must exist among core leaders within a given single church."[14] This is because core leaders are charged with ensuring control of a ministry's mission and message. You might find help in considering who needs to be on the same page and to what degree in Henson's dynamic inclusion model.[15]

The issues of employment include legal dimensions that I will not address in this book.[16] When it comes to legal issues, I encourage churches to consult a good church attorney. All your documents, from constitution and bylaw to facility policies and hiring practices, should all be unified and consistent with each other.

According to 1 Timothy 3 and Titus 1, an elder or church leader must be above reproach, blameless. If you are blameless, then you are above reproach. The root meaning of the Greek word for *blameless* is "to lay hold upon." The point is that there is nothing in your life that is a handle someone could grab hold of and use to bring an accusation against you. The focus is not so much on specific activities as it is on character and consistency of life. Many people have a handle that other people grab on to, to describe them: she's such a flirt; he's always looking for a fast buck; he'll lie at the drop of a hat if it makes him look good; you can't trust that guy; she's a drunk; he's got a quick temper. A church leader should not have such a negative handle.

This raises the issue of just how blameless you have to be. If the standard is Jesus Christ, none of us would ever serve as leaders. Each church has to make judgments in their particular situation as to who are the most blameless people to serve as leaders. Different leadership positions require different levels of blamelessness. Different regions of the world view certain behaviors as more or less blameworthy in terms of a person's reputation. Godly people defer leadership to others who are more mature. All of us are in process; none of us have arrived at Christlike maturity.

So how does all this apply to a person's sexual past and present? If a person had an adulterous affair or was sexually promiscuous when they were single, does that disqualify them? The answer is that it depends on how long ago it happened, if they've repented, and whether they've built a reputation as a "one woman kind of man" (1 Tim. 3:2). In terms of LGBT+ people, the decisions should be no different than with the sexual past and present of a straight person. The same kinds of judgment and wise consideration should apply to both.

So, would you have a LGBT+ on your church leadership team?

It's so important to recognize the various ways the term *gay* is used. Remember the discussion in chapter 5. You would want to have conversations with that person to know what he or she means by describing themselves as gay. In one case the answer might be that they absolutely can be considered with a person such as Wesley Hill. But in another case, with a person who is engaging in casual sex with multiple partners, the answer is obviously that they should not be considered, whether they are gay or straight.

Some have asked, if the child of a pastor or elder "comes out," is that leader now disqualified because they don't have "their own house in order"? Here, in addition to sexuality, as with other ways in which children might behave, the issue is about how that dad or mom is parenting, not the choices of the child. Each person stands before God. A godly parent can have a prodigal child. Are they parenting that prodigal well? And that is not to say that just because a child "comes out" that they are being "prodigal." They may be quite spiritually mature.

There are other difficult questions to answer that each local church leadership team may need to address, such as:

- Besides positions of teaching and leadership, would you consider hiring the partner of a monogamous same-sex couple for any of your staff positions, including nonteaching roles or facility management roles?
- A beloved youth leader comes out as having same-gender attractions but has also vowed to remain celibate before the Lord and supportive of monogamous heterosexual marriage. Do you allow him to continue in ministry without restriction? Do you apply new restrictions but still allow him to continue in the role?
- An elder or staff member is exploring his or her theological position and leaning toward moving to an affirming position

in favor of same-sex marriages. Do you remove them? Work with them over time? Ask them to continue but only if they will refrain from sharing their views?

In no way do I claim to have the answers to these and dozens of other questions and scenarios that may arise in our churches. At this time in church history, we do not have so many answers. But I know we will be guided by grace *and* truth in full measure. Love will be our core. We will prayerfully seek the Lord and listen to each other and to each person. Our focus will not be on sexuality, but on Jesus.

Discussion Questions

1. How does love serve as an overarching principle for how we minister well to LGBT+ people? How does this truth apply to our tone and posture, regardless of our theology and position?
2. How can we help our people break through the sad and paralyzing confusion that showing love would be condoning sin, that compassion equals affirmation, or that proximity conveys approval?
3. What are the merits and dangers of writing policies and position papers? What seems best for your church in terms of what to put, and not put, into writing?
4. How could you lead or suggest to an appropriate person that they lead the leaders of the church (elders, pastors, deacons, staff) through a study on this topic? What needs to take place for it to actually happen?
5. Why is training on language so important? In your context what words and phrases are helpful and which are hurtful?
6. How could you preach or teach about this topic in your church? What venues would be appropriate and what timing?

7. What are factors related to the question of whether to attend a same-sex wedding? What is your view? Do the leaders of your church need to share the same view about attending weddings? Why or why not?

8. What is your church's approach to employment and leadership for LGBT+ people?

CHAPTER 13

SEXUAL QUESTIONS AND COMMON ISSUES

Leading Wisely

After he read an early draft of this book, a straight, single man in our church who lives with his male life partner sent me these beautiful words: "Let us not fold our arms in smugness but open our arms wide to all, while we practice and present the sparkling gems of uncompromising truth on shining silver platters of grace. Many are looking for the treasure: it's ample, available, and to be given." He asked, "Has Christians' condemnatory language outspoken the sparkling springs of divine truth and love?"

As we consider practical matters of church ministry, once again as leaders of the body of Christ we look to Jesus as the embodiment of grace and truth, not in balance, but each in full measure. Our center and focus is Jesus, not sexuality. And as stewards of Christ's church, we join him by the Holy Spirit in extending grace to those on the margins, while holding firm to truth. As his ambassadors, we offer his love to hurting people and communicate his charge to give up our lives for him—all in, holding nothing back.

Many of the ministry questions we will address in this chapter circle around the deep issue of "belonging." Joshua Ryan Butler rightly said, "There is perhaps no question more central to the human heart than this: Can I belong? We are made for communion with God and others. We are created for relationship, crafted to know and be known, designed to walk with others—made to belong."[1] So when we sit around tables in our church offices discussing membership and more, remember that when LGBT+ people ask about joining the church, baptism, service, and communion, these are more than questions about doctrinal beliefs; they are also about belonging. Am I wanted? Will I be included in the family? Can I be part of this faith community?

A temptation in these discussions is to focus on the boundaries, about what we will *not* allow. And yet it would be better to shift our minds to what we are *for*, rather than to specify what we are *against*. God offers all of us humans life in Christ, the fruit of the Spirit, and much more. We are *for* marriage and fidelity. Butler provided a practical example: "Rather than saying, 'We welcome gay and lesbian people, but we don't allow them to engage in same-sex sexual relations,' it's better to focus on the institution of marriage, something like: 'We believe that marriage is a one-flesh lifelong union between two sexually different people, and that God intends all sexual relations to be expressed within this covenant bond.'"[2] The leaders in your church can apply your unified efforts to clarify and express how God is *for* all of us; he wants good for us, and we want good, blessing, for *each* member and guest in our churches.

How we form our responses to complex ministry questions about local church practices in relation to LGBT+ people is shaped by how we understand being gay, and how we understand what it means to join or be part of a local church. In chapter 5 we talked about five ways the term *gay* is commonly used: gender roles, behavior, identity, attraction, and orientation. When we come to questions of membership and serving in various church ministries, it can be easy to forget these distinctions and as a result make huge mistakes that hurt people. In terms of gender roles, just because a man appears culturally feminine or a woman comes across as culturally masculine is no reason to treat them differently in any way. Simply because one person is attracted to another is no reason to prevent them from serving as a leader in the church. Think of denying leadership status to the straight man who is attracted to *any* woman other than his wife. If you applied this standard, 99 percent of the straight men would be excluded.

This fact raises the important principle of not holding to a double standard. However you construct your approach to baptism or your approach to who can volunteer in children's ministry, it's a matter of integrity that you apply the same standard to all people—in the case of this book, to LGBT+ people and to straight people alike. For instance, when persons refer to themselves as gay or lesbian in terms of their identity or orientation, does that prevent them from engaging in church life or even church leadership? If it does, then you need to consider how you will consistently apply that standard to other identities and orientations: such as to a ten-year-sober alcoholic. Of course our primary identity should be in Christ. And we know that lust is sin, yet if we try to police internal sinful thoughts, we head off down a dangerous road. When it comes to sinful sexual behavior, whether of straight people or LGBT+ people, the same pastoral discernment should come into play. Was this a onetime event or chronic rebellion? Does this person evidence a hard heart, or are they showing a broken and contrite heart?

Our approach to practical ministry issues is also shaped by how we understand what it means and what is required to "join" the local church. While this is overly simplistic, you can think of churches as "high-bar" and "low-bar" when it comes to belonging. How hard is it to get in, and what are the requirements for staying in? In this discussion, I am not siding with one approach or the other. Both can be biblically appropriate, and most churches are somewhere on a continuum from high-bar to low-bar, or might even slide to one side on one issue and on another issue slide the other way. In either case, joining a church is more like joining a family than joining a club. Membership is not a matter of paying dues, enjoying services, and having privileges; it is rather about relationships and responsibility as a family member.

A family includes all the members, even those who are hard to be around. We open Christmas presents with the sister who borrowed a dress and never returned it. We eat Thanksgiving dinner with the uncle who cracks inappropriate jokes and the cousin who makes awkward political comments. Family membership is not based on performance. Families include infants who can't yet talk and grand-mothers who can no longer cut their own meat at dinner. We take special care of the disabled and differently abled in the family. In healthy families we support those who have been hurt or have hurt themselves with bad choices, yet we resist enabling them. Loving families welcome guests to the Thanksgiving table to join our feast, and loving churches welcome guests to our worship services to taste and see that God is good.

Another overarching factor in discussions of who can be involved in a local church is the difference between *believing* and *living* in a way that conflicts with your church's position. What I mean is the differ-ence between a person engaged in sexual behavior that violates your church's teaching and a person who affirms behavior that is opposed to your teaching. For instance, how would you handle a straight man who tried to set up a date between a lesbian in his small group and another lesbian he knows at work? The apostle Paul critiqued not only those who practice immorality but also those who "approve" of those who practice it (Rom. 1:32). In Revelation the apostle John quoted Jesus Christ speaking to the churches against those "who hold to the teaching of Balaam who taught Balak to entice the Israelites to sin so that they ate food sacrificed to idols and committed sexual immorality" (Rev. 2:14). Jesus rebuked not only people who commit sexual immorality but also those who agree with a teaching that allows it. A little later in the same chapter, Jesus rebuked those who "tolerate that woman Jezebel. . . . By her teaching she misleads my servants into sexual immorality" (Rev. 2:20).

While Jesus was concerned not just about living in sexual immorality but also about believing in teaching that affirms immoral behavior, he provides grace for those who are in process. Remember, for example, the story of Peter in Acts 10, which we discussed earlier. We want to show grace for people to grow in their understanding. And once again it's dangerous to try to police people's internal thoughts and beliefs because we cannot read minds. Yet the situation is different when a person actively teaches or counsels against the teaching of your church. That can be divisive, and unity is a serious issue. If a person engages in a campaign to overturn your church's teaching, that person must be confronted. On the other hand, if a person is thinking through sexual ethics and not sure where they land, or is simply questioning your church's position personally, that is no reason to limit their access to church ministry and service. We want to give people gracious space to grow in their understanding and maturity in Christ.

Another temptation we want to avoid is lack of up-front clarity, because it can bite both us and the person when they feel like there has been a bait and switch. Personally, in opening conversations with LGBT+ people in our church, I sometimes find myself holding back on the full conversation about our sexual ethics out of a desire to provide a warm welcome, and yet at times I am simply avoiding a hard conversation. This advice could sound in apparent conflict with previous counsel not to front-load conversations with what the Bible says on same-gender sexual relations. And there is a tension you want to hold. On the one hand, you want to be up front, so that later a person does not say, as a woman once said to me, "I thought I was loved and accepted at your church, until I found out about the 'homosexual clause.'" On the other hand, you do not want to throw Bible verses at an LGBT+ person when you first meet them. Negotiating these opening conversations requires spiritual wisdom and discernment for each individual person and their unique situation.

That realization of uniqueness is central to the advice that follows on membership and more. Generic advice never quite fits each unique person and a specific moment in their journey. Such advice is more like the wisdom in Proverbs that applies in a general way but is not a promise or a law. And some wisdom principles we hold in tension: Do not defend yourself, but do explain yourself. Love overlooks sin, and love confronts sin. General wisdom needs to be applied with prayerful spiritual discernment in each particular case.

To wisely make that personal application requires listening. Too often we hear only a little of a person's story or the start of their questions and then begin answering before we have really understood. Take a long time to listen. Ask questions. Seek to really understand the nuances of their story, the emotions, the hurts and dreams, the wounds and joys, the hopes and disappointments. Look for what is under the surface. Do not assume that you know. Listening is not agreeing. Listening is loving. Without listening it is difficult to really love. Inviting people to your family dinner table or to share a meal at a local restaurant just to listen to their story will distinguish you as a person who is genuinely invested in the well-being and care of those you shepherd.

Finally, before we get to specific questions, it's important to remember the backdrop of our tattered history in regard to LGBT+ people. As a fact, whether we think it is right or wrong, they have felt largely excluded by churches. In these conversations, when Christian leaders say we want our churches to be a safe place for LGBT+ people, and then add, "But where do we draw the line?" that question itself can be healthy. But it can also reveal an intention to keep LGBT+ people at a distance, to protect ourselves from "those people." Ty

Wyss, founder of Walls Down Ministry, wrote the following, which I think well expresses a Christlike heart for how to approach practical church ministry matters around belonging.

We also must recognize that the church's history with LGBT people has been one of exclusion and non-engagement and that the main question in response to reaching them has been "Where do we continue excluding?" rather than "How can we make people we've previously excluded feel welcome and included?" . . . I'm ready for something different. I'm ready for restoring dignity to LGBT people in our communities and in our churches. And I'm ready to proclaim the Gospel that declares that in God's Kingdom there's no longer any dividing lines that create fallen hierarchical systems. There's one community, a new community that shouts an equitable "You belong!"

So how do we shift our posture without shifting scripture? I believe focusing on how to make people feel welcome rather than where we might have to "draw the line" one day is important. I believe this can happen when we acknowledge the fact that LGBT people have so much to offer the Christian community. . . .

Again, I hope you don't hear me saying "anything goes" and that no one teaches the sexual ethic God has put forth in His word, but rather a radical shift from focusing on dividing lines to actively looking for places LGBT people can serve, be connected, and truly feel "at home" in a church body.[3]

Frankly I'm intimidated by trying to offer general wisdom for these ministry decisions because I am so aware that I do not have all the answers, or even very many answers at all. Each scenario can be so complex with theological issues, cultural dynamics, and individual church factors. There is no one right answer to most of these questions. Each church leadership team needs to make their own choices before God among a range of God-honoring options. In any case, we all want to be guided by the Spirit as we bathe decisions in prayer and focus on Christ. All decisions should be grounded in love and full of grace and truth. We wrestle first with what is right and good before the Lord and then only second with how we will communicate our approach to a person, and potentially to our church community. How a direction will be received should not be the basis for decision but should be a major factor in how we communicate our decision.

Membership

Can an LGBT+ person become a member of your church? We want to base our answer on God's Word. But looking in the Scripture, we do not find clear instructions on church membership. In fact, the early churches were informal gatherings, not official organizations. Churches vary significantly in their approach to membership. Some have rigorous guidelines and an extensive process with high expectations of members. Usually the thought is that you need to believe before you belong. Others do not have an official membership at all but simply consider as members those who are involved by their activity. The prior thought is reversed: you can belong before you believe. We can use the "high-bar, low-bar" analysis to see local churches on a spectrum. Your theology of membership impacts how you will answer the opening question about LGBT+ people.

Broadly speaking, one approach is to tighten your membership policy to exclude people in some kind of serious sin, but if you go that route, you want to be sure you apply your guidelines in a fair and even way to straight people as well as to LGBT+ people.

Personally, I encourage a missiological approach that sees offering a place of belonging for LGBT+ people as an opportunity, rather than as a threat.[4] In Acts 15, on behalf of the Jerusalem Council, James said,

"It is my judgment, therefore, that we should not make it difficult for the Gentiles who are turning to God" (v. 19). In a similar way we should remove as many barriers as possible to enable LGBT+ people (and all people) to turn to God. All the church members we already include in our church are sinning people, including leaders. It's worth a look back at how Jesus treated people in the crowds that followed him (who were not all believers by a long stretch). He fed them, healed them, touched them, and taught them. He rarely rebuked them for their sins.[5]

In one of his parables, Jesus told how the weeds and the wheat will grow together until the harvest (Matt. 13:24–30). By application we could allow in our church all kinds of people to belong without our trying to sort the weeds from the wheat. If a person is not in your church, you do not have nearly the opportunity to minister to them that you have if they are involved with your fellowship. And in his frequent farming metaphors, Jesus encouraged us to water and tend to fragile planted seeds so they can grow even as they are battered by the Devil and the world (weeds) early in their faith.

Whatever your decisions on this issue and others, it's important that your leadership be of one mind so that you speak with one voice. Be honest and clear about your answers so that you do not confuse people, send mixed messages, or create false expectations.

Baptism

As with membership, churches have a high-bar and low-bar approach to adult baptism. Some require courses and commitments before baptizing, while others will immediately baptize someone who confesses faith in Christ. They might point to Pentecost, when about three thousand were baptized. And following that story, we read about the Ethiopian eunuch being baptized by Philip (Acts 8), and the

Philippian jailer by Paul the very day they believed (Acts 16). Those with a high bar point to common practices in the ancient church in the centuries just after the New Testament requiring a person to go through catechism before being baptized.

As with membership, whatever your approach, it should be consistent. If you require that baptized people simply make a confession of faith in Christ, that's one thing (and would not exclude LGBT+ people), but if you require them to repent of all known sin (or ones you view as serious) or demonstrate a transformed life, then you will be making harder judgment calls with each person no matter their sexual lives.

Lord's Supper

As with baptism, I am attempting to avoid the significant and important theological issues and differences among Christians in regard to the Lord's Supper, but your particular theological tradition and personal position will impact how you make decisions on this church practice. In general, some churches practice closed communion and others an open table, but, as with most issues, there is a spectrum of how closed and how open. Basically, a closed approach requires that a person be a member of that particular church or denomination (such as be an Episcopal or Roman Catholic member in good standing). An open-table approach welcomes anyone to the table of the Lord's Supper, but leaves the decision to participate or not to each individual's conscience.

At our church we invite people to make their own decisions based on their awareness of what this sacred act means. Even with an open approach, it is not uncommon for church leaders to recommend to people in unrepentant rebellion that they abstain until they repent and return to Christ. Be careful not to conclude that a person is living in sin just because they identify as LGBT+. That would be like concluding that a heterosexual male must be using pornography. Statistically, it is quite possible, but we don't go around presuming what people are doing in private. I mention this because many gay people report that Christian leaders too quickly presume that they are actively sinning when all they did was share about their sexual orientation. Once again it's important to be consistent.

Baby Dedication and Baptism

Some churches baptize infants while others dedicate them. Without getting into that dispute of which is the more biblically fitting way to go, in either case, at issue is whether you would allow a married (or unmarried) same-sex couple to dedicate or baptize their child at your church. We have responsibilities to the parents, to the child, and to our church community. Theologically, we want to ask, what is the meaning of the baptism or dedication? Specifically, does this act endorse the parents as being Christians, moral, upstanding, godly people? For consistency we should ask if we are evaluating the fitness of *all* parents who bring children to be dedicated or baptized. Is each couple married, or might some be living together? Or perhaps a single mom who had a baby out of wedlock wants to pledge to raise her child in God's ways.

One factor to consider is the setting. Some churches do dedications outside their worship services, even in private ceremonies. At issue is the congregation's reception. If you have two women standing on the platform on a Sunday morning before the watching church body with their infant, it could miscommunicate that you endorse gay marriage when you do not. However, if you have a private ceremony with a lesbian couple but not with other couples, then it could look like you are trying to hide something rather than acting in the open. If you routinely offer private ceremonies for different kinds of couples, then you increase opportunities to respond positively to gay couples and their babies.

In our church we believe that dedicating a child is a good act for a parent even if at that moment a mom or dad is struggling with being faithful to Christ. It's noble to publicly pledge to raise your child in God's ways, even if you are currently running away from God. We are working at communicating that baby dedication is open to *all* parents no matter where they are with Christ at the moment, so that our church learns we are not endorsing parents but are rather providing an avenue for them to make a sacred pledge. And as a church family we pledge to support and help parents raise their children, knowing we all fail in many ways. We are a community of forgiven sinners, not perfect people or perfect parents. More recently, along with some other churches, we are encouraging the extended family to stand with the parent(s), and close friends as well, including members of their small group. This symbolizes that we are committed to investing in the next generation as a church community and reduces the singular focus on the nuclear family.

One last point: babies are not aware of what is happening in a dedication ceremony. Their parents, however, will always remember the moment. If you decline to dedicate a child because of how you measure the status of a parent, you place a mark of rejection on this family. The story line of this family may be filled with one rejection after another, with some of the rejection coming in the name of the Christian faith. Declining to dedicate a child could be the seed of rejection that propels that child away from the Christian faith. Stories of judgment or rejection (as later recounted by the mom and dad) will impact a child's ideas of how his or her family is viewed by the church. Imagine a child hearing, "When you were a baby, that church refused to dedicate or baptize you."

Volunteers: Serving and Leading

Who can serve in the church in what roles? Most every church has some sort of requirements for various positions of service. For instance, choir members should know how to sing. Those who work in technology need to be capable of running the soundboard, working the lights, or running the slides on whatever software you use. For a teaching role, you may likely require that teachers agree to your statement of faith so you know that what they teach does not conflict with your doctrine. For elders or deacons you may require a high level of spiritual maturity, following 1 Timothy 3 and Titus 1. Here is where I think the consistency principle helps us. Why would you add anything to your requirements for serving in a specific role merely to address LGBT+ people who desire to serve, whether they are affirming, sexually active, or celibate?

Many churches, including ours, differentiate between serving and leading. While the two overlap, they can be distinguished. Leading refers to those roles involving teaching or holding a position of significant influence, such as pastor, elder, teacher, director of a ministry, and sometimes leader of a group. Service includes other volunteer roles, such as playing in the worship band, being a greeter, serving in the nursery, running sound, or serving in a soup kitchen. These roles are just as important as leadership roles. The Bible says every member of the body is equally valuable and important. However, service roles do not carry the same degree of influence as leadership roles. Many people in a church would assume that the leaders, paid or unpaid, represent and speak for the church. So it makes sense for church leaders to be in agreement.

Toward that end many churches create a leadership covenant or agreement that spells out in advance what they expect of leaders in the church and what support they will provide for leaders (regardless of whether a leader is straight or gay). You want to be up front so you do not create hard feelings down the road.

Children's and Student Ministry

Leadership roles in children's and student ministry carry extra sensitivity, and they should. Along with many churches, we require a background check if a person wants to serve with children or students, because we want to protect our kids from predators. We want to know if a person has a criminal record. We have a higher standard for anyone who wants to serve with kids. Sadly, in many cultures LGBT+ people have falsely been seen as being unsafe with kids, as if they would prey on them in a sexual way. This is simply incorrect. Straight people are just as likely or unlikely to be a risk, if not more so for straight men.[6] Other church members may be concerned about the model being set for their children by a same-sex couple.

In student ministry, churches face many more issues as students are coming to grips with their own sexuality and with that of their peers. Most high school students have a LGBT+ organization in their school. According to Mark Yarhouse, there is consensus in the scientific community that, on average, a person first realizes their lesbian, gay, bisexual, or transgender orientation in early adolescence, which means around thirteen years of age.[7] This age puts a boy or girl in seventh or eighth grade.

In Andrew Marin's research, he found that 96 percent of his study's participants had prayed for God to make them straight when as teenagers they first realized they were not straight.[8] A common thread in many stories was that after praying in the privacy of their bedroom and still feeling the same way, a teenager would go to church or a church student ministry in the hopes that God would answer their prayers and remove their sexual desires.[9] That teen might show up in your church without their parents, and you might not realize they are desperate inside because they will be covering it up on the outside.

How will leaders in your church's student ministry respond when a teenager comes out to them? Do students feel safe to talk about their sexual feelings in your church? Have you trained your leaders in how to respond? Check out the resources available from Preston Sprinkle, Bill Henson, and Mark Yarhouse, all of whom have books and guides for students, as well as families of LGBT+ students, and those who serve in student ministries. I especially recommend Bill Henson's *Guiding Families of LGBT+ Loved Ones*, second edition, available at leadthemhome.org. His material on providing sustainable support will be invaluable to you if you want to care well for the kids in your church who are coming out, and provide resources for their families. Henson offers practical tools and tips for parents and those serving students.

In student ministry, churches face other complex issues, such as what to do when an openly gay high school student wants to go to youth camp or on the overnight campout. Are there any restrictions or guidelines? We've had parents ask if they should pull their child out of our student ministry because their kid declared a noncomforming sexual identity on Facebook. We want to keep ministering to these students and their entire families. In this arena we need to remember the uniqueness of each person and situation. What seems wise in one case does not work well in another. Remember we are not talking so much about issues as about real people with personal stories that matter.

If an LGBT+ teen demonstrates spiritual interest, then wouldn't it be wise to keep nourishing their faith identity? Isn't it worth finding a role for them to serve in and exercise their God-given talents? If we reject LGBT+ teens simply because of their sexuality, it can deconstruct a young person's entire sense of worth as well as his or her spiritual identity. Inclusion is necessary to foster spiritual growth. This is true for all of us.

Counseling and Relationship Events, Workshops, and Retreats

With adults, your church will likely face decisions about counseling. Presumably you would counsel any person in need, but you might not provide premarital counseling to a same-gender couple.

Yet what do you do for the married same-sex couple who asks for relationship counseling? On the one hand, you have the opportunity to minister to them. On the other hand, you do not want to endorse a marriage you believe to be unbiblical. In looking back at Jesus' example, he seemed to have no sin filter for who he ministered to. It seems to me we should take every opportunity available to bring the message of Jesus and the comfort of the Spirit to each person. If a same-sex couple is seeking counseling from your church, you have a wonderful open door to share hope and truth and grace with them from God's Word.

In men's and women's ministries, issues can arise with marriage seminars and overnight retreats. Suppose a married same-sex couple who has been attending your church wants to come on your annual weekend marriage retreat. Do you allow them to sign up? If so, are there any conditions? Why or why not? A lesbian couple wants to attend your women's retreat. Do you allow them to sign up? If so, are there any conditions? Is there any difference between these two situations? In these kinds of situations, each church will struggle with tensions between being open to everyone yet avoiding miscommunicating what they believe to others. With these kinds of events it's good to communicate in advance the goals of the event and what will be taught so people know what to expect. And, if you know LGBT+

people will be present, prepare your leaders to show grace and stand for truth in love.

It's wise to do some training with your lay leaders yourself or bring in experts who offer this kind of training for churches. Because these issues are so highly charged, you will need more than a few minutes or one sermon to equip your leaders both to hold to biblical truth and to show Christ's amazing grace. Your church members need to be secure in the church's theological position and learn how to minister well to people on the margins who have often been excluded.

Church Discipline, Dealing with Sin

As leaders of a church we want to lead the people whom we shepherd to live holy lives, and at times that involves confronting sin. In the case of nonstraight sexual sin, the situations are often complex and freighted with emotion from our cultural moment. In conversations among church leaders about sexual sin, someone will inevitably ask about "church discipline" and how it might apply to same-sex sexual sin. Often at this point everyone goes quiet or puts their head down because this is a hard topic!

While the phrase "church discipline" is not in the Bible, it provides a title under which people often arrange the Bible's teaching on how a local church should handle serious sin within its own fellowship. I, however, find the phrase unhelpful and distorting because it conjures up in our minds the legal process of a formal organization. Fundamentally the church is people, and the New Testament is describing not an organizational policy with legal overtones but a relational dynamic among close friends in small home churches.

All believers sin on a regular basis, but we do not confront all those sins, nor do they impact our membership, service, or leadership in a local church. Every leader of a local church, every pastor and elder, sins. All of us have stubborn sins to which we continually and sadly fall prey. And each of us has a responsibility to encourage one another to holy living, to turn from sin and turn to Christ. We are to admonish one another, *if* we have the relational bond to have that kind of conversation. Importantly, we should guard against Christians confronting someone they see doing something they think is sinful or inappropriate when they lack the relational connection for that kind of communication. Is it really every Christian's obligation to tell gay people—or any other group of people—what they think or believe?

There are occasions when certain kinds of sin need to be addressed by the leader of a church community. Examples could include heresy, when sound doctrine is threatened (meaning core truth is at stake— the gospel—not a secondary doctrine such as the timing of end-time events). This should be more than a misunderstanding, or about a person in process of growing, but rather about a person knowingly teaching heresy (Galatians 1 vs. Philippians 1). Another example is divisiveness, when the unity of the body is at stake, when sin hinders the work of God by bringing confusion or division. At times leaders should confront public immorality when the witness of the church is at stake with serious sin that mars God's holy character and hurts Christ's reputation in the community. This action is particularly vital if the exposed person is a church leader. For a person's own sake, when the sin is threatening that person's life or someone else's life, as when abuse or violence is involved, leaders need to step in.

One classification scheme that might guide your church is to distinguish among toleration, restoration, and expulsion based on Romans 14, Galatians 6, and 1 Corinthians 5. For some behaviors we show compassion to weaker brothers (Rom. 14); for others we restore gently because they are caught in a sin (Gal. 6); for still others we exclude them to motivate them to repent (1 Cor. 5).

When we consider behaviors that some Christians see as sin but others do not, such as watching media with sex scenes, smoking, drinking, or gambling, we can agree to disagree. Rather than condemn each other, we tolerate each other. We show compassion to the weaker brother or sister for whom a certain act might be sin. There are those in our church who think it's wrong to go trick-or-treating on Halloween, and others who think it's totally fine. We agree to disagree.

But there are other behaviors that are clearly sin. Our brother or sister may be caught in a trap, and we need to help them get out. Paul told us to gently restore each other (Gal. 6:1–2). Love helps a friend to repent. "My brothers and sisters, if one of you should wander from the truth and someone should bring that person back, remember this: Whoever turns a sinner from the error of their way will save them from death and cover over a multitude of sins" (James 5:19–20).

At times, however, leaders must deal more severely with people involved in unrepentant and serious sin. A person who is harming others should be removed from the fellowship. At our church we've had to remove men who were seducing women. A shepherd must distinguish a wolf from the sheep, and protect the sheep from a wolf. In all cases our goal is to restore an unrepentant brother or sister. We are driven by love for the person, for the church body, and for the watching world. The reasons we address a person in sin are first for their own sake so they will repent and be restored (Matt. 18:15; 1 Cor. 5:1–13; 2 Cor. 2:5–11; Gal. 6:1–5; 2 Thess. 3:6–15; 1 Tim. 1:20; James 5:19–20). A second reason is to protect the purity and unity of the whole church family in life, doctrine, and relationships (Josh. 7; Acts 5:1–11; Acts 20:29–30; 1 Cor. 5:1–13; 1 Tim. 5:17–22; Titus 1:10–14; and consider the metaphor of the body in Rom. 12 and 1 Cor. 12). A third reason is so that a local church will continue to be a bright witness to the community, the watching world.

Recently the #MeToo movement has exposed some churches and ministries that did not deal effectively with sexual sin, men who were abusing women, including some in leadership roles. The Roman

Catholic Church has been wrestling for years with their previous inadequate handling of priests who abused their authority by acting as sexual predators, even among their own flocks, and how to prevent recurrences (Acts 5; Rom. 2:24; 1 Cor. 11:27–34; Heb. 12:5–11; Rev. 2:14–15, 20). Their toleration of sexual abuse and cover-up has damaged their reputation worldwide, and hurt the overall cause of Christ.

The Special Case in 1 Corinthians 5

"It is actually reported that there is sexual immorality among you, and of a kind that even pagans do not tolerate: A man is sleeping with his father's wife. And you are proud! Shouldn't you rather have gone into mourning and have put out of your fellowship the man who has been doing this?" (1 Cor. 5:1–2).

Is the incest situation in 1 Corinthians 5 parallel to same-sex marriage today? Many pastors have had members of their churches use this text to demand that church leaders put same-sex couples out of the church. Is that right?

In the Corinthian situation, a man in the church was having sex with his stepmother. The Greek phrase indicates it was an ongoing relationship, not a onetime affair. It was a crime of incest according to Roman law. Some sexual sins, such as a married man having a woman or boy on the side, were acceptable to the Romans, but incest was not. How could the church tolerate what even the pagan society condemned as deviant? Based on this text and others, we can assume this man was a believer involved in the church and that he had not repented of his sin. His stepmother with whom he was sleeping may not have been a believer since Paul explicitly said his instructions did not apply to those outside the church.

What is striking is that the man himself was never directly

addressed by Paul. Rather, Paul's concern was with how the church was mishandling the situation by ignoring it. The burden of 1 Corinthians 5 was to explain why the church should remove the immoral person from their fellowship. Why should they take such drastic action? In our day we really need to understand why, because for most of us this is a very challenging command, not because it is hard to understand the specifics of the required action, but because it is hard to understand the value of doing it.

Comparing the issue with similar situations in other contexts helps me appreciate Paul's counsel. Picture a family living room, a school classroom, a team locker room, and a work conference room. Let's start in a home.

Moms and dads have had to exercise tough love with their adult children. (Note: before you read this example, please know that I am *not* endorsing parents kicking their LGBT+ teen out of their home because they have come out. That is horrifying.) As a good parent, you set clear guidelines for staying in your home. If these guidelines are willfully and consistently broken, this would mean your adult child has chosen to leave. When your child defiantly violates the rules (sadly, sometimes with criminal or immoral behavior), parents cry many tears on the day they must bring the news to their child that they have chosen to leave. It is incredibly painful, but it can be the right decision to exercise tough love, to help your child face consequences and learn to take responsibility for himself or herself, as well as protect younger siblings.

As a teacher, you may have had to remove a student from a classroom. Sometimes their behavior was so disruptive that the rest of the class suffered until they left. Maybe you played on a sports team, where one person's bad behavior wrecked the chemistry of the whole team; sometimes it happens with the most talented player on the team. Or in a work environment, have you endured a coworker whose negativity or immorality made you not even want to go to work? There are times when an employee needs to be fired, a player released from the team, a student removed from the classroom, and even an adult child removed from the home. In the church there are times when a member needs to be removed from the fellowship.

Paul was shocked not only at the sin but also at the attitude of the church. They were proud. What sense does this make? Status was very important to the Corinthians. It is possible that this man was wealthy. Let me be blunt. Many people would advise a pastor, "You do not want to tick off a wealthy donor." Maybe this man hosted the church in his large home and was an influential person in the city. Because of who he was, they may have been slow to address the embarrassing situation that would shame a powerful, wealthy person. The Corinthian church may have been proud that this "famous" or wealthy man was in their church. This happens on athletic teams. Leadership hesitates to release the superstar. In work environments it might be the supersmart engineer or the top salesperson. In a classroom it may be the daughter of the principal.[10]

Instead of being proud, they should have mourned. Mourning implies not just feeling but actions. Rather than saying, "We're fine; we're great," they should have faced the sin, filled with anguish over what the man was doing and how it was hurting the church. That mourning should have led them to put the man out of their fellowship. The debacles at Penn State, Baylor, the University of Tennessee, Florida State, and others are poignant reminders of what happens when you ignore sin.[11]

Think about a family. Sometimes when one family member is in serious sin, family and friends will come together for an intervention. An intervention is not a legal decision but an act of love by those who are closest to a person and love them the most. I've been involved in several interventions that have literally saved someone's life. A man in our church has thanked me over and over for loving him enough to meet with his family and friends to confront his alcohol and drug abuse that was killing him and destroying his family. It is powerful when a whole football team together confronts a teammate over his bad behavior and says it must cease or he is off the team.

Paul's point had nothing to do with people outside the church but only with those inside. Your relationship with your own kids is very different from your relationship with the kids down the street. You are responsible to discipline your own kids. In fact, Paul explicitly said that it is not our business to judge those outside the church (1 Cor. 5:12). God will do that. Our responsibility is to love those outside the church, to serve them with the gospel of Jesus, to share his love and hope. Our problem is that we do the opposite, and too often we are lenient with ourselves and judgmental of those outside the church. This text does not apply to those who are not Christians. It applies only to those who are members of a specific local church of which those involved are also members.

So, does this text apply to every professing believer in a local church who is actively engaged in same-sex sexual relations? In harmony with some others who have studied this passage carefully, I do not believe it applies in every case.[12] When it does apply, then to be consistent, church leaders need to apply it much more widely, to more sins than most do. Listen to the people Paul included in this chapter:

> I wrote to you in my letter not to associate with sexually immoral people—not at all meaning the people of this world who are immoral, or the greedy and swindlers, or idolaters. In that case you would have to leave this world. But now I am writing to you that you must not associate with anyone who claims to be a brother or sister but is sexually immoral or greedy, an idolater or slanderer, a drunkard or swindler. Do not even eat with such people. (1 Cor. 5:9–11)

Few of us are discussing disassociating from greedy, materialistic people who abuse consumer debt, those who drink too many margaritas, or those who make slanderous Facebook posts. When we apply this text today in our churches, however, we should apply it evenly to all those mentioned: "sexually immoral or greedy, an idolater or slanderer, a drunkard or swindler." If we selectively apply the text, then we are being hypocritical and unjust. In terms of being sexually immoral, a common analog to a same-sex union is a straight unmarried couple living together.

Biblical commentators have identified how Paul's instructions in 1 Corinthians 5 draw from the Mosaic law in Deuteronomy.[13] In addition to the texts in Deuteronomy, I wonder if the sin in view is "defiant" sin, which in a Hebrew word picture describes sin with "a high hand." The image is of a fist raised against God in rebellious defiance. In his commentary on Numbers, Jewish scholar Jacob Milgrom described what this image conveys: "The upraised hand is therefore poised to strike; it is a threatening gesture of the Deity against His enemies or of man against God Himself. Thus, this literary image is most apposite [appropriate] for the brazen sinner who commits his acts in open defiance of the Lord (cf. Job 38:15)."[14] If there is a correlation between Numbers 15 and 1 Corinthians 5, then perhaps the sin Paul is concerned about is a brazen, prideful one committed in defiance against God. The Hebrew word in Numbers 15:30 describes "a person acting in deliberate presumption, pride, and disdain."[15] In Numbers 15:31, this sin of obstinate rebellion is also called blasphemy against the Lord.

In addition, I wonder if another dynamic involved here in 1 Corinthians 5 is much akin to the #MeToo movement where institutions have ignored sexual abuse and not held people accountable to a sufficient degree. Paul specifically said that this sin is of a kind that not even the pagans tolerate (1 Cor. 5:1). Because the church was ignoring the issue, they were compromising their witness to the community.[16] As it was in the first century, so today there are sexual sins that our culture tolerates, such as adult pornography, adultery, and sex before marriage, but there are others our society will not tolerate, such as child pornography, sexual violence, and abuse of authority, namely, a teacher, coach, boss, or priest taking sexual advantage of a person under their authority, whether male or female. Of course, biblical justice and morality should always be of paramount importance to the church. We must support victims abused by those in power over them. But particularly when the reputation of our Savior is at risk because the sin is abhorrent not just in the church's eyes, but in the eyes of society as well, church leaders must address it, and quickly. By taking swift action to deal with unrepentant sinners, the church is agreeing with our culture that such people should be held accountable. But that does not mean the church allows the culture to define what is sin. The Word of God does that.

Given this analysis of 1 Corinthians 5, the text does not apply to every same-sex couple. It applies only if a person is a Christian, and a member of a local church, and then only to those few who are acting defiantly and thus blaspheming God, negatively impacting the church's unity and its witness to the community. If a person, or couple, is aggressively disruptive to the unity of a church community by their sinful behavior, then that behavior needs to be addressed in a 1 Corinthians 5 fashion. In addition, other factors must be considered, which I address in the next section. Having said this, 1 Corinthians 5 remains a difficult passage to handle well, and I respect those who differ from me on how to interpret and apply this text.

How Do We Minister Well to Same-Sex Couples in Our Church?

Let's presume you believe that a same-sex marriage is against the Bible. A married same-sex couple begins attending your church and comes to the point of repentance and surrender to Christ. They approach you for help in how best to proceed. Do they get a divorce legally, or does divorce even apply if you don't consider their relationship to be a biblical marriage? Do they continue in their monogamous relationship? Do they continue in their marriage but commit to being celibate, meaning they stop having sex? What direction do you give them? At the risk of overgeneralization, four broad categories exist into which same-sex couples at your church most likely fit.

If a person is not yet a believer in Jesus Christ, then your primary focus is to share the gospel and love them unconditionally just as Jesus loved us while we were still sinners. As Peter did at Pentecost, we invite people then to repent and believe in Jesus for eternal life. We do not judge unbelievers (1 Cor. 5:12).

If a person is a new believer, or a growing believer, then we patiently walk with them as the Holy Spirit convicts them of sin. At appropriate times, we share biblical truth, encouraging them to follow Jesus even when the implications are difficult. We see this modeled by Jesus in his conversations with the woman at the well (John 4), the woman caught in adultery (John 8), and the prostitute washing his feet with her hair (Luke 7).

If a person is convinced they are right and wants to make an issue out of it, aggressively teaching a position contrary to the church's beliefs, then we must confront the divisiveness.

The more difficult case is a couple who sincerely want to follow Christ and obey the Word of God but who interprets the texts differently, even after extensive conversation. This could also apply to a single gay person who would like to enter a same-sex marriage one day. They believe that a same-sex, committed, one-flesh, monogamous marriage is acceptable before the Lord. To make the case as difficult as possible, assume that as much as one can know, they are spiritually mature in most respects. They know the Bible well and share the gospel with others. They want to do everything possible to guard the unity of the Spirit in the fellowship with a humble posture. They strongly believe they are in God's will and living in his blessing. Is there room for us to disagree agreeably?

To think this difficult case through well, we need to examine theology about levels of sin in the body of Christ. While it is true that any sin is enough to make us guilty before a holy God (Gen. 2:17; Rom. 5:16; Gal. 3:10; James 2:10; 1 John 3:4), not all sins bring equal consequences. For instance, murder is worse than hate, rape worse than lust, and stealing worse than envy. Consider biblical references to worse sins or ones deserving more severe action, such as the seven sins God hates (Prov. 6:16–17), the "unpardonable sin" (Matt. 12:31–32; 1 Tim. 1:20), sins of leaders (Ezek. 8:8–13; 1 Tim. 5:20; James 3:1), and leading others into sin or heresy (Matt. 5:19; 18:6).

We can apply several layers of analysis to bring clarity to a sin's seriousness.

- *Intentional vs. accidental* (murder vs. involuntary manslaughter)
- *Defiant vs. naive* (defying God when you know what you are doing is wrong vs. not being aware that what you are doing is wrong). The Old Testament distinguishes sins of ignorance (Lev. 4:2; Num. 15:22–24; 35:11–12 vs. 20–21) from sins of defiance (Num. 15:27–31; Ps. 19:13).[17]
- *Intent to harm vs. intent to help* (breaking a phone in anger vs. breaking it when trying to repair it)
- *Premeditated vs. spontaneous reaction* (embezzlement vs. a crime of passion)
- *Coercive vs. consensual* (sexual assault vs. sex between unmarried consenting adults)
- *Lustful vs. loving* (being with a prostitute vs. unmarried couples living together)
- *Faithless vs. faithful* (adultery vs. sex before marriage when engaged)

- *Persistent vs. onetime* (ongoing repeated adultery vs. one-night stand)
- *Ignorant vs. knowing* (Num. 15:22–24; Matt. 11:20–24; Luke 12:47–48; John 19:11; Heb. 10:26–27)

So how serious is the sin of a same-sex couple who are in a faithful, Christ-centered marriage? Which of the above categories apply? It is intentional but consensual, loving and faithful, but persistent and likely with knowledge, and yet likely not defiant.

When a Christian is convinced that certain behavior is biblically acceptable, and yet their church sees this behavior as sinful, depending on the severity of the sin and a person's response, we either agree to disagree or part ways in terms of fellowshipping at the same church. Often that person chooses to leave the church of his or her own accord. If we disagreed about the morality of dressing up as a ghost for Halloween or regularly driving five miles over the speed limit, we would likely agree to disagree, given that the person was not going on a crusade that harmed unity. If a person is poisoning the body, being divisive, hurting another person, or damaging God's reputation, after several appeals and no repentance, we may ask that person to leave the church. The church could (and often does) allow a person whose behavior we see as morally wrong (even though they do not) to participate in the church (to the extent we would anyone else). It can be an uncomfortable situation, but with mature people, all of whom are hoping and praying that the other will grow in their understanding, it offers a gracious way forward.

In terms of levels of sin, this is not a Romans 14 tolerance issue because, unlike meat offered to idols, which was not intrinsically sinful, same-sex sexual behavior is sinful. Galatians 6 applies even though a couple may not believe they are caught in a sin. So we should gently help that couple see their sin and get free from it. Given that a couple is being humble and not creating division, 1 Corinthians 5 may not apply, especially if they are actively seeking to obey the Lord in other matters, and want to work well with church leadership, and make every effort to keep the church unified.

In terms of seriousness, their sinful union does not come from a heart of lust or violence. There is no intent to harm, but their behavior is premeditated and persistent. Their sin does not fit the categories of overtly threatening themselves or others, destroying the unity of the church, or impairing the church's witness in the community. Depending on how they handle themselves and how the church responds, however, unity could be at stake. While the truth of what God says on this matter is at stake, the gospel itself is not involved in terms of being saved (justification). This is not a salvation, gospel issue, such as Paul addressed in Galatians 1. I realize that the gospel addresses all our sin, however, and we should all be in the process of sanctification in the power of the Holy Spirit. Having acknowledged that point, even though the couple's position is biblically wrong, it is not heresy and will not prevent them from being born again. To guard against confusion, the senior or lead teaching pastor has every opportunity to appropriately clarify the church's biblical position on marriage and sexuality from the pulpit.

Therefore, in most cases the best response in a local church will be to walk with this couple over time, praying with them to see truth as long as unity can be preserved. We also need to give time for complicated issues to be worked out, such as, if a couple is legally married, would we ask them to get legally divorced? Who raises the children? For analogous situations see how the church has handled polygamy in Africa. Does a man divorce all his wives but one? Does he still bear responsibility for each wife's well-being, and what about the children? Other parallels can be found in the cases of a couple who remarries after a clearly unbiblical divorce, and those who live in the United States without proper immigration status. All such people are usually welcomed to belong to our churches, and so should same-sex couples be welcome to be part of our church families. A related challenge is how to come alongside same-sex couples who want to foster or adopt children, especially if your church has a vibrant foster/adoption ministry. Importantly, this is a pastoral posture decision, not a change in moral position about our theology of marriage and sexuality.

How do you respond when someone asks about the church's stance on homosexuality or the LGBT+ community or asks if they would be welcome at your church? Offer to briefly defer your answer to a lunch or coffee in a face-to-face setting where you take an active interest in hearing the person's story and why this question is important to them. If there is not such an opportunity and you must respond on the spot, then I think Josh Butler offered a good model response that you could modify for your personality and context:

> Thanks for your inquiry! We believe that LGBT+ individuals are created in the image of God, loved radically by God, with inherent dignity, value and worth, with great gifts to bring to God's world and to the body of Christ, and that Jesus calls all who follow him to honor and treat them as such. And we have several LGBT+ people who are part of our church. We celebrate their gifts, delight in their humanity, and call them brother and sister. We also believe Jesus calls all of us who follow him, gay or straight, to a sexual ethic in which sex is reserved for the lifelong covenant of marriage between one man and one woman (what is often called the "traditional," as opposed to "affirming," sexual ethic), a "one flesh" union between two sexually different persons. If you're interested, this is a sermon our lead pastor gave a while back that goes into more depth. Also, I know this can be a polarizing conversation in our culture today and an extremely personal one for many people, and I'd love to be available to listen or share more if that's helpful to you.[18]

✱

At the end of the day, these conversations over leading a church in a time of sexual questioning matter because of Jesus Christ. Jesus came and gave his life for each of us, straight and LGBT+ alike. As church leaders, we carry Jesus' mission to bring his message to a hurting world ravaged by sin and hammered by the Devil. Jesus offers living water, the bread of life, and joy in his presence, a joy that exceeds every sexual pleasure. One day soon through Jesus we can each be with God, restored and renewed. He will resurrect our bodies and transform them. Each person has the opportunity to receive God's gracious love gift of eternal life in Jesus Christ. And we have the privilege of offering this divine gift freely to every single person without distinction. What an awesome, joy-filled mission! In this messy, dark world, we shine the light of life in Christ as we share his love with *all* people.

Discussion Questions

1. Why do you think belonging is such a deep issue for many people?
2. Are there ways your church might inadvertently be expressing a double standard in regard to LGBT+ people in some aspect(s) of your ministries?
3. How do you understand the difference between "believing" and "living" in a way that conflicts with your church's position? And how might you approach a person differently depending on whether the conflict was doctrinal or behavioral?
4. Would you say your church is more high-bar or low-bar in regard to church membership? How do you intend to approach church membership for LGBT+ people?
5. How will you handle baptism for LGBT+ people? What about the Lord's Supper? What about baby dedication or baptism?
6. How will you approach serving and leading opportunities for

LGBT+ people? Would you create a leadership covenant agreement? For whom?

7. How will you approach children's and student ministries in terms of LGBT+ people serving?

8. How will you take care of LGBT+ students and their families?

9. What will be your approach to counseling, workshops, and retreats?

10. How will you handle what has been called "church discipline"— that is, how will you care for sinning people?

11. How will you minister to and with same-sex couples in your church?

12. What are your biggest takeaways from this book? What are your hardest remaining questions? What do you sense God is saying to you the loudest?

ACKNOWLEDGMENTS

I thank the triune God for the grace to write for his honor. Writing for me is a way to worship, as prayerfully the Spirit flows words that will be true, good, and beautiful. My precious wife, Tamara, has been a constant encouragement throughout, assuring me that God is active in this project. She is God's gift to me.

While all errors are mine, I give credit to Craig Vogel, who volunteered to do the early editing on the manuscript before it went to Thomas Nelson. Craig's attention to detail in form, punctuation, and style is remarkable. He put the endnotes together in proper form. In addition, Craig has an eagle eye for clarity and precision, so the book is better because of his careful work.

I'm grateful to several nonstraight friends who spent tremendous emotional energy to read the manuscript, give me quality feedback, and ask hard questions. You improved the book and, more importantly, blessed me. I thank God for you.

Although a number of people read early versions of the manuscript, three people gave extensive expert feedback. I'm deeply grateful to Bill Henson, Preston Sprinkle, and Greg Coles, who corrected and challenged me on multiple points, as well as provided sensitivity to avoid misunderstandings and offense.

The team at Thomas Nelson has been a blessing to work with. Joey Paul has both encouraged me and challenged me. His veteran publishing experience has been invaluable and instructive.

APPENDIX: SAMPLE SERMON SERIES PREPARATION

Series Title: *Sexuality: Guided by the Word*

Preview to the Church

Sexuality is one of the most widely debated topics today. But as Christians we must ask, what is God's view of sexuality?

So, yes, we're going there—we're going to talk about sexuality. In this series we're going to discuss issues that may make us uncomfortable. Our study may challenge our desires and long-held views, but because we want to live out what we say we believe and are called to represent Christ to our world, we have to wrestle with these issues. And because we are people guided by the Word, we're going to the Bible for answers.

The Bible will help us understand God's design for sexuality, but we want to come away with more than a set of principles. The Holy Spirit uses God's Word to transform our hearts. Our prayer is that through this series, we may grow closer to Jesus, reflecting both his purity and compassion. Pray that we will be people who receive, live out, and represent his amazing grace and his timeless truth. At Christ Fellowship we are all about Jesus.

Training We Provided to Small-Group Leaders in Advance

Goal of this session: to prepare you to confidently lead your life group well in a biblical study of sexuality in connection with the sermon series.

- By giving you a draft copy and preview of the sermon outlines, discussion questions, list of resources, and study guide.
- By equipping you for how to talk with your group in advance to encourage them to do the series.
- By equipping you with how to handle difficult or awkward situations that might arise in your life group.

Introduction and Context

We want the people of Christ Fellowship to develop the mind of Christ and demonstrate the heart of Christ. Our goal is to provide you with a solid biblical framework. We can develop the mind and heart of Christ on sexuality by prayerfully studying God's Word.

We live in a messy world ruined by sin and at war with the Devil. While we would like nice, clean formulas, real-life people are not mathematical equations; they are complicated, in need of compassionate listening to truly understand and apply biblical wisdom. Married people and singles both wrestle with distorted sexuality. Many of us have gay family and friends. How do we reconcile our experience with the great guy or woman at work who is gay if we think the Bible says it is a terrible sin?

Why Do This Series?

1. *To grow in Christ (spiritual maturity).* Sexuality is a major issue. Distortions and misunderstandings about sexuality are damaging our lives, marriages, and families. Many are trapped in some kind of sexual sin or shame. We need to grow in Christ in our sexuality. Most Christians at Christ Fellowship do not have a robust biblical theology of sexuality beyond some simplistic moral codes. We need to grow in our biblical knowledge of sexuality.

2. *To care for the hurting (compassion).* Nearly every person in our church knows a person, often a family member, dealing with sexual issues. Most are ashamed, confused, and disturbed. They need biblical guidance. Many people dealing with sexual sin feel unwelcome at churches. We need to grow in grace and compassion in this area so that at Christ Fellowship we offer a gracious welcome for those caught in sexual sin. We are all welcome, people of grace.

3. *To advance the gospel (witness).* Sexuality is one of the top sociopolitical issues in our culture today, and we have not yet addressed it directly. It would be irresponsible to avoid it in fear rather than compassionately bringing God's truth to bear. Currently same-sex issues are one of the sharpest cultural divides between Christians and the secular society, creating both barriers and opportunities for the gospel. We must equip our people to share the gospel well on this topic.

Series Overview

Point: Develop the mind and heart of Christ on sexuality by prayerfully studying God's Word.

- Goodness and Sexuality
- Sin and Sexuality
- Same-Sex Issues: Part One
- Same-Sex Issues: Part Two
- Grace and Forgiveness

Series Plans

Warning to parents: topic sensitivity level sixth grade and above. Avoid political issues, same-sex marriage, hiring, health benefits. Make the simple point that there should be justice for all people. No one should be abused or mistreated.

Q&A sessions: follow up on two *Sunday nights from 5:00 to 7:00* midway through the series.

Student ministries: We will cover the topics over three weeks with high school students but not with middle school students. We will talk with parents in advance. If parents prefer, middle school students can serve in Promiseland (our children's ministry) during this series on Sundays.

Parents: We will offer a seminar on how to talk to your kids about sex with an outside expert.

Time for open Q&A

Time of prayer for the series

An Email Letter to Our Life Group Leaders in Preparation

Bruce and I [our pastor of small groups] were chatting last week about the value of being prepared as staff and elders for people who may be confused or even upset over the topics addressed in the sexuality series. These are times when Satan can blind or distract people who then express their feelings in a variety of unhelpful ways (venting in a small-group setting, writing nasty texts or emails, threatening to leave the church, and so forth). It is wise for us to be in special prayer for this time and to be prepared to respond to people in a mature manner. Also know that these guidelines can be helpful beyond the sexuality series whenever people make potentially hurtful statements.

Following are several suggestions for us to consider:

1. As already mentioned, all questions or comments from outside media sources should be directed to our pastor of communications.
2. We must speak with one unified voice as we listen to concerns, being careful not to add fuel to the fire or throw anyone under the bus.
3. If you have the chance to speak directly to a person, consider the following:
   - Thank them for sharing and validate their feelings.
   - Express openness to hear and a desire to listen and understand.
   - Ask questions to be sure you understand them.
   - Ensure they have not misunderstood (which is common).
   - Share our mutual desire to honor Christ and the Word in all we do.
   - Encourage people to take their concerns directly to God in prayer.
   - Urge them to study the Scriptures before forming premature conclusions.
   - Bless them if they decide to leave, and keep a wide-open door to return.

4. Always offer people the chance to sit down face-to-face with one of our pastors or elders to express any concerns and get clarification.

5. If you are hesitant to talk over people's concerns personally, please let another leader know so we can follow up with them.

6. Keep your eyes and ears open to our people so we can shepherd well the flock of God that he has entrusted to all of us.

7. Most importantly, let's commit to pray for our people that their ears and minds will be open to truth and that they will grow in compassion for others.

Thanks for preparing your own hearts to be ready to receive what God has in store for us and to serve our people well in this and every season.

NOTES

Introduction

1. This "hope" in no way diminishes the historic Christian teaching that marriage should be between a man and a woman for life, and that sexual activity is reserved only for marriage.

Chapter 2: Better than Sex

1. See Jonathan Grant, *Divine Sex, A Compelling Vision for Christian Relationships in a Hypersexualized Age* (Grand Rapids: Brazos, 2015), for an incisive cultural analysis.

2. Todd Wilson, *Mere Sexuality: Rediscovering the Christian Vision of Sexuality* (Grand Rapids: Zondervan, 2017), 38.

3. Biblical scholars differ on how to divide the phases of God's work through time. For a good recent discussion, see Kevin Vanhoozer, *Faith Seeking Understanding: Performing the Drama of Doctrine* (Louisville: John Knox, 2014), 97–98, who argues for a five-stage approach that I find compelling. However, for this exercise on sexuality, it's helpful to distinguish between creation and the fall.

4. See Dennis P. Hollinger, "The Christian's Worldview and Sex," in Hollinger, *The Meaning of Sex: Christian Ethics and the Moral Life* (Grand Rapids: Baker, 2009), 69–92, for a similar but more detailed analysis; and Denny Burk, "Introduction," in *What Is the Meaning of Sex?* (Wheaton, IL: Crossway, 2013), where he interacts with Hollinger on the purposes of sex.

5. Although some Christians struggle over how to read the scientific

and historical details in Genesis, the main theological teaching on sexuality and marriage remains valid.

6. I'm aware that a small percentage of people are born intersex, in which their external anatomy (phenotypic sex) does not match their chromosomal sex. See the research of Dr. Leonard Sax in "How Common Is Intersex? A Response to Anne Fausto-Sterling," in the *Journal of Sex Research* 39, no.3 (August 2002): 174–78.

7. Mark Yarhouse, *Understanding Gender Dysphoria: Navigating Transgender Issues in a Changing Culture* (Downers Grove, IL: IVP Academic, 2015).

8. Preston Sprinkle, "A Biblical Conversation About Transgender Identities" (pastoral paper, Center for Faith, Sexuality, and Gender, 2018), www.centerforfaith.com /resources?field_product_category_tid=1.

9. While some, such as James Bronson, argue against the fact that our genders are complementary in Genesis, see the great, brief discussion by Kevin DeYoung on the resonances of our complementary genders with all of creation in his chapter "One Man, One Woman, One Flesh" on Genesis 1–2, in DeYoung, *What Does the Bible Really Teach About Homosexuality?* (Wheaton, IL: Crossway, 2015). Also note Preston Sprinkle's balanced treatment in which he acknowledges Bronson's point about kinship. Preston M. Sprinkle, *People to Be Loved: Why Homosexuality Is Not Just an Issue* (Grand Rapids: Zondervan, 2015), 30.

10. K. A. Mathews, *The New American Commentary*, vol. 1A, Genesis 1–11:26 (Nashville: Broadman and Holman, 1996), 216. See Matthews for more on helper, "She is called Adam's "helper" (*'ēzer)*, which defines the role that the woman will play. In what way would Eve become a "helper" to the man? The term means "help" in the sense of aid and support and is used of the Lord's aiding his people in the face of enemies (Ps. 20:2 [3]; 121:1–2; 124:8). Moses spoke of God as his "helper" who delivered him from Pharaoh (Ex. 18:4), and the word is often associated with "shield" in describing God's protective care of his people. There is no sense derived from the word linguistically or from the context of

the garden narrative that the woman is a lesser person because her role differs (see more at 2:23). In the case of the biblical model, the "helper" is an indispensable "partner" (REB) required to achieve the divine commission. "Helper," as we have seen from its Old Testament usage, means the woman will play an integral part, in this case, in human survival and success. What the man lacks, the woman accomplishes. As Paul said concisely, the man was not made for the woman "but woman for man" (cf. 1 Cor. 11:9). The woman makes it possible for the man to achieve the blessing that he otherwise could not achieve "alone." And, obviously, the woman cannot achieve it apart from the man.

11. See Sprinkle, *People to Be Loved*, chap. 2.
12. Sprinkle, "A Biblical Conversation," 2.
13. Ryan T. Anderson, *When Harry Became Sally: Responding to the Transgender Moment* (New York: Encounter Books, 2018), 149.
14. There is some dispute about Paul's marital status. Most likely, when he was serving as an apostle, he was a single widower. See Denny Burk for a good brief argument. www.dennyburk.com /was-the-apostle-paul-married.
15. See Anthony C. Thiselton, *The First Epistle to the Corinthians: A Commentary on the Greek Text,* New International Greek Testament Commentary (Grand Rapids: Eerdmans, 2000), on 1 Corinthians 7 for an excellent analysis.
16. See, for example, Kutter Callaway's *Breaking the Marriage Idol: Reconstructing our Cultural and Spiritual Norms*, IVP Books, 2018.
17. Hollinger, *Meaning of Sex*, 15.
18. Ed Shaw, *Same-Sex Attraction and the Church: The Surprising Plausibility of the Celibate Life*, 87, loc. 982–983, Kindle.
19. Shaw, *Same-Sex Attraction*, 112, loc. 1303–1306, Kindle.
20. Shaw, *Same-Sex Attraction*, 91, Kindle.

Chapter 3: More than Pleasure

1. Hebrew scholars have recently pointed out that the Hebrew phrase here refers more broadly to a kinship bond, but even so, sexual intercourse celebrates and expresses that bond for a married couple.

2. See Hollinger, *Meaning of Sex*, 199–222, for a good discussion.

3. Richard Foster, *Money, Sex and Power: The Challenge of the Disciplined Life* (San Francisco: Harper and Row, 1985), 92.

4. In the context "weaker" refers not to women being inferior to men, but rather to the fact that most men have more physical strength, and perhaps in the culture of the day, that women had less social empowerment. Author Thomas R. Schreiner expands this point very effectively: "In what sense are women 'weaker'? Nothing else in the New Testament suggests that women are intellectually inferior, nor is it clear that women are weaker emotionally, for in many ways the vulnerability of women in sharing their emotions and feelings demonstrates that they are more courageous and stronger than men emotionally. Nor did Peter suggest that women are weaker morally or spiritually than men. Such a view would suggest that men are actually better Christians than women, which is not taught elsewhere in the Scriptures, nor is it evident in history. The most obvious meaning, therefore, is that women are weaker than men in terms of sheer physical strength. Peter used the word for 'female' or 'woman' (*gynaikeios*) rather than 'wife.' He directed attention to what is uniquely feminine about women, pointing husbands to the knowledge that God would require them to have of the female sex." Thomas R. Schreiner, *The New American Commentary*, vol. 37, *1, 2 Peter, Jude* (Nashville: Broadman and Holman, 2003). And see also Karen Jobes: "In the context of 1 Peter, the weaker vessel is primarily understood as physical weakness relative to men's strength. Therefore, Peter's exhortation indirectly addresses the issue of physical abuse. However, the immediate context makes it clear that the female is also weaker in the sense of social entitlement and empowerment. Peter teaches that men whose authority runs roughshod over their women, even with society's full approval, will not be heard by God." Karen Jobes, *1 Peter*, Baker Exegetical Commentary on the New Testament (Grand Rapids: Baker Academic, 2005).

5. Lisa Scheffler, *Sexuality: Guided by the Word* (McKinney, TX: Christ Fellowship, 2014), 12, cfhome.org/xmedia/guides/sexuality-guided-by -the-word-pdf.pdf.

6. Sprinkle, *People to Be Loved*, 169, loc. 2701–2703, Kindle.

7. Some scholars have developed much more robust biblical theologies of singleness, such as Barry Danylak, *Redeeming Singleness: How the Storyline of Scripture Affirms the Single Life* (Wheaton, IL: Crossway, 2010). See also Jana Marguerite Bennett, *Singleness and the Church: A New Theology of the Single Life* (New York: Oxford University Press, 2017); Christine A. Colón and Bonnie E. Field, *Singled Out: Why Celibacy Must Be Reinvented in Today's Church* (Grand Rapids: Brazos, 2009); Barry Danylak, "Secular Singleness and Paul's Response in 1 Corinthians 7" (PhD diss., University of Cambridge, 2012); and Barry Danylak, *A Biblical Theology of Singleness*, Grove Series B45 (Cambridge: Grove, 2007).

8. Roman Catholics have long appreciated the value of singleness, although demanding celibacy for clergy as was insisted at the Council of Elvira in AD 306 is unwise and without biblical basis.

9. Sprinkle, *People to Be Loved*, 169, loc. 2703–2705, Kindle.

10. Wilson, *Mere Sexuality*.

11. Debra Hirsch, *Redeeming Sex: Naked Conversations about Sexuality and Spirituality* (Downers Grove, IL: InterVarsity, 2015), 50.

12. Wilson, *Mere Sexuality*, 50.

13. Shaw, *Same-Sex Attraction and the Church*, 108, loc. 1259, Kindle.

14. Shaw, *Same-Sex Attraction and the Church*, 109, loc. 1266–69, Kindle.

15. Shaw, *Same-Sex Attraction and the Church*, 110, loc. 1283–86, Kindle.

16. See a good discussion in Stanley Grenz, "The Single Life," *Sexual Ethics: An Evangelical Perspective* (Louisville: Westminster John Knox, 1990), 181–199, esp. 194–95.

17. Grenz, *Sexual Ethics*, 195 (see also 218).

18. Grenz, *Sexual Ethics*, 212.

19. Lewis B. Smedes, *Sex for Christians: The Limits and Liberties of Sexual Living* (Grand Rapids: Eerdmans, 1976, 1994), 113.

Chapter 4: Same-Sex Sexuality

1. Kelly Bayliss, "Gay Couple Beaten in Possible Hate Crime Attack Police," NBC10, September 13, 2014, www.nbcphiladelphia.com /news/local/2-Gay-Men-Attacked-by-Group-Center-City-274964621 .html.
2. Sprinkle, *People to Be Loved*, 9, loc. 133–34, Kindle.
3. Andrew P. Marin, *Us versus Us: The Untold Story of Religion and the LGBT Community* (Colorado Springs: NavPress, 2016), 6, loc. 353–55, Kindle.
4. Marin, *Us versus Us*, 34, loc. 668–70, Kindle.
5. Marin, *Us versus Us*, 53, loc. 898–99, Kindle.
6. Marin, *Us versus Us*, 65, loc. 1030–32, Kindle.
7. "What Millennials Want When They Visit Church," Millennials & Generations, Barna, March 4, 2015, www.barna.com/research /what-millennials-want-when-they-visit-church/.
8. Sprinkle, *People to Be Loved*, 17, loc. 261–65, Kindle.
9. For a recent accessible, fair, and scholarly reading, see Sprinkle, who interacts with revisionist interpretations and takes them seriously. See Gagnon for a comprehensive reading and Burk and DeYoung for a recent short, careful interpretations of these texts.
10. Sprinkle, *People to Be Loved*, 30 grants this point.
11. See Michael L. Brown, *Can You Be Gay and Christian? Responding with Love and Truth to Questions About Homosexuality* (Lake Mary, FL: Front Line, 2014), 132, who points out that Jesus used the plural referring comprehensively to all sexual acts outside of marriage. And DeYoung, *What Does the Bible Really Teach About Homosexuality?*, 74–75, who quotes lexical scholars making this point. *The Standard Greek Lexicon*, BAGD, 854, defines *porniea* as "unlawful sexual intercourse, prostitution, unchastity, fornication."
12. N. T. Wright, "What Is Marriage For? Tracing God's Plan from Genesis to Revelation," *Plough Quarterly* 6, accessed July 24, 2018, www.plough.com/en/topics/life/marriage/what-is-marriage-for.
13. See also Ezekiel 16:49–50. In their pride, they did detestable things.
14. I am aware that Ezekiel describes the sin as arrogance and lack of

concern for the poor. "Now this was the sin of your sister Sodom: She and her daughters were arrogant, overfed and unconcerned; they did not help the poor and needy" (Ezek. 16:49).

15. If you are a teacher, you may want to know how revisionists read these laws as applying only to temple prostitutes. See the following authors, who quote revisionists and counter their arguments. Gagnon, *Bible and Homosexual Practice*, 111–42; Brown, *Can You Be Gay and Christian?* 106–27; Sprinkle, *People to Be Loved*, 44–51.

16. See DeYoung, "Taking a Strange Book Seriously," in *What Does the Bible Really Teach About Homosexuality?* for a good treatment of these passages and their relevance today. By using the term *arsenokoite* in 1 Corinthians 6:9 and 1 Timothy 1:9–10, a combination of *arsen* and *koite*, which come from Leviticus 20:13, Paul communicates that Leviticus 20:13 is relevant for Christians.

17. If you are a teacher in the church, you should be familiar with the debate over the term *unnatural*; see Sprinkle, Burk, Gagnon, DeYoung for good analyses.

18. Sprinkle, *People to Be Loved*, 89, loc. 1388–91, Kindle.

19. NIV footnotes on 1 Corinthians 6:9, e9. For more on these two words, see Gagnon, *Bible and Homosexual Practice*, 303–36. For a recent extensive discussion see Sprinkle, "Lost in Translation: Homosexuality in 1 Corinthians 6:9 and 1 Timothy 1:10," in *People to Be Loved*.

Chapter 5: Same-Sex Sexuality

1. See Thiselton, *First Epistle to the Corinthians* on these verses: "[Paul] is not describing the qualifications required for an entrance examination; he is comparing habituated actions, which by definition can find no place in God's reign for the welfare of all, with those qualities in accordance with which Christian believers need to be transformed if they belong authentically to God's new creation in Christ. Everything that persistently opposes what it is to be Christlike must undergo change if those who practice such things wish to call themselves Christians and to look forward to resurrection with Christ."

2. Rosaria Butterfield, *Openness Unhindered: Further Thoughts of an Unlikely Convert on Sexual Identify and Union with Christ* (Pittsburgh: Crown & Covenant, 2015), 83.

3. Butterfield, *Openness Unhindered*, 137–46.

4. See Owen Strachan's post for recent discussion of this issue in view of the 2018 Revoice Conference in St. Louis. Owen Strachan, "On the Revoice Conference, 'Gay Christianity,' and the Apostle Paul's Showstopper Words to the Corinthians," Patheos, *Thought Life* (blog), June 1, 2018, www.patheos.com/blogs/thoughtlife/2018/06/on-revoice-gay-christianity-and-the-apostle-pauls-showstopper-words-to-the-corinthians/.

5. Bruce Miller, *Sexuality: Approaching Controversial Issues with Grace, Truth and Hope* (McKinney, TX: Dadlin, 2016). Currently out of print but available from the author at www.brucebmiller.com.

6. Gregory Coles, *Single, Gay, Christian: A Personal Journey of Faith and Sexual Identity* (Downers Grove, IL: IVP, 2017), loc. 991, Kindle.

7. Nate Collins, *All but Invisible: Exploring Identity Questions at the Intersection of Faith, Gender, and Sexuality* (Grand Rapids: Zondervan, 2017), 300, loc. 6149–53, Kindle.

8. For other points of view see Bridget Eileen's thoughtful blog: Bridget Eileen, "Gay or Same-Sex-Attracted, *Meditations of a Traveling Nun* (blog), www.meditationsofatravelingnun.com/gay-same-sex-attracted/ and in contrast, Daniel Mattson, *Why I Don't Call Myself Gay: How I Reclaimed My Sexual Identity and Found Peace* (San Francisco: Ignatius Press, 2017).

9. Sprinkle, *People to Be Loved*.

10. Butterfield, *Openness Unhindered*, 76–77.

11. Denny Burk, "Is Same-Sex Orientation Sinful?" (Unpublished paper, 66th Annual Meeting of the Evangelical Theological Society, San Diego, CA, November 2014).

12. Butterfield, *Openness Unhindered*, 83.

13. Collins, *All but Invisible*, 122, loc. 2323–25, Kindle.

14. Sprinkle, *People to Be Loved*, 144, loc. 2304–5, Kindle.

15. Sprinkle, *People to Be Loved*, 145, loc. 2325–26, Kindle.

16. Sprinkle, *People to Be Loved*, 146.

17. Sprinkle, *People to Be Loved*, 148, loc. 2371–73, Kindle.

18. American Psychological Association, "Answers to Your Questions: For a Better Understanding of Sexual Orientation and Homosexuality," American Psychological Association, 2008, accessed May 12, 2018, www.apa.org/topics/lgbt/orientation.pdf.

19. Nate Collins, *All but Invisible*, 120, loc. 2280–82, Kindle.

20. Simon LeVay, *Gay, Straight, and the Reason Why: The Science of Sexual Orientation* (New York: Oxford University Press, 2011), 20.

21. Michael W. Hannon, "Against Heterosexuality," *First Things*, March 2014, www.firstthings.com/article/2014/03/against-heterosexuality.

22. Hanne Blank, *Straight: The Surprisingly Short History of Heterosexuality* (Boston: Beacon Press, 2012).

23. Jonathan Katz, *The Invention of Heterosexuality* (Chicago: University of Chicago Press, 1995).

24. Butterfield, *Openness Unhindered*, 96.

25. Butterfield, *Openness Unhindered*, 106–7.

26. "Being gay is, for me, as much a sensibility as anything else: a heightened sensitivity to and passion for same-sex beauty that helps determine the kind of conversations I have, which people I'm drawn to spend time with, what novels and poems and films I enjoy, the particular visual art I appreciate, and also, I think, the kind of friendships I pursue and try to strengthen." Wesley Hill, *Spiritual Friendship: Finding Love in the Church as a Celibate Gay Christian* (Grand Rapids: Brazos, 2015), 80.

27. See the insightful papers delivered at the 2014 Evangelical Theology Society by Denny Burk, Preston Sprinkle, and Wesley Hill; also note the three good principles in the appendix "Same-Sex Attraction: Three Building Blocks" in DeYoung's book *What Does the Bible Really Teach about Homosexuality?*, "Same-sex Attraction: Three Building Blocks" Denny Burk, "Is Homosexual Orientation Sinful," Journal of the Evangelical Theological Society 58, no. 1 (2015):95–115. "Sexual Orientation in Paul's World: It's Not What You Think," Preston Sprinkle ETS 2014. "Is Being Gay Sanctifiable?"

Wesley Hill ETS 2014. See commentary on the conversation at at the 2014 annual meeting of the Evangelical Theological Society by S. Craig Sanders, "Burk: Experience of Same-Sex Attraction 'Occasion for Repentance,'" *Southern Baptist Theological Seminary Southern News*, December 5, 2014, news.sbts.edu/2014/12/05 /burk-experience-of-same-sex-attraction-occasion-for-repentance/.

28. Wesley Hill, "Is Being Gay Sanctifiable?" (Unpublished paper, 66th Annual Meeting of the Evangelical Theological Society, San Diego, CA, November 2014).

29. Nils Hammarén and Thomas Johansson, "Homosociality: In Between Power and Intimacy," *SAGE Open*, January 10, 2014, sgo.sagepub. com/content/4/1/2158244013518057. According to Wikipedia, "In sociology, homosociality means same-sex relationships that are not of a romantic or sexual nature, such as friendship, mentorship, or others."

30. Butterfield, *Openness Unhindered*, 31–32.

31. Nate Collins, *All but Invisible*, 148, loc. 2859–65, Kindle.

32. Collins, *All but Invisible*, 148, loc. 2866–72, Kindle.

33. Collins, *All but Invisible*, 144, loc. 2774–76, Kindle.

34. Sprinkle, *People to Be Loved*, 146, loc. 2346–49, Kindle.

35. Collins, *All but Invisible*, 149, loc. 2881–82, Kindle.

36. Collins, *All but Invisible*, 150, loc. 2895–98, Kindle.

37. See Nate Collins and Greg Coles, "Is Same-Sex Attraction (or "Being Gay") Sinful?" The Center for Faith, Sexuality, and Gender, accessed April 20, 2018, centerforfaith.com/.

38. Collins, *All but Invisible*, 146.

39. Hill, "Is Being Gay Sanctifiable?," 4.

40. Hill, "Sanctifiable," 3.

Chapter 6: Same-Sex Sexuality

1. Shaw, *Same-Sex Attraction and the Church*, 97, loc. 1103–4, Kindle.

2. Shaw, *Same-Sex Attraction and the Church*, 100, loc. 1147–48, Kindle.

3. Wesley Hill, *Washed and Waiting: Reflections on Christian Faithfulness and Homosexuality* (Grand Rapids: Zondervan, 2010), 72.

4. Shaw, *Same-Sex Attraction and the Church*, 64, loc. 684–85, Kindle.

5. Shaw, *Same-Sex Attraction and the Church*, 68, loc. 738–40, Kindle.
6. Coles, *Single, Gay, Christian*, loc. 1296, Kindle.
7. Shaw, *Same-Sex Attraction and the Church*, 10, loc. 46–49, Kindle.
8. Coles, *Single, Gay, Christian*, loc. 1379, Kindle.
9. Shaw, *Same-Sex Attraction and the Church*, 150, loc. 1796–1801, Kindle.
10. Coles, *Single, Gay, Christian*, loc. 1388, Kindle.
11. Sprinkle, *People to Be Loved*, 174ff.
12. See Hill, *Spiritual Friendship*, spiritualfriendship.org.
13. Wesley Hill, Evangelical Theological Society, 2015 Plenary address paper.
14. Alan Bray, *The Friend* (Chicago: University of Chicago Press, 2003), introduction.
15. Bray, *Friend*, 316.
16. Hirsch, *Redeeming Sex*, loc. 1787–94, Kindle.
17. Collins, *All but Invisible*, 97, loc. 1820–23, Kindle, also see pp. 92–98.
18. See Wendy VanderWal-Gritter, *Gracious Spaciousness: Responding to Gay Christians in the Church* (Grand Rapids: Brazos, 2014), 6.
19. Hirsch, *Redeeming Sex*, loc. 1682, Kindle.
20. See Collins, *All but Invisible*, 273–82, on the history and experience of reparation—refer to his section, pp. 273–282.
21. See Christopher Yuan and Angela Yuan, *Out of a Far Country: A Gay Son's Journey to God, A Broken Mother's Search for Hope* (Colorado Springs: Waterbrook, 2011), for a powerful expression of this point.

Chapter 7: Jesus' Conversations with Sexual Sinners

1. Sprinkle, *People to Be Loved*, 82, loc. 1297–99, Kindle.
2. While we may dispute the wisdom of the term *gay*, it is gracious to use the term that people use to describe themselves.
3. I'm aware this passage is not included in many early manuscripts.
4. Glenn T. Stanton, *Loving My (LGBT) Neighbor: Being Friends in Grace and Truth* (Chicago: Moody, 2014), 32, loc. 363–64, Kindle.

Chapter 8: Hot Potatoes, Logs, and Stones

1. Fyodor Dostoyevsky, *The Brothers Karamazov* (London: Dent, 1927), chap. 41.
2. Sean McDowell and John Stonestreet, *Same-Sex Marriage: A Thoughtful Approach to God's Design for Marriage* (Grand Rapids: Baker, 2014), loc. 140, Kindle.
3. Stanton, *Loving My (LGBT) Neighbor*, 77, loc. 1109–11, Kindle.
4. I encourage you to read Wesley Hill's story in Wesley Hill, *Washed and Waiting: Reflections on Christian Faithfulness and Homosexuality* (Grand Rapids, Michigan: Zondervan, 2016).
5. Susan Cottrell, "You Love Gay People? That's Great. Prove It," Patheos, *FreedHearts* (blog, post by Justin Lee), March 11, 2014, www.patheos.com/blogs/freedhearts/2014/03/11 /you-love-gay-people-thats-great-prove-it/.
6. Cottrell, "You Love Gay People?" See also Bekah Mason, "Finding My 'True Self' as a Same-Sex Attracted Woman," *Christianity Today*, accessed May 14, 2018, www.christianitytoday.com/women/2017 /june/finding-my-true-self-as-same-sex-attracted-woman-obergefell .html for five practical suggestions.
7. Butterfield, Openness Unhindered, 21.
8. Mark A. Yarhouse, *Understanding Sexual Identity* (Grand Rapids: Zondervan, 2013), develops the metaphor of competing scripts.
9. Wendy VanderWal-Gritter's book by this title (*Gracious Spaciousness*) inspires us to grace even though I disagree with her biblical interpretation.

Chapter 9: Not in My Church

1. Collins, *All but Invisible*.
2. Collins, *All but Invisible*, 146, loc. 2817–18, Kindle.
3. See Collins, *All but Invisible*, 196.
4. Collins, *All but Invisible*, 264, loc. 5314–21, Kindle.
5. Marin, *Us versus Us*, 81, loc. 1232–34, Kindle.
6. Marin, *Us versus Us*, 1.
7. Sprinkle, *People to Be Loved*, 14, loc. 211–12, Kindle.
8. Kyle Rohane and Andrew Finch, "Kyle Idleman: God Never

Wastes What We Go Through," CTPastors, March 2017, www
.christianitytoday.com/pastors/2017/march-web-exclusives
/kyle-idleman-god-never-wastes-what-we-go-through.html.
9. Collins, *All but Invisible*, 31, loc. 471–73, Kindle.

Chapter 10: Sexual Sin and Healing

1. Coles, *Single, Gay, Christian*, loc. 644, Kindle.
2. Coles, *Single, Gay, Christian*, loc. 648, Kindle.
3. Coles, *Single, Gay, Christian*, loc. 651, Kindle.
4. See also an excellent exposition of this passage by Denny Burk in "Glorify God with Your Body," in Burk, *Meaning of Sex?*.
5. William Arndt, Frederick W. Danker, and Walter Bauer, *A Greek-English Lexicon of the New Testament and Other Early Christian Literature*, 3rd ed. (Chicago: University of Chicago Press, 2000), 555: "to join closely together, *bind closely, unite* τινά τινι *someone with* or *to someone;* fig. extension of the lit. mng. 'to glue' or 'join' substances, act.
6. Rachel Gilson, "Two Marvelous Truths Help Me Say No to Sexual Sin," *Christianity Today International*, December 14, 2017, www
.christianitytoday.com/ct/2017/december-web-only/rachel-gilson
-marvelous-truths-help-me-say-no-sexual-sin.html.
7. *PCUSA Book of Common Worship*, 88.

Chapter 11: All in the Family

1. Bill Henson, "Posture Shift," Lead Them Home, accessed May 21, 2018, www.leadthemhome.org/. Used by permission.
2. This is the case even though the Bible evaluates Solomon as less than righteous and honorable (1 Kings 11).
3. VanderWal-Gritter, *Generous Spaciousness*. Also see her website Generous Space Ministries, www.generousspace.ca/.
4. For more on this view see Thiselton's commentary, "*He is not describing the qualifications required for an entrance examination; he is comparing habituated actions, which by definition can find no place in God's reign for the welfare of all, with those qualities in accordance*

with which Christian believers need to be transformed if they belong authentically to God's new creation in Christ. Everything which persistently opposes what it is to be Christlike *must undergo change if those who practice such things wish to call themselves Christians and to look forward to resurrection with Christ.*" Thiselton, *First Epistle to the Corinthians,* emphasis mine.

5. Henson, "Posture Shift."
6. Henson, "Posture Shift."
7. Marin, *Us versus Us,* 46, loc. 813, Kindle.
8. Sprinkle, *People to Be Loved,* 150, loc. 2408–11, Kindle.
9. Sprinkle, *People to Be Loved.*
10. There are many "one another" commands in the Bible, such as to love one another, accept one another, and greet one another.
11. Henson, "Posture Shift."
12. Marin, *Us versus Us,* 100, loc. 1455–59, Kindle.
13. Hill, *Spiritual Friendship.*
14. Shaw, *Same-Sex Attraction and the Church,* 74, loc. 817–18, Kindle.
15. Tim Otto, *Oriented to Faith: Transforming the Conflict over Gay Relationships* (Eugene, OR: Cascade, 2014), 6. As quoted in Sprinkle, *People to Be Loved,* 20, loc. 326–29, Kindle.
16. Shaw, *Same-Sex Attraction,* 50, loc. 520–22, Kindle.
17. Collins, *All but Invisible,* 166, loc. 3311–13, Kindle.
18. Collins, *All but Invisible,* 167, loc. 3318–20, Kindle.
19. Marin, *Us versus Us,* 85, loc. 1285–88, Kindle.
20. Sprinkle, *People to Be Loved,* 140, loc. 2247, Kindle.
21. Henson, "Posture Shift."
22. Rosaria Butterfield, *The Secret Thoughts of an Unlikely Convert: An English Professor's Journey into Christian Faith,* 2nd ed. (Pittsburgh: Crown & Covenant, 2014).
23. For practical and inspiring comments on hospitality, see Butterfield's chapter "Openness Unhindered."
24. Sprinkle, *People to Be Loved,* 178, loc. 2826–28, Kindle.
25. L. E. Durso and G. J. Gates, Serving *Our Youth: Findings from a National Survey of Service Providers Working with Lesbian, Gay,*

Bisexual, and Transgender Youth Who Are Homeless or At Risk of Becoming Homeless (Los Angeles: The Williams Institute with True Colors Fund and The Palette Fund, 2012), cited in Bill Henson, *Guiding Families of LGBT+ Loved Ones: For Every Pastor and Parent and All Who Care*, 2nd ed. (Acton, MA: Posture Shift Books, 2018), 16.

26. M. A. Schuster, L. M. Bogart, D. J. Klein, et al. "A Longitudinal Study of Bullying of Sexual Minority Youth," *New England Journal of Medicine* 32 (2015): 1872–74; and C. Ryan, S. T. Russell, D. Huebner, R. Diaz, and J. Sanchez, "Family Acceptance Project. Family Rejection as a Predictor of Negative Health Outcomes in White and Latino Lesbian, Gay, and Bisexual Adults," *Pediatrics* 123, no. 1 (2009): 346–52, cited in Henson, *Guiding Families*, 16.

27. Durso and Gates, *Serving Our Youth*.

28. Collins, *All but Invisible*, 171, loc. 3399–3401, Kindle.

29. J. G. Kosciw, E. A. Greytak, N. M. Giga, C. Villenas, and D. J. Danischewski, *The 2015 National School Climate Survey: The Experiences of Lesbian, Gay, Bisexual, Transgender, and Queer Youth in Our Nation's Schools* (New York: GLSEN, 2016).

30. Sprinkle, *People to Be Loved*, 181, loc. 2869–71, Kindle.

31. Elizabeth Leland, "Forsyth: Mother Faults Condemnation by Church Leader for Triggering Son's Suicide," *Charlotte Observer*, October 12, 2016, www.charlotteobserver.com/news/special-reports/permission-to-hate/article105746141.html, accessed July 27, 2018.

32. Collins, *All but Invisible*, 309, loc. 6327–30, Kindle.

Chapter 12: Sexual Questions and Church Ministry

1. Sprinkle, *People to Be Loved*, 150, loc. 2406-08, Kindle.

2. Bill Henson, *Posture Shift Implement Tool*, DVD, available at www.leadthemhome.org/get-resources/posture-shift-implement-tool, chap. 4.

3. Henson, *Guiding Families*, 29–30.

4. Preston M. Sprinkle, *Grace/Truth 1.0: Five Conversations Every Thoughtful Christian Should Have About Faith, Sexuality and Gender* (Amazon Digital Services, 2017), 24, Kindle.

5. Sprinkle does a good job of discussing these in *Grace/Truth,* 117ff.

6. Collins, *All but Invisible,* 170, loc. 3389–90, Kindle.

7. Sprinkle, *People to Be Loved,* 179, loc. 2840–42, Kindle.

8. Henson, *Posture Shift Implement Tool,* 11–13.

9. Henson, 12.

10. Bruce Miller, *Same-Sex Wedding—Should I Attend: A Wise Way to Develop Your Own Response* (McKinney, TX: Dadlin Media, 2018).

11. Smedes, *Sex for Christians,* 122.

12. For more input see my book *Same-Sex Wedding* as well as Sprinkle, *Grace/Truth,* 63–71. Sprinkle's website, centerforfaith.com, also has a recommended resource in Pastoral Papers, "Should Christians Attend a Same-Sex Wedding Ceremony?"

13. Henson, *Posture Shift Implement Tool,* chap. 26.

14. Henson, *Posture Shift Implement Tool,* chap. 26.

15. Henson, *Posture Shift Implement Tool,* chap. 25–28.

16. See Henson, *Posture Shift Implement Tool,* chap. 31–41, for some information.

Chapter 13: Sexual Questions and Common Issues

1. Joshua Ryan Butler, "Guidance for Churches on Membership, Baptism, Communion, Leadership, and Service for Gay and Lesbian People" (pastoral paper, Center for Faith, Sexuality, and Gender, 2018), www.centerforfaith.com /resources?field_product_category_tid=1.

2. Butler, "Guidance for Churches," 17.

3. Tyler Wyss, "Include Them," WallsDown.org, May 2, 2018, www .wallsdown.org/blog/2018/4/27/29-include-them.

4. Henson, *Posture Shift Implement Tool,* chap. 16.

5. Henson, *Posture Shift Implement Tool,* chap. 22–23.

6. Gregory M. Herek, "Facts About Homosexuality and Child Molestation," University of California–Davis, 1997–2018, psychology.ucdavis.edu/rainbow/html/facts_molestation.html.

7. Marin, *Us versus Us*, 133, loc. 1843–47. See also Caitlin Ryan, *Helping Families Support Their Lesbian, Gay, Bisexual, and Transgender (LGBT) Children.* (Washington, DC: National Center for Cultural Competence, Georgetown University Center for Child and Human Development, 2009).

8. Marin, *Us versus Us*, 135, loc. 1866–67, Kindle.

9. Marin, *Us versus Us*, 136, loc. 1883–84, Kindle.

10. See more discussion on this point in David E. Garland, *1 Corinthians* (Grand Rapids: Baker Academic, 2003).

11. Jake New, "The 'Black Hole' of College Sports," *Inside Higher Ed*, February 9, 2017, www.insidehighered.com/news/2017/02/09 /baylor-not-alone-shielding-athletes-accused-misconduct-punishment.

12. See Sprinkle, *People to Be Loved*, 153–55, Kindle.

13. See a fuller discussion in Roy E. Ciampa and Brian S. Rosner, *The First Letter to the Corinthians*, Pillar New Testament Commentary (Grand Rapids and Cambridge, UK: Eerdmans, 2010).

14. Jacob Milgrom, *Numbers*, JPS Torah Commentary (Philadelphia: Jewish Publication Society, 1990).

15. Ronald B. Allen, "Numbers," in *The Expositor's Bible Commentary: Genesis, Exodus, Leviticus, Numbers*, vol. 2, ed. Frank E. Gaebelein (Grand Rapids: Zondervan, 1990), 830.

16. "If the church tolerates sin that even pagan society condemns as deviant, it torpedoes its moral witness in the world. If its standards of sexual morality sink below those of the unconverted society around them, something is badly amiss." Garland, *1 Corinthians*.

17. The Hebrew word indicates "Obstinate rebellion is described by the phrase 'high hand' (Num 15:30)," *Theological Wordbook of the Old Testament*, eds. R. Laird Harris, Gleason L. Archer Jr., and Bruce K. Waltke (Chicago: Moody, 1999), 363.

18. Butler, "Guidance for Churches."

ABOUT THE AUTHOR

Bruce Miller has been the pastor of Christ Fellowship Church in McKinney, Texas, since 1997. He founded Centers for Church Based Training and helped develop The WISDOM Process©, a systematic way to think through issues and make decisions. Bruce taught theology at Dallas Theological Seminary and is the author of six books. He speaks at churches, organizations, and conferences about the culture's changing views on human sexuality and the impact on the church. Bruce and his wife, Tamara, have five grown children and live in McKinney, Texas.